ESKIMO STAR

From the Tundra to Tinseltown: The Ray Mala Story

LAEL MORGAN

EPICENTER PRESS
ALASKA BOOK ADVENTURES™
www.EpicenterPress.com

Epicenter Press is a regional press publishing nonfiction books about the arts, history, environment, and diverse cultures and lifestyles of Alaska and the Pacific Northwest.

Publisher: Kent Sturgis
Editor: Ellen Wheat
Proofreader: Karen Olson
Indexer: Cathy Dyer
Cover & text design: Victoria Michael, Michael Designs
Printer: Consolidated Press, Seattle

Cover Photos: *Front cover*: (Top) Ray Mala portrait by Melbourne Spurr, Mala Family Collection. (Bottom, from left) Gloria Saunders and Ray Mala in *Red Snow* (1952), Mala Family Collection; Actor Nick Stuart and cameraman Ray Mala, photo courtesy Lorena Coats; Ray Mala in *Igloo* (1932), photo courtesy Anna Jobson; Ray Mala and Lotus Long in *Last of the Pagans* (1935), Mala Family Collection. *Back cover*: Astor Theater marquee, premiere of *Eskimo* (1933), photo by John Jobson, Mala Family Collection.

Library of Congress Control Number: 2011922362
ISBN 978-1-935347-12-5

10 9 8 7 6 5 4 3 2 1
Printed in the United States of America

To order single copies of ESKIMO STAR, mail $19.95 plus $6 for shipping (WA residents add $2.35 state sales tax) to Epicenter Press, PO Box 82368, Kenmore, WA 98028; call us day or night at 800-950-6663, or visit www.EpicenterPress.com.

For those who, despite hard times,

have the courage to dream that life might be fair

OTHER BOOKS
BY LAEL MORGAN

Good Time Girls of the Alaska-Yukon Gold Rush

Art and Eskimo Power:
The Life and Times of Alaskan Howard Rock

The Kotzebue Basin

Alaska's Native People

And the Land Provides:
Transition of Alaska Natives from a Subsistence
to a Money Economy

CONTENTS

FOREWORD

I t doesn't get much better than this. A dedicated author, Lael Morgan, spent years researching the life of the most famous Eskimo actor in history. Here she has fashioned an immensely readable, valuable document that presents Ray Mala's life in the perspective of the times and milieu into which he was born, and in which he functioned so well.

This book sets the scene by describing the harsh arctic world of the Inupiat people, in which Ray's grandparents were successful survivors. His parents fared much better in that world. They were all self-made people. Whatever achievements they accomplished in life were self-generated, sometimes against fierce odds. And this, in spite of being a member of a minority regarded by most visitors to their native land as primitive aborigines with nothing to show for their advantage except the ability to digest whale blubber.

Ray Wise Mala rose so far above this image that he became not only a highly respected cameraman in Hollywood, but also an internationally recognized performer, able to portray Natives of almost any land in the world. He starred in a number of films, played the romantic interest in others. And in between he became the "go-to" guy for filming in Alaska and the Arctic.

Producers would not consider filming in the Frozen North without his help, consultation, and advice.

This life was not without its difficulties. Ray was a movie star, sure. He was also, to most Hollywood folk, an Eskimo. This was both advantage and hindrance. Advantage in that he had a unique talent and appearance that made him marketable in a world that was just beginning to discover exotic lands and peoples for screen depiction. A hindrance in that because he was unique in the Hollywood social scene, he was at first something of an outsider. Germans, Hungarians, British, Chinese, all had their friends of like heritage with whom they could spend off-work hours. My dad had a group of German, Austrian, and Hungarian friends who would come over for weekend gatherings. The exiles. But how many Eskimos were there in Hollywood?

Because of Ray's outgoing personality and cheerful spirit, he overcame any cultural differences over time and was fully integrated into Hollywood society. It took time, but it happened.

I remember Ray as a big, handsome man who visited my father in his home, bringing his son, and his visits were always welcome. His genial smile could light up the entire house in the blink of an eye. His cheerful demeanor and sparkling humor made his visits a treat.

Just as important, Dad enjoyed Ray's work on the set. His camera work was always excellent. He was reliable, professional, and had an excellent aesthetic sense. Joe LaShelle, the director of photography, recognized this and kept Ray at his side for years. Dad, knowing the value of the team, made films with Joe and Ray whenever possible. They complemented each other.

There is a drive in the Mala family that cannot be held back. It runs in the blood. Ted Mala, Ray's son, is one of the most highly regarded physicians in Alaska, specializing in

Native medicines and practices. Ted Mala Jr., Ray's grandson, is following in his famous grandfather's footsteps in the performing field, as is his granddaughter, Galina, an actress-producer. And both, like their Eskimo forebear, are adept at fielding two worlds.

More than anything else, this book is a testament to survival and the unconquerable will of one determined individual who always saw something better ahead. It is a great object lesson for those many naysayers who cannot imagine a better life, and who consequently do nothing to better their condition. Ray always saw a light at the end of the tunnel and strove for it. There was always the chance that the light might turn out to be a different color than when Ray first reached for it, but he always knew it was there.

Most importantly, this book is a treat to read. Lael Morgan paints a marvelous word picture equally well of the bleak white landscape of Northern Alaska and the glitz of Hollywood. Many larger than life characters long gone live again in this book. The men and women who carved a destiny in the ice of Nome and Point Barrow, the hardy souls who kept themselves and each other alive in spite of all the odds, the movers and shakers of early Hollywood are all portrayed brilliantly against the backdrop of Ray Mala's life story.

Ray's life is an inspiration for us all to be the very best we can be. It is a book to read and then to pass to your children to read. We are all richer for Lael Morgan's memoir about Ray Mala's odyssey.

—ROBERT J. KOSTER
Veteran Production Manager and Producer
Directors Guild of America since 1961
Son of Director Henry Koster

A BRUTAL LOVE STORY. Publicity for *Last of the Pagans* made much of the fact Ray captured his unwilling bride, Lotus Long, but soon convinced her he'd make a good husband. Long, who was married to one of Ray's fellow cameramen, was not in his list of real-life romances, however. *Mala Family Collection*

ACKNOWLEDGMENTS

M y thanks to the direct descendants of Ray Wise Mala, not only for their encouragement, but for their determination to maintain a hands-off editorial approach, letting the chips fall where they would.

Without the assistance of Ray's sister, the late Lorena Herbert McConnell Coats, we would know little of Ray's early life. Lorena's stepsisters, Mildred Herbert Richey and Doris Herbert Wright, of the Seattle area, were also valuable in providing information on family background, and on early Candle, where they were raised by their father, John Herbert, and their mother, Hilda, who was Lorena's stepmother.

It was through the Herberts' former neighbor, Mary "Betty" Teters, now of Wilsonville, Oregon, that I managed to locate Doris and Mildred. It was with the help of Willie Hensley that I located Teters. And it was with the help of Hensley's recent book, *Fifty Miles from Tomorrow: A Memoir of Alaska and the Real People*, that I gained considerable insight into their early lives. Although born of an Eskimo mother and a Jewish trader in the Kotzebue region nearly four decades after Mala was raised there, Hensley's thoughtfully recorded account of his tumultuous childhood appears remarkably similar to Mala's because their tradition-bound Inupiat culture was so slow to change. Much is also owed to Mala's first wife, Gertrude Becker

Lundstam, who, like Hensley and Mala, was of mixed parentage, raised in the Arctic with a foot in both cultures, and spoke openly of the conflicts that drove them.

The descendants of Frank Kleinschmidt—Ruth Sarrett of Brick, New Jersey, and Peggy MacGowan of Windsor, Colorado—were equally objective in supplying information on Mala's swashbuckling mentor, as was Kleinschmidt's grandson, Olney Webb of Ketchikan, Alaska.

I am indebted to the late Miles Brandon, who thirty years ago unsuccessfully tried to explain to me the special bond his Eskimo parents, Jimmie and Trixie Ahkla, had with the Mala family, but left the door open for me to figure it out myself. Finally, Brandon's nephew, Paul Ayotte of Anchorage, tracked down enough family history to provide the vital links.

Ann Whipple of Nome furnished fascinating information on her grandfather, Bert Merrill, warts and all. Hans Olav Løkken, a distant relative of boat captain and dog-mushing champion John Hegness, helped define his life. Laura Samuelson, director of the Carrie M. McLain Memorial Museum in Nome, who put me in touch with both of them, worked hard to locate additional information.

Much of my Hollywood research was done just after I got my private detective's license there in 1981, but it was Dr. Ted Mala's family friends who provided the most help. High on that list are Maxine Shean, whose mother married Ray's father; Maxine's husband, Bob; and Allen Handler, Ted's godfather, and his wife, Jane, who were neighbors to the Mala family. The late Joseph LaShelle was also generous with his time for this project, as was Bob Koster in sharing history partially documented by his father, Henry.

Steve Kline, then a screenwriter and now the owner with wife Bo of the Typhoon! Restaurant chain in Washington and Oregon, provided a base of operations and local knowledge to drive my California research in the 1980s. My friend and former student, Robert Basille, Golden Retriever research service, filled in the gaps working at the Hall of Records and elsewhere around Los Angeles..

Special thanks, as well, to Tami J. Suzuki at the San Francisco History Center, San Francisco Public Library, for digging out an unsuspected clipping file on Ray's father, William Wise.

Travel writer Lawrence Millman, of *Northern Latitudes* and a dozen more books, provided copies of long-forgotten correspondence from Peter Freuchen to artist Rockwell Kent during the making of *Eskimo*, a treasure Millman generously shared before publishing it himself.

I owe considerable debt to Ann Fienup-Riordan of Bethel, Alaska, who researched Mala in a day before electronic databases and the Internet made things easier. Her careful work, *Freeze Frame: Alaska Eskimos in Movies* (University of Washington Press, 1995), provided an excellent foundation for later research.

Thanks to Gay Salisbury of Fairbanks, Alaska, for locating the first movie footage Ray Wise shot on his own, a documentary he sold to Pathé News on the diphtheria serum run to Nome. Salisbury's book on the 1926 epidemic, *The Cruelest Miles: The Heroic Story of Dogs and Men in a Race Against an Epidemic*, written with Laney Salisbury, was not only an enormous help in documenting this period of Ray's life but a great read.

James McKee Rawley, Redlands, California, provided excellent material on his beautiful mother, the late Mamo Clark Rawley. The research of Linda Graf, of Sun City, Arizona, on Rex the Wonder Horse and Buck the Saint Bernard provided considerable insight into the production of *Robinson Crusoe of Clipper Island* and a movie John Wayne and Ray never got to finish. Former child star Sally Martin Marks, who appeared in *The Barrier* and now a resident of Milwaukee, added solid information on that film, which has never made it into VCR or DVD.

THE ISLAND PRINCESS WHO REALLY WAS. A member of the Hawaiian royal family, Mamo Clark had received good reviews in *Mutiny on the Bounty*, in which she had recently starred with Clark Gable. *Mala Family Collection*

Special thanks, too, to Gillian Smythe of Anchorage, who chased down notice of Mala's first wedding and filled other research gaps when I was several thousand miles from the sources. I'm indebted to Irene Rowan of Anchorage, who provided shelter, encouragement, and some excellent contacts. And to Barbara Swartzlander, head of the library at the University of New England, who proofread the finished manuscript before I had the courage to pass it on.

Finally, it should be noted that my publisher, G. Kent Sturgis, supported this book even in the bad old days when it wasn't much bigger than a flyer because he believes that Ray Wise Mala has an important place in Alaska history. My thanks to him for making it happen and making sure it was right.

PROLOGUE

I n 1980, in the process of interviewing villagers for a book on Alaska's Kotzebue Basin, I kept seeing photos of an extraordinarily handsome young Eskimo prominently displayed in a number of homes.

"Who is that?" I finally asked.

"That's cousin Ray, the movie star," the homeowner replied, meaning Ray Wise Mala, who was born and raised traditionally in the region but went on to become a movie star in the 1930s. Then, shortly thereafter, Dennis Corrington, an ivory trader I'd met in Nome, asked me to write a chapter on Mala for a book he was planning on famous people of the Far North. When Congress passed the Sea Mammal Protection Act of 1972, Corrington had been caught with a fine collection of walrus tusks that he could no longer sell legally because the law forbids all but Alaska Natives to traffic in them. Knowing local artists, Corrington commissioned them to etch each tusk with the portrait of a famous Alaskan. The artwork would be great to display in his shop, and he planned to use a photo of each to begin the chapters of his book.

When I accepted his assignment in 1982, I contacted Mala's only child, Dr. Ted Mala in Anchorage, who had inherited his father's photo collection and scrapbooks but knew little of his family history because he'd been orphaned before he reached the age of seven. Dr. Mala was in touch with a few family friends and Ray's sister Lorena, so he passed their addresses on to me, suggesting I interview them. The majority lived in California where, fortunately, I had just taken an assignment with the *Los Angeles Times* and could easily track them down. In addition, I haunted Hollywood film libraries and wrote to a number of famous stars Ray had worked with.

Unfortunately, Ray Wise Mala had been a very private man, and I soon discovered that most who had gotten close to him had long since died. I did learn enough about him to turn out a decent chapter for Corrington's book, but the former ivory trader was so successful at expanding his business to attract the tourist trade, he never got around to publishing it, and I went on to other projects.

Over the years that followed, I would occasionally run into Dr. Mala, who would ask if the project was still in limbo and, on hearing it was, would gently suggest I expand my chapter into a book. But I didn't have enough material for a book and, given Ray's penchant for privacy plus the fact that few personal papers survived, I doubted that I ever would.

The Internet had not yet come into its own. What few records survived on Ray Wise Mala were scattered. And I had come up against a wall in learning anything about Frank Kleinschmidt, an early moviemaker and big game guide, who had discovered the Eskimo and trained him as an actor and cameraman.

I didn't give the subject much more thought until 2003, when Dr. Mala's son, Ted Mala Jr., phoned me with questions about his famous grandfather. I was working in Texas and my files were in storage in Maine. I could remember a lot of the unpublished facts I'd unearthed about Ray, but I couldn't give Ted Junior a well-rounded picture of his famous forebear without my old files. Since I was teaching on contract at the University of Texas at Arlington, I promised I'd take a look at what I had when I returned to Maine in the spring, but that didn't happen because I extended my contract and didn't return to the Northeast for three more years.

During this period, Ted Junior was working as an ad salesman for the *Los Angeles Times* while trying to break into the movie industry and was collecting memorabilia—movie posters and lobby cards—on his grandfather. Always polite, never nagging, he stayed in touch, calling a couple of times a month just to remind me he was still interested and excitedly sharing each new discovery he made concerning his grandfather's career. As I grew fonder of him, I came to realize that if I didn't do something with the material I'd gathered on Ray Wise Mala and the unusual era that spawned him, it would be lost. And most of the people I'd interviewed were already gone. Ted Junior's enthusiasm for the project was so infectious, in fact, that when I finally got my records out of storage one afternoon in 2006, I immediately sat down at my computer to see if I could fill some of the gaps via the Internet. Five hours later, I had located enough good material, including some

ON THE LOOKOUT FOR THE MISSING MANUSCRIPT

After he became an international star—even bigger in Europe than in the United States because of his magnificent performance in *Eskimo*—Ray discovered to his chagrin that his studio, MGM, wasn't planning to keep him under contract. There was some thinking that he was "too exotic" to qualify for regular movie parts, but the Inupiat was as optimistic as he was patient, and he decided to wait for a chance to prove himself. Meanwhile, he used his enforced downtime for networking, improving his acting portfolio, knocking out a movie script, and writing the story of his life. The screenplay, preserved in his family's collection, is remarkably solid for a first-time screenwriting effort, which makes would-be biographers unusually eager to unearth his long-missing autobiography.

provocative facts on Frank Kleinschmidt, to realize that a book might be possible.

There was, however, one more question. Was Ray Wise Mala a hero, as Dennis Corrington had insisted when he talked me into researching the Eskimo's unusual life? For certain, Mala had been a movie star, but that profession is often deemed shallow and self-serving. As for his work as a cinematographer, Ray pioneered a highly innovative

ONE TOUGH GRANDMOTHER

An attractive child and not robust, Ray suffered abuse from full-blooded Eskimo peers who taunted him because his father was a white man and not around to protect him. Happily, his Inupiat grandmother, Nancy Armstrong, was determined to rescue him when few others seemed to care. Wresting him from the white man's world that had so captivated his young mother, she taught him everything she knew about her traditional subsistence lifestyle, which was considerable.

Without resources to purchase modern weapons, she trained him to become an accomplished hunter with a spear and with bow and arrow, making incredibly long marches in the dead of winter with only caribou furs for warmth and shelter. It must have been tough duty for a small, scrawny youngster who was also enrolled in the local Quaker school with marching orders from his mother to acquire a white man's education. But Ray thrived in both environments, perfecting his English, writing skills, and Western social graces as he grew to be over six feet tall with the incredibly able body of an Adonis.

period and was well respected in that field . . . but a hero? I didn't think so.

Not until I came to understand the depth of the struggle he faced for early survival and the guts required to follow his genuinely improbable dream did I begin to realize that Ray Wise Mala really did qualify for hero status at least a thousand arctic miles beyond the celluloid stereotype. He had come of age at a time when those of his Eskimo race were viewed by most whites as subhuman, or at best semicivilized. In addition, he was forced to deal with discrimination by his own people and his stepmother for the all too well-publicized facts that his Jewish father was an outsider, who had abandoned his teenaged Eskimo mother, and that Ray, himself, was a mixed-breed love child.

Happily, the youth realized early that to challenge the racial slurs he encountered would prove useless, for in his era they were a given and there was zero tolerance for militancy with an eye to self-defense, let alone fighting for equal rights. Instead, with the patience of Gandhi, Mala focused on excelling in areas where he found his strength, quietly disproving the stereotypes through his own good example. Although focused on acculturation, he was proud of his Native survival skills at a time when most Alaskans simply took them for granted, and he championed the ways of his Eskimo people every chance he got.

Shortly after his first big movie success (*Eskimo*, 1933), while still in his twenties, Mala wrote an autobiography. Never published, the manuscript is lost, despite my strenuous attempts to locate it because I would love to know how Ray portrayed himself. One might guess, however, from the many interviews he gave and his only surviving written work—a movie treatment based on the Eskimo reindeer industry that flourished in the 1920s—that he credited his Eskimo upbringing in the harsh world of the Arctic with his remarkable staying capacity and the success he later enjoyed.

At the time, the American public had become fascinated with the Eskimo culture, initially through a staged documentary titled *Nanook of the North* released in 1922, followed by several similar productions. Mala's movie *Eskimo*, though more accurate than most, still included a number of misconceptions about the Eskimo culture, portraying its subjects as living in snow houses, rubbing noses as a sexual overture, and involved in overzealous wife swapping. Yet while the parts Ray played usually perpetuated these myths, and he was sometimes portrayed in studio handouts as an Eskimo bumpkin, when questioned he made an articulate effort to explain his people and their traditions accurately, occasionally at the cost of disappointing the press.

Once Mala became a father, he became openly critical of Alaska's substandard education system for Natives, and other voices rose to join him from within the territory. The Eskimo's acting career, stalled earlier, had rekindled with offers from entertainment movers and shakers like Cecil B. DeMille. Had he lived longer, I suspect he would have used his new prominence to become more vocal in the fledgling fight for Native rights.

But what I like best about Ray Wise Mala is that while most "heroes" available as role models for Native people of the North were preachers and politicians, he was an original: a generous, sophisticated, self-made man from the humblest of beginnings, who gamely straddled cultures yet never forgot the debt he owed his own.

CANDLE, ALASKA, A REMOTE TUNDRA OUTPOST. Established as a white man's mining camp, Candle boasted a post office by 1902, when Russian trader Bill Wise arrived to stake a gold claim. His son, Ray Wise, was born in a nearby sod house, probably belonging to the child's Inupiat grandparents, in 1906. Later Ray's Eskimo mother wed Swedish entrepreneur Johnny Herbert, whose dancehall and hotel were on the waterfront with his false-fronted saloon, just left of center. *Photo courtesy of Mary Teters*

One
ON EVERY MARQUEE

T he evening of November 14, 1933, was unseasonably warm, and America was gripped by the Great Depression, but ermines and sables were in vogue with the high-end crowd that jammed the entrance of the plush Astor Theater in New York City. Its marquee, blazing with 70,000 lights and hyped as the largest billboard in the world, announced the premiere of *Eskimo*, THE BIGGEST PICTURE EVER MADE.

No room for names of the cast. Just the five-foot-high brag line followed by "*ESKIMO*" in letters that had to be forty feet high.[1] But soon every moviegoer in America and Europe would know that twenty-seven-year-old Ray Wise was a movie star. A star against odds so great he actually found them amusing.

He was of mixed descent: part Eskimo—a race long stereotyped as subhuman—and part Russian Jew, which he quickly discovered was also considered low on the social scale. Born out of wedlock in a small, isolated Alaskan village in 1906, he'd been on his own since age twelve, shortly after the Great Flu Epidemic took his Eskimo mother. Armed with a fifth-grade education, a fair command of English, quiet charm, and a desire to be anywhere but where he had grown up, he worked his way out—first as a dishwasher and later a deck hand—to Nome, the Far North's largest city. Then, crewing for a diversified group of white adventurers, he fell into a career as a moviemaker, when it was discovered that he could hand crank a camera in numbing arctic cold when white men quailed. Eventually, the young man made it to Hollywood, where he became assistant cameraman at Fox Studios during its pre-Depression glory days. Acting seemed the next logical step, for he was uniquely handsome, and a lifetime of hard manual labor had provided him with an enviable physique.

In the press blitz for *Eskimo*, the film's writer, Danish explorer Peter Freuchen who had a bias for fiction, made his success sound fairly simple. "Ray had played some bit parts for a small film company which had brought him to the United States and left him behind in Seattle, penniless and jobless," the bearded writer told reporters. "As soon as he heard about

◀ **THE BIGGEST PICTURE EVER MADE.** The marquee at the Astor Theater blazed with 70,000 light bulbs for the New York City premiere of *Eskimo*. The show opened to good reviews and a full house and also did well in Europe. *Photo by John Jobson, Mala Family Collection*

BUCKING THE ESKIMO STEREOTYPES

Robert Flaherty's *Nanook of the North*, a carefully staged movie on Greenland Eskimos premiered in 1922 and later dubbed "visual anthropology," was the first, feature-length, commercially successful documentary. Not only did it spark intense international interest in peoples of the Arctic, but it established a broad range of inaccurate stereotypes still being protested by northern Natives. Most damaging was Flaherty's portrayal of the Canadian aborigines as totally primitive, in the same way they had seemed to explorers two centuries earlier.

In reality, while Flaherty's people still did live by subsistence hunting and fishing, as did their Alaskan counterparts, they were also well adapted to the white man's culture, hunting with modern firearms and traps, and exchanging their furs for cash and trade goods.

Even more annoying to Alaskans was the fact that their forebears had never lived in snow houses, as had their Greenland cousins. Nor did they rub noses to show affection, or swap wives with the gusto shown in Flaherty's flick.

Because *Eskimo* was about Greenland Eskimos, it featured a number of these clichés—snow houses, nose rubbing, serial wives—but they never seemed to anger Ray, as they did many others. Given a chance, the actor was quick to correct silly misconceptions about the land that he loved, but he knew there was nothing to be gained by reacting harshly. A naturally quiet man, Ray just let it slide.

the MGM film to be made in Alaska, he walked all the way to Hollywood and turned up just before I was due to leave. He was ragged, dirty, and half starved, but we saw at once he could be used. Before giving him a screen test, [Hunt] Stromberg let him have money enough to clean up, sleep, and eat for a few days. We could hardly recognize him when he turned up again. He was good looking, intelligent, and he spoke the Eskimo language. He was engaged at once and I was ready to leave."[2]

Actually, director Woodbridge Strong Van Dyke Jr. had turned Wise down flat, not because the well-paid, card-carrying union member was ragged and dirty, but on the grounds that he was part Jewish. The talented director had made a name for himself using indigenous people in his popular films—*White Shadows in Tahiti*, and *Trader Horn* in Africa. Despite studio pressure and the fact Ray spoke fluent Inupiat, Van Dyke refused to consider a leading man who was a half-breed. No matter that the leading ladies he'd lined up had not a drop of Eskimo blood. While never even hinting that indigenous beauties might not be up to American taste, he argued that everyone knew Eskimo women couldn't act, so he had no choice there. This, in fact, was the reason *Eskimo*'s female stars were not at this night's world premiere. It was easier to explain to the press that they weren't free to leave their Alaskan igloos than to admit that the lovely LuLu Wong was pure Chinese and Lotus Long, the accomplished costar, was of French, Hawaiian, and Japanese descent.

Ray had gotten his leading role only after the "pure" aborigine Van Dyke had chosen to star in *Eskimo* quit two months into production because someone in the movie crew was making passes at his wife.[3] But it ended well. Studio executives, discovering Wise looked "exotic," were now shamelessly promoting him as pure Eskimo. They already knew from earlier sneak previews in Los Angeles that the film would be well reviewed. Ray's friend, John Jobson, had done one hell of a fine job on East Coast publicity, managing to place a formidable number of favorable press releases everywhere, including several in the *New York Times*. Jobson must have seen the movie at least fifty times, but his enthusiasm was still contagious. People, including Ray, believed him when he insisted that *Eskimo* would become a classic.

Then writer Freuchen, trading on his fame as an adventurer, arrived in New York City early to give innumerable talks to organizations of all kinds. Peter electrified reporters with a tale about how Ray had survived stalking by a hungry wolf during filming. But actually, getting the world premiere launched was proving to be a challenge.[4] When Ray had last seen the frenzied Dane, he was trying to talk New York promoters out of sending a flock of penguins on stage, on the grounds there were no penguins in the Northern Hemisphere. The promoters were doubtful.

"Penguins would be expected," one of them argued.

Ray chuckled quietly and headed for one last look at Broadway before the opening curtain. A troupe of classical musicians dressed in furs was just winding up its concert, ready to head for the warmth of the Astor's magnificent orchestra pit. Another northern fantasy of the publicity men. All day a team of reindeer had been driven around the streets of New York advertising the show, and there was not one empty seat.[5] Nor was there even one dark bulb in the 70,000-light marquee, Ray noted. You could hear them; almost smell the electricity in the air. Tuxedo-garbed director Van Dyke arrived and Ray hurried to join him, resplendent in his own $2,500 Eskimo dress parka of sealskin trimmed with bird

feathers and fox. The audience loved them and, although the primitive reality of the film proved disturbing to many, there was no arguing its beauty or the power of its acting.[6]

Early the next morning, when reviews were read at the cast party, they were solid. "It is a remarkable film, one that often awakens wonder as to how the cameramen were able to photograph some of the scenes and record the impressive sounds," *New York Times* critic Mordaunt Hall wrote.

As for the uncredited, mostly Eskimo cast, who delivered their lines in Inupiat (with subtitles), Hall was as surprised as he was condescending. "The acting of the Eskimos, and their ability to do what was asked of them by the director is really extraordinary. Several of the girls are very good looking and deliver performances which are wonderfully natural," he noted. "The Eskimo in the leading male rôle actually gives one the impression of the moods and feeling of the character."

It was a night to remember always. Ray Wise had proved himself as an actor beyond a doubt. He realized it without any help from Mordaunt Hall. And in the heady excitement of that glittering premiere, he tried not to think of the personal cost of his triumph. Yet, in truth, despite the lovely blonde starlet on his arm, and the congratulations of *Eskimo*'s extraordinary cast and crew with whom he had lived and worked for many months, he was as lonesome as he'd ever been in an unusually lonesome life. ∎

Two

HALF-BREED BAGGAGE

eing born a bastard carried little stigma in Ray Wise's Eskimo culture. The Inupiat word for the condition is *aapailaurat*, which gently translates "without a father."[1] Despite the teaching of their missionaries to the contrary, most Eskimos still viewed sex as a natural phenomenon. Children, especially boys, were an asset to any family and were welcomed.

"An Eskimo baby's feet never touch the ground" is still a favorite Inupiat saying, for someone is always cuddling the young ones. And if Ray's pretty, young mother sometimes preferred white man's pleasures to Eskimo family responsibilities, his nomadic grandmother, Nancy Armstrong, was delighted to provide the child with a thorough indoctrination into her culture, which took bitter cold and occasional famine in stride.

Being a mixed breed—the son of a white man—might not have proved a problem either, had his father William "Bill" Wise been around to stand up for him. For Candle, Alaska, where Ray was born, was a white mining town. Bill Wise had been a pioneer, and a highly successful trader who was well liked. Born into a wealthy Russian family in 1886, he was rumored to be related to the tsar through his aristocratic mother, Dena Wolsch. His father, Mendel Weisbleeth, although part Jewish and part Siberian Eskimo, was welcomed in the royal court until he became an outlaw for reasons that remain a family secret.

Although the assassination of Tsar Alexander II touched off anti-Jewish riots and massacres backed by the government,[2] the Weisbleeths continued to live a charmed existence until about 1889 when they angered the royal family. Son Bill was only four, his two sisters slightly older. With the tsar's troops in close pursuit, the Weisbleeths fled with only the clothes on their backs and whatever jewels they could sew into the seams.

They may have escaped through the snows of Siberia to Alaska or elsewhere on North America's remote West

◄ **KARENAK ELLEN "CASINA" ARMSTRONG.** Unusually tall, and graceful, Casina (left) was drawn to the white man's culture to which miners introduced her in Candle around the turn of the century. Here she posed with friends for Nome-based photographer O. D. Goetze, who labeled a similar photo simply "Eskimo Beauty." This undated photo was probably taken about the time Casina met Bill Wise, a Russian-born trader of whom no early pictures can be found. *Photo courtesy of Lorena Coats*

Coast, for no record can be found of their entry into the United States. But by 1900, Dena and the children had taken up residence in San Francisco as naturalized citizens under the name of Wise.[3] What happened to Mendel is a matter of conjecture. If he was a revolutionist, perhaps he traveled back to Europe, for he is not listed at their modest rental at 212 Fourth Street or in any government record. Dena declared herself head-of-household and claimed "merchant" as her profession in that year's census, but the poverty the family faced was dire. Son Abraham, twenty-two, who had immigrated to San Francisco earlier, barely made a living playing his violin in music halls and restaurants.[4] Nettie, the oldest, had apparently gone out on her own, but sixteen-year-old Theresa was still dependent. So when Bill quit high school to join the gold rush to Alaska, no one stopped him. Solemnly he swore he would not return until he had made a million dollars so his near-desperate mother could live in comfort.[5]

How Bill Wise made his way north or where he landed is unknown. Only fifteen at the time, he later claimed to have earned his first money running errands and "making deals" in the gold camps.[6] But Wise was also a clever gambler, especially at poker, which is probably how he acquired the considerable capital necessary to establish himself as a trader in the Kotzebue Sound region after about 2,000 miners flooded the area. The supply center was Kotzebue village, then known as Kikiktagamute,[7] the largest Native settlement, which had already attracted a considerable number of outsiders. There was an enclave of white whalers who had jumped ship, a Japanese colony that had drifted in after the Klondike and Nome rushes, and resident traders from several nations. Earlier, newcomers had introduced the Eskimos to deadly diseases and alcohol, while systematically wiping out large populations of the sea mammals and game on which aboriginal peoples had long depended. Times were tough. Quaker missionaries of the Friends Church had just arrived to save the surviving Natives, but many Eskimos had grown wary of outsiders who assumed they were savages.

Their arctic settlement was an impromptu jumble of tiny, unpainted tarpaper shacks, tents, traditional sod houses, and four primitive trading establishments, canting in various directions on wavering, treeless permafrost, with no electricity or other amenities, not even a reliable source of potable water. The population was about 200, which increased each summer when about a hundred or more migrant Eskimos and a little fleet of schooners arrived to barter. Wise fit in comfortably, as many of the outsiders were European, including trader Hugo Echardt and his mail-order bride from the Vienna Opera, who gave impromptu concerts on the tundra. But because the Russian was late to the rush and just getting established, he found Kotzebue competition stiff.[8] Happily, a new discovery was soon made on the south side of the Sound, nine miles up the Kiwalik River, and Wise was among the first to the remote location.

They named the place "Candle" after the candlewood willows that grew in the otherwise barren land. By 1902, the settlement had a post office and, although the population never got much over 200,[9] the area proved a good, steady gold producer for those lucky enough to stake claims. So good, in fact, that Johnny Herbert, a short, genial Swede who had established a bar and hotel on the Sound in Kiwalik at the mouth of the river, moved up to build the Candle Hotel, Dance Hall, and Saloon. Ornate, with a full rosewood-backed bar, and relatively comfortable although unplumbed, Johnny's establishment soon became the center of community activities,[10] so Bill Wise made it his headquarters, too. He was seven years Herbert's junior, but both were out to get rich quick. With several years of privation and arctic experience under his belt, Wise knew what Herbert and his other customers needed for supplies and had the capital to buy wholesale. Traveling downriver by boat in the summer to meet every ship and making the long trip north to Kotzebue via dog team in winter for special orders and to fill the gaps, he built a lucrative trade. And he was equally industrious at the all-night card games Herbert hosted, gambling big and winning often.

Which is how, by 1905, Bill Wise came of age in Candle. From a spindly youth, he had matured to six feet of well-muscled manhood. Extraordinarily handsome, with hazel brown eyes, brown hair, a warm smile, and polished manners, he also had the advantage of his profession. While there were other Candle miners who were young, handsome, and wealthy, Wise not only had ready cash but trade goods, too, including calico fabrics and trinkets much coveted by females.

There were few white women in the area, but race was not an issue at that time and place, especially after Casina captured the trader's attention. Her Inupiat parents, Nancy and Isskosk Armstrong, lived by subsistence, moving often between sod houses and seasonal hunting and fishing camps, trapping furs occasionally for cash to buy a few white man's goods such as guns and camp stove fuel. This was the way of most Eskimos in the area, but not so, Casina.

Perhaps the girl was different because she was a product of her mother's earlier marriage to Preston Keyakpuk Mills, who may have been attracted to the new culture.[11] Her Eskimo name was Karenak;[12] the Christian name she was given was Ellen and her last name was Armstrong.[13] However, her love of bright lights and partying earned her a nickname variation of "casino" early on. At five feet eight inches tall, she literally stood out among her Eskimo peers, who were generally short in stature. She was also a genuine beauty with a lovely figure. She could be funny and she was fun, but it was her high enthusiasm for excitement that captured a man's attention, and she captured Bill Wise.

FOLLOWING THE GOLD RUSHES

Alaska endured dozens of gold rushes starting about 1880 when pioneering prospectors struck pay dirt in Juneau. For that reason and because, like his father, Bill Wise shied away from inclusion in public records, we don't know where in Alaska the young Bill was headed when he left San Francisco to seek his fortune. Nome would have been his most likely destination because the gold there was in the beach sands and easy pickings, but exactly where Wise would have gone when that strike petered out in 1901 is harder to guess. There were plenty of small finds in that region and a big new discovery in Fairbanks in 1902, but by then Wise was established in the Kotzebue region and had staked a claim at Candle.

It is interesting to note that during this era when many stampeders used aliases, Wise was up front about his name and background. Had this not been the case, Casina Armstrong would never have been able to encourage the son he had unknowingly fathered with her to locate Wise later in life.

Although the trader vanished from record after leaving Candle in 1906, his lucky strike during Alaska's last great gold rush at Iditarod in 1909 made him high profile again, and he would remain in touch with Alaska mining buddies after he left the territory to settle in San Francisco.

RAY WISE MALA'S FIRST PHOTO OP IN 1907. Most Eskimo babies during this era had no need for clothing because they snuggled inside their mother's parka. However, Casina Armstrong made sure her firstborn was lavishly outfitted in clothing favored by the parents of white children, hoping perhaps to move him into the world of his Caucasian father. *Photo courtesy of Lorena Coats*

She had no interest in skin sewing or crafting Eskimo boots, skills that were sure to attract a good Eskimo husband but required crimping home-tanned leather with one's teeth, which soon wore them down to nubs. What whites referred to gingerly as the "true Eskimo smell"— a pungent mix of urine-tanned furs and seal oil, a diet staple, heightened by prudent avoidance of soap and water in the arctic cold— appalled the girl as well. Casina much preferred store-bought goods and white men. She enjoyed using soap. She avoided the Friends missionaries, for they were against dancing and she loved to dance. Nor had she any interest in the government school, although she was quite smart. Her English was fair, and she could do basic math when it came to the trade goods she wanted. Johnny Herbert, a widower,[14] so favored the girl that he let her have the run of his dance hall, but Casina was dead set on Bill Wise from the moment she laid eyes on him, probably at about age thirteen. She would have no other.[15]

For some time, it seemed to be a genuine love match, but in the spring of 1906, Wise's luck failed. He was still making good money trading. Enough so he sent some home to his family every month and had a sizable cushion in the bank. But the really big money lay in gold, while his claim had produced so little it became a local joke. The "sucker" to whom he finally sold this "useless" mining property immediately struck it rich, and there was no other land in the area worth staking. Wise wasn't even close to accumulating his million, and he was determined not to go home (which he still thought of as San Francisco) until he had.[16] What he needed, he decided, was a fresh start.

He didn't tell Casina where he was going because he didn't know. Just off to the next gold rush, and nobody knew where that would be. Young and fairly inexperienced with men, she hadn't seen it coming and had no idea how to hold him. Later, she would wonder if he might have stayed or taken her with him if they had known she was pregnant. But they didn't.

Although there was a hospital in Candle, Ray Wise was delivered in a sod house by his grandmother and a niece on a ruthlessly cold morning two days after Christmas in 1906.[17] His mother named him Ray and provided him with a fine layette traditional for white babies.[18] His Eskimo name, Ach-Nachak, or Chee-Ak, translated "young woman," although even as a newborn, it was quite obvious that he was not. But Inupiats often handed down the names of ancestors with no regard for gender, and he was a very pretty baby—winning enough to curb his mother's appetite for partying. She adored him to the point that she continued to breast feed him until he was seven, he would recall with embarrassment. But his upbringing was that of the Inupiat culture she hoped to abandon, because she had to turn to her family for support. Finally, since nothing had been heard from Bill Wise, Johnny Herbert had convinced Casina to marry him, and so she gave the lad over to the care of a great-grandmother to be weaned.

The old woman elected to take Ray hunting with her, walking some distance from the town to make sure he really worked up an appetite. Finally, when he was exhausted and crying for his mother, she produced a can of peaches, the first he'd ever tasted, while she enjoyed some whale fat and skin called *muktuk*, which he had refused. Later, after she'd drifted off to sleep, he tried to wake her without success. Ray was too inexperienced to know she was dead, but he was smart enough to worry about the vicious polar bears which often prowled on their coast. Helplessly, he stayed beside the corpse, not knowing what else to do. When hunger overtook him again, he foraged in her little food bag and ate the last of her frozen muktuk. By the time trappers found them two days later, Ray Wise was thoroughly weaned and ready to eat anything.[19]

The marriage of Casina to Johnny Herbert provided Ray with a beautiful baby sister, Lorena, and some semblance of family. The new husband was shorter than Casina, and famous in the region for his rebel yell and Civil War uniform, despite the fact that he still spoke with a heavy Swedish accent and had made his way north via the West Coast when he immigrated in 1896. Before heading out to the Alaska gold rush at the turn of the century, he'd worked for a wealthy family as a butler, which proved fine training for the hotel business.[20] After Casina took up with Bill Wise, Herbert had moved in with an older Native girl named Anna, whom he listed in the 1910 census as his "partner." She did, indeed, help him operate his hotel and bar in Kiwalik so he could give more attention to his Candle investments.[21] However,

his parents disowned him for marrying outside his race. Anna had ended up as a patient in Morningside Hospital for the insane in Oregon,[22] and Herbert wanted children. He wasn't a demonstrative man, but he treated Casina like a queen and showed young Ray deference as a son.

Knowing his wife's penchant for dance halls, the practical Swede moved the family to the old hotel he owned in Kiwalik, now closed except for the annual landing of supplies to ship upriver to Candle after the ice went out in July. Otherwise, the once lively coastal settlement had been pretty much abandoned except for old John Hamburg, who had been "shanghaied" into the whaling fleet and jumped ship there around 1890. The only other permanent resident was his Eskimo wife, Molly. In summer, Casina's parents came with other Eskimo families to fish, as was their tradition. They called the place "Keehkech-Taguruk," or Big Sand Spit, and it was also where they had long left their dead, laid out in their finest on driftwood platforms to freeze-dry in the sharp arctic air, raised above the ground so wild animals would leave them in peace. Ray found the burial place spooky and the spit itself unnerving, for in heavy winter storms it seemed a sure bet it would wash out to sea, taking the old hotel with it. Not that they'd miss the building. His grandmother's sod house was easier to heat, and everyone was convinced the dank second-floor bunkhouse of the hotel was haunted.[23] Ray preferred Candle, which was a lot livelier and had a government school. But Johnny Herbert refused to move Casina there and didn't want the responsibility of raising her son in his bar. As a result, when Ray reached school age, the Armstrongs arranged for him to stay with his mother's older brother John, who based his successful fur trade out of Kotzebue.[24]

Which is how Ray found himself enrolled in the Quaker school, for John Armstrong was a lay preacher of that faith.

CAN YOU FIND RAY WISE? This photo was taken outside the Quaker school in Kotzebue between 1913 and 1916 when Ray Wise was enrolled. Unfortunately, none of the children were identified by photographer Herbert N. T. Nichols, so we can only guess. *Photo from Nichols Collection, courtesy of Mark Ocker*

He was doing well enough to take on an extra family member, in part because his church had worked with Natives to pull together a fur trading cooperative, which helped them keep their prices high in the face of white competitors.[25] The Quakers had also backed reindeer herding as a Native industry, which was bringing added prosperity to the region. But their major focus was education, and since Kotzebue had a much larger Native population than Candle, the government had found it feasible to farm out their schooling to enterprising missionaries. The teachers were strict. Burly educator Charles Replogle, who had previously run a sawmill in Indiana, spoke out strongly against vices, which included just about everything that went on at Johnny Herbert's Candle bar. Replogle maintained that nobody

could be a Christian if he smoked. It was also Replogle's policy to beat unfortunates on the hands with a ruler if they lapsed into speaking Inupiat, for the school's goal was total acculturation.

Ray, already fairly fluent in English, escaped this punishment. Nor was he in need of the Friends' constant lectures on cleanliness, targeted to classmates whose families were not convinced that bathing should be a requirement in the high Arctic. However, Ray was far less successful with peers who tormented this handsome newcomer, calling him "half-breed," "whitey," and "pretty boy." Unused to dealing with gangs of cocky young Eskimos hardened by living off the land, and yet to get his growth, Ray often returned from school bloody and bruised. Uncle John gave him some pointers on self-defense, but, surprisingly it was his grandmother who made the real difference.

Despite the usual stereotypes, Nancy Armstrong was as skilled a hunter as almost any man, and she quietly began training her grandson, not with a gun—which was favored when his uncle, John, took him trapping—but with traditional spears and arrows that required no expensive bullets. They lived on wild game, sea mammals, and fish. Even in winter they occasionally camped on the ground, sleeping in the surprising warmth of reindeer skins, and they traveled hard, over rough terrain for long distances to find their prey.

Proud of their culture, Nancy also coached Ray for the Eskimo games, which were held each Christmas holiday and included Olympic-style events like high kicking and long-distance running. No one expected much from the scrawny kid with his fancy white ways, but under his grandmother's tutelage he grew stronger and wiser. "I would stick with the oldest man in the race until I felt sure I could leave him," he explained, recalling the first long-distance race in which he finally made a name for himself. "Then I did, and I found that others who hadn't followed the veteran were so exhausted that they couldn't keep up with me."[26]

Winning improved his standing among Kotzebue peers and earned him the admiration of Emma Black, a cousin who was also enrolled at the missionary school and who became his closest friend. A natural athlete, he also did well at white man's sports like football, ice skating, and skiing, as well as tennis, which was introduced by outsiders on the Kotzebue beach.[27] With relatives, he traveled to several government-sponsored reindeer fairs in neighboring villages—wonderful events that included reindeer races and tests of other skills required by herders. The annual events drew hundreds of Eskimos from many miles around.

ESKIMO GAMES INVOLVE ENDURANCE AND TOLERANCE TO PAIN

Despite the fact that they struggled for survival in one of the world's harshest environments, often migrating seasonally in small family groups, it was customary for many Eskimos to gather in mid-winter and occasionally in the summer to trade and socialize. During such periods, games that tested athletic skills, endurance, and tolerance of pain were often featured, and many of them have come down to us today. A revival of interest in this tradition followed the founding of the Alaska Eskimo, Indian, Aleut newspaper, *Tundra Times*, in the 1960s, which began promoting an event called the Eskimo Olympics. Known today as the World Eskimo-Indian Olympics, it has become one of Alaska's most popular sporting events.

Ray also visited the Friends school upriver at Noorvik, a model Eskimo settlement in timbered country that boasted a sawmill, modern houses with electricity, a forty-bed hospital, and an equally modern school where typing was part of the curriculum.[28] He favored geography classes over the religious instruction the missionaries offered. And, ever curious about the world that lay beyond his region, he sought out well-traveled sailors from what locals called the "mosquito fleet" of small boats that serviced Kotzebue Sound.

Still, Ray was happy to return to Keehkech-Taguruk every summer to help his family, for he greatly missed his mother and his baby sister, Lorena, of whom he'd grown extremely fond. In the spring of 1916, there was a new baby, Margaret, also known as Harriet, who was as pretty as the first. Johnny Herbert appeared much pleased with his growing brood, and Casina also seemed happy, although there were times when Ray noticed a faraway look in her eyes. From the beginning, she had been honest with him about his real father, always insisting that Bill Wise never would have vanished if he'd known about Ray. Bill Wise had talked a lot about his family in San Francisco, she said. Maybe some day, when Ray had grown to be an important man, he would find his father there.

Ray returned to the missionary school the next fall with renewed determination. But there was widespread sickness in the spring, and one day John Armstrong appeared to tell him that Casina was dead.[29] It was the beginning of the great flu pandemic of 1918, which would wipe out whole Native villages and leave hundreds of youngsters orphaned. It killed 72 out of 82 at Teller Mission down the coast and 176 out of 300 Alaska Natives with a fair number of whites at nearby Nome.[30] Luckily, Mr. Replogle's son, Delbert, had built a wireless radio and, working with local leaders, helped quarantine their area so that Kotzebue and the neighboring village of Noorvik were spared. But it was too late for Casina, and Ray was so despondent he dropped out of school.[31]

His grieving stepfather, who was in no position to take care of two young daughters, placed them with neighbors and returned to Sweden to visit his family, while Ray was sent to live with Nancy Armstrong. But much as he loved his grandmother and wanted to watch over his two sisters, he was so utterly miserable he decided to run away. He was only

twelve, but since he could easily pass for fifteen and had experience working at Herbert's hotels, he had no trouble getting hired as kitchen help in a Kotzebue restaurant. It was a miserable job. The white owner treated him harshly, but his small wage saved him from the charity of his uncle, John, who badgered him to accept God's will and return to school.

Then, in late fall, he was taken on as galley help by the captain of a little schooner who was headed south. The job involved more dishwashing and taking orders from an evil-tempered cook, but when the cook got drunk and Ray covered for him, the captain took notice. When a crewman jumped ship, Ray again proved a nimble substitute. He was good in the engine room, too, and absolutely fearless in any weather.

Eventually he landed at a lumber camp, probably in Oregon, where he was hired to run errands. This took work from some of the older boys in camp, who retaliated by beating him up until some sympathetic loggers taught him how to box.[32] Still, Ray wasn't comfortable working in the woods. Having been raised on the open tundra, he found the forest stifling. The southern winter was a treat—seldom below zero—but he missed the ocean and the Arctic. He missed his little sisters and even Johnny Herbert. So, finding a berth on one of the last boats going north for the season, he returned to Kotzebue late in 1919 to discover the Sound frozen and the landscape covered with snow.

Equipping himself with snowshoes and some dried fish, he walked the long peninsula that backed Kotzebue and then followed the coast to the Kiwalik River and inland to Candle, a trip of about 100 miles. Here, he learned to his dismay that Johnny Herbert had married a Swedish woman named Hilda, 38, whom he had met on the boat during his visit to Sweden a year earlier. She'd been living in America almost as long as Herbert, working as a maid for a wealthy Chicago family, who allowed her to return to Sweden every two years for a vacation.

Never married, she was delighted when she received a letter from Herbert following his return to Alaska, suggesting that she become his wife.[33] Herbert considered himself lucky, since his plump little bride had a head for business and would be so much help raising his daughters.

Hilda was not as pleased. Although quick to laugh and generally easy going, she had no idea until she arrived in Candle that Herbert had two daughters, one an infant. In fact she was still struggling with that problem when Ray, another unknown, showed up. She had been raised to disapprove of half-breeds, but at least the sisters had Herbert's blood. It didn't take long for her to realize that her new husband was open handed to a fault, but she wasn't going to let him feed another man's son. As for Ray, she refused to speak with him or allow him in their house.

Johnny Herbert tried to reason with her. Ray was a strong and willing worker. They had the hotel and bar to run, with tons of freight to haul up from Kiwalik after the ice went out each spring. Someone had to care for the horses used for freighting and help work the family mining claim. Someone had to shovel snow after every storm so they would not be buried in it. But Hilda was pregnant with their first child, and it was no use. Resigned, Herbert quietly let the boy sleep in the back of the bar so he could finish school.

Ray's studies went well. He was the only student in fifth grade, which could have been boring, but the Snyder kids and Ann Thomas were in the sixth grade of their one-room school, so he got to study their lessons, too. Unfortunately his sisters were too young to attend. He only got to see Lorena if she managed to sneak out of the house to talk to him. Harriet, who was not yet two, had been farmed out to Marie and Tom Roust, owners of a roadhouse down the street, who had no children of their own and were very protective of her.[34]

Finally, well before spring, Hilda ordered Ray gone. Herbert protested that his stepson was only fourteen and the winter was still severe, but Ray Wise strapped on his snowshoes. Without family support, he knew he could not survive where he was, or even in the Eskimo culture of his aging grandmother where close ties with relatives would not ensure success for a half-breed. Embarrassed, Herbert slipped the boy fifteen dollars, and Ray set out alone for Nome, the largest settlement in the Far North and its major port, which lay more than 100 miles away over rugged mountain country and down a frozen, rocky coast.[35] He'd visited that town during his earlier travels and knew the ice of that Bering Sea roadstead would break well before it went out into Kotzebue Sound. He was a good cook and a pretty good sailor, and he knew something about engines, too. His plan was to hit the beach early, so maybe someone would hire him. ∎

Three
ON HIS OWN AT FOURTEEN

Even at a distance, Nome looked like a frighteningly big city to young Ray Wise as he descended a snow-filled Kigluaik Mountain pass en route from Candle to the Seward Peninsula in the early spring of 1920. Although considerably less than a mile wide, the settlement's Front Street was strung out for a good five miles along the Bering Sea coast, with an impressive number of two- and three-story buildings plus a dazzling assortment of telephone and telegraph poles. Above them towered the 100-foot steeple of Saint Joseph's Catholic Church, with its electrically lighted six-by-eight-foot cross, a beacon for travelers—believers or not—caught on the tundra during the fearsome storms of the region's seven-month winter.[1] There were street lights,[2] too, and occasional automobile headlights among the horse-drawn wagons and dog teams that mushed in the cold dusk of the Far North's largest settlement.

Looks were deceiving, however, for although some 30,000 souls had rushed to the settlement after gold was discovered in the sands of its beaches twenty years earlier, the population had dwindled to about 800. Only one in ten of the buildings was occupied. Most were in serious disrepair, and the wooden street paving and boardwalks were rotting.[3]

Still, Nome remained a viable white man's town, with four times the population of Kotzebue, all strangers to Wise, the fourteen-year-old thought grimly. The Natives were bound to be territorial. He'd heard that most of Nome's Eskimos had died in the flu epidemic, but he soon encountered a threesome who proved as hostile as the Kotzebue boys had been when he was a newcomer there. Fortunately, a tough Eskimo from out of town named Jimmie Ahkla, who was twenty-two, joined the fray on Ray's side, and fighting back to back, they licked the locals.[4] Pleased with themselves, Wise and Ahkla soon discovered they had

◀ **RAY WISE'S SECOND FAMILY.** Nome area reindeer herder Jimmie Ahkla, with his wife, Trixie, and their children, Billy, in his mother's parka, and Miles on his father's lap, provided Ray with a much needed family when he had none. Like Ray, the Ahklas went into show business but later returned to Alaska to live by fishing and hunting. They would remain lifelong friends.
Photo courtesy of Paul Ayotte, a grandson of the Ahklas

RAISED IN THE REINDEER ERA

After the exploitation of sea mammals and Alaska Native hunting grounds by outside whaling crews and later by gold prospectors had left many Eskimos close to starvation in the 1890s, missionary Sheldon Jackson introduced reindeer herding to the region with the help of government agencies. Jackson imported the animals, which are nearly identical to caribou and are sometimes referred to as "old world" caribou, in small numbers from Siberia. They adapted well to the Alaskan Arctic and, under the tutelage of experienced herders from Lapland, Eskimos soon owned large herds.

During the era in which Ray Wise grew to manhood, reindeer herding was viewed as one of the most promising industries of his region. Annual fairs featuring reindeer races and social events, as well as training for herders, were highly popular. However, overgrazing and inept political wrangling on the part of white administrators caused this unusual agricultural venture to wane almost as quickly as it had materialized. Although the animals had once numbered 600,000 in northern Alaska, by the end of World War II there were only a half-dozen small herds left. Spasmodic attempts to revive the industry since that time have not been productive.

much in common despite the difference in their ages. Jimmie's father also was a white man, a doctor of Irish origin from the states who had come to the Arctic on a whaling ship and stayed there to prospect.

Early on, Dr. Cole Brandon, Jimmie's father, had befriended Presbyterian missionary Sheldon Jackson, who had just imported reindeer from Siberia in the hopes that Alaskan Eskimos might raise them for food and profit. The wildlife and sea mammals on which the Natives depended were being decimated by hordes of whalers, sealers, and prospectors who were flocking into the country.[5] Dr. Brandon became so interested in the preacher's attempt to help them that he manned the Teller Reindeer Station for Jackson in the winter of 1898, when there was too much snow for prospecting.[6]

Jimmie said little about his Eskimo mother, except that she had worked on Dr. Brandon's whaling ship as a skin sewer before moving with him to Teller, where Jimmie and his younger sister, Alakook, were born. Apparently the doctor intended to settle permanently in Alaska, for he became a reindeer commissioner and, in 1900, was one of five men who had helped found Anvil City, which later became the gold rush town of Nome.[7] But like Ray's father, Brandon became restless and moved on to an unknown destination, leaving Jimmie's mother to raise his children on her own. After her early death, the children were moved to the mission Presbyterians had established in Teller.[8] Having grown up around the reindeer station, Ahkla become a herder and trainer of sled deer for racing, but Ray was surprised to learn that reindeer men on the Seward Peninsula did not shepherd their herds, as was the custom in his region. Instead, they let the animals wander in the wild until the annual roundup for branding and butchering of meat to sell, which left the herders plenty of time to hunt and fish.[9]

In town to buy supplies for arctic fox trapping, Ahkla invited Wise to team with him at his camp at Igloo near Teller, and Ray's problem of what to do for the two months until shipping opened was solved. The two bachelors proved unusually compatible. Ahkla, who was outgoing, found Ray unusually quiet, seldom volunteering information. However, the Candle youth was not at all shy about responding to questions. In fact, he proved to be an excellent storyteller, and he also enjoyed practical jokes. Both men were well educated for their race at the time and, curious to learn about the world from which their fathers had come, they were enthusiastic readers. Skilled trappers, they worked well together. In addition, they picked up a post office contract of sorts, occasionally joining Harold Miller, a friend of Jimmie's, to skate from Teller to Igloo and back with the mail.[10]

When the ice finally went out, Captain Jack Hammer agreed to give Ray a berth on the mail boat *Silver Wave*. Nome was a tough home port because it had no harbor or protection from storms. Small boats could tie up at the mouth of the Snake River, but the *Silver Wave*, which was fifty-five feet long with a six-foot draft,[11] had to anchor more than a mile out, while goods and passengers were lightered to within thirty feet of shore and then let drift through the breakers. Women were carried ashore on the backs of men who waded out to the lighters. Lives and valuable goods were often lost in the rough surf,[12] but Wise fared well with Captain Hammer, who was an excellent seaman and careful with his landings.

Wise also found a friend in John Becker, who owned the local machine shop and a saloon on Nome's Front Street. The boy wasn't a bar patron, having seen enough drunks at Johnny Herbert's to avoid alcohol, but Becker let the newcomer hitch occasional rides on his flatbed

FRONT STREET, NOME. This view of Nome's main street is how it looked in winter about the time of Ray Wise's arrival. A boomtown of 30,000 during the turn-of-the-century gold rush, the population had dwindled to 852, but it was still nine times bigger than Ray's hometown of Candle and about four times larger than Kotzebue, where he had earlier attended school. *Photo by O. D. Goetze, Dr. Daniel S. Neuman Collection, courtesy of Alaska State Library*

wagon, and Ray always kept an eye out for him when he got shore leave.

Born in Canada of German parents who spoke French, Becker had packed a piano in pieces over Chilkoot Pass to get to the Dawson gold rush in 1898. Then he moved to the Seward Peninsula when gold was discovered there and became an American citizen. His Eskimo wife, Ella, spoke no English, but she wouldn't allow their eight children to speak anything else, and Becker was proud of the fact that they were all fluent.

YOUNG RAY WISE AT WORK. This shot, probably taken in Nome in about 1922, is the first known photograph of the young Eskimo as a cameraman. In addition to being able to hand crank a camera at 50 below zero, Ray had a natural eye for sharp focusing. *Mala Family Collection*

Wise met one of them, Gertrude, when he jumped on the wagon one afternoon to find her riding home from school with her dad, eating a candy bar. Although only eight, she was indeed fluent, introducing herself and then confiding with a giggle that her own mother couldn't pronounce her non-Eskimo name. Ray, however, was determined to remember it because Miss Becker was as beautiful as she was amusing.[13]

Because the mail boat was constantly on the go once the ice cleared, Wise saw little of Nome until midsummer, and then he scarcely recognized it because the population had swelled to about 2,000. The beaches on both sides of town, so lonesome when he had left in late May, were white with tents, and the streets were crowded with hundreds of Eskimos from all parts of the Arctic. The entire population of King Island was camping there. Natives came in from the Seward Peninsula and Cape Prince of Wales. There were the Ungalardlermiut, Yupik Eskimos who lived much like the Inupiats, from Norton Sound and the mouth of the Yukon, and Yupiks from Nunivak and Saint Lawrence Islands whose language was difficult for Inupiats to understand. They had arrived in large skin umiaks[14] and small, open wooden boats, to socialize and trade. Many were carving walrus ivory but, although there were plenty of white tourists for them to sell to, they seldom peddled their curios on the streets. Instead, quite businesslike and decently dressed, they dealt directly with shop owners, selling to them for wholesale prices.[15]

Nome prided itself on allowing Native people "complete equality," so they enjoyed a free run of the town. Of course, churches and the movie theater were segregated, and so was the Golden Gate Hotel,[16] but no one with other options would stay in that motley old barn at three dollars per night. Despite the hostelry's ornate, gold rush era decorations, it canted in about five directions, had paper-thin walls, and was so musty the air there was almost impossible to breathe. Ray preferred to camp on the sand spit where most of Nome's Eskimo population resided.

But he was seldom there for long, for the *Silver Wave*'s run included Kivalina, Point Hope, and Barrow as well as Kotzebue and, twice a summer, Kiwalik. There he found Hilda Herbert running Johnny's old hotel. She wouldn't speak to him, of course, but from former neighbors he learned that his sisters were doing well.[17] So when summer ended, Ray elected to stay in Nome, where he got a job delivering for the Nome Water Company, "Pure Water from Moonlit Springs, Foot of Anvil Mountain," which turned off the town's few running water taps after freezeup.[18] Clean and neatly dressed, well aware of his place in the nearly all-white community but cheerful and friendly, he came to know most of the townsfolk, making a good impression that would later serve him well.

Better yet, he discovered Nome's Dream Theatre, a 400-seat movie palace that opened once or twice weekly. Despite a metal stove in one corner, the place was incredibly drafty at 50 below zero, and the piano played to accompany the silent films was sadly out of tune.[19] As a half-breed, Ray was required to sit in the Eskimo section, but he was oblivious to everything but the latest Hollywood epic. He enjoyed the actors and the insights that plots provided into the lives of outsiders, but what really fascinated him was the seemingly magic camera work.[20] How did they do it?

Come spring, Wise quit his job to go trapping again with Jimmie Ahkla, arriving back in Nome too late in the season to connect with Captain Hammer, who was taking four members of explorer Vilhjalmur Stefansson's expedition to Russia's Wrangel Island. This was a business venture the able skipper would regret, because the group tried to claim the desolate real estate formally for Canada and Great Britain while Hammer planted the Stars and Stripes. Angered, the Soviets vowed revenge. In the aftermath of the Russian Revolution, the relationship of America with the Soviet Republic was strained at best, and to make matters worse, Alaskan sea captains were slipping past the Soviet border guards to avoid paying the license fees the new officials required to trade in their territory.[21] Many

Alaskans also had dealings with the White Army, which was still trying to fight the revolutionists. So when Soviets captured a white Russian colonel who had a $500,000 check in his pocket from Olaf Swenson, who had chartered Hammer's ship to barter for furs along the Russian coast, they shot the colonel and then managed to capture the *Silver Wave* along with Captain Hammer and crew, keeping them in a Soviet prison for nearly a year.[22] Wise, meanwhile, signed on with Captain Frank Kleinschmidt, a short, wiry filmmaker and lecturer with a heavy foreign accent, who mounted a movie-making expedition to the Siberian side and *didn't* get caught.

Like Ray's friend, John Becker, Kleinschmidt had come north during the Dawson rush. German, but a naturalized American citizen and merchant marine, he did well enough to start his own shipping company in partnership with Captain Louis Lane, one of Nome's richest citizens, after gold was found there. He based their two power schooners, the *Diamond L* (for Lane) and the *Diamond K* (for Kleinschmidt), at Teller, which was about 150 sea miles from Nome and the only natural harbor in the area. Marriage to Margaret "Alaska" Young, daughter of the local Presbyterian missionary, brought Kleinschmidt additional prominence, which he used to good advantage.[23] By the time the northern rush had slowed, he had sold his company and connected with the Seattle Chamber of Commerce, recruiting a group of rich businessmen to go big game hunting with him in Alaska and Siberia. Serving as captain of the *P. J. Abler*, a three-masted power schooner he chartered out of Seattle in 1913, Kleinschmidt also shot 2,000 feet of motion picture film of arctic wildlife and Eskimos, while collecting 2,000 specimens for the prestigious Carnegie Museum in Pennsylvania. On return, he edited the film to show with lectures, producing what is regarded today as Alaska's first travelogue.[24]

The venture proved so lucrative and his film showings so successful that Kleinschmidt chartered again in 1914, this time returning with a live polar bear and a walrus for Woodland Park Zoo in Seattle. The *New York Times*, which had earlier printed notice of his motion picture showings, ran several features on him, including one about his dining with Russian explorers off eastern Siberia, where one of them showed up all dressed in white.[25]

By now, there were a number of professional moviemakers visiting the Arctic.

Lowell Thomas discovered the territory in 1914 and returned in 1915.[26] Pathé movie man Will Hudson, who had made a name for himself shooting footage for Seattle's Alaska-Yukon-Pacific Exposition of 1909, accompanied a Harvard-Smithsonian expedition in 1913 to shoot in Siberia. He later found himself locked in arctic ice on Captain Louis Lane's *Polar Bear*, which was near the *Karluk* carrying a Stefansson expedition that had been reported missing. With Lane, Kleinschmidt's former partner, Hudson managed to walk out over moving ice and some of the most rugged terrain in Alaska to Fairbanks, bringing with him news that Stefansson was still alive and having movies to prove it.[27] Then there was Fred LeRoy Granville's well-received film, *Rescue of the Stefansson Arctic Expedition* (1914).[28] But it was World War I and not his competition that had nearly destroyed Kleinschmidt's career.

Making the most of his German connections and America's neutrality, Kleinschmidt joined the Austro-German forces in November 1914 to cover the fighting. Traveling on a mine sweeper in the Adriatic, shooting from airplanes and a dirigible over Belgrade, and moving with ground forces to the Russian front, he got marvelous footage.[29] He also garnered favorable coverage by the *New York Times*, after assuring an audience that the German officers were gentlemen. But on April 6, 1917, the United States entered the war against Germany, and Frank Kleinschmidt was in trouble.

The *New York Times* was silent when a showing of Kleinschmidt's film, *War on Three Fronts*, at Carnegie Hall caused a riot in 1917,[30] but when government agents found him armed and arrested him, hoping to prove treason in November of that year, it was news.[31] Friends successfully defended him. Kleinschmidt announced that he would donate proceeds from his war film to the German-Austrian-Hungarian Relief Association while denying indignantly he was pro-German. Margaret Kleinschmidt sued for divorce, asking support for their three daughters. The Carnegie Museum, with which Kleinschmidt had worked since 1909, declined to sponsor another Alaskan expedition, and no backing was forthcoming from the Seattle Chamber of Commerce.

What apparently saved the moviemaker was the sale of his German footage to Hollywood director D. W. Griffith, who incorporated it into a feature titled *Hearts of the World*, "a love story of the Great War."[32] Stopping only long enough to marry Essie, a well-rounded young beauty with an intriguing French-Canadian accent, Kleinschmidt chartered an old sub chaser he christened *The Silver Screen* and headed north in 1922.[33] There he enlisted Ray Wise, a capable crewman he noticed when he was a passenger on the *Silver Wave*.[34] If Kleinschmidt had been better financed, he probably would have confined the fifteen-year-old to galley and deck duty, but the filmmaker was as desperately short-handed as he was short of money. "I had to think up scenes, write the scenario or story, construct everything, teach the Eskimo what to do, how to act, and then photograph it, all by myself without assistance, help or suggestions from anybody except my wife, which makes it hard and difficult to judge what you are really accomplishing, no criticism, no counter balance," he would later remark to a niece.[35]

Ray Wise was more than happy to fill the gaps. When Kleinschmidt's hands got too cold to operate his old hand-cranked 35-mm De Brie camera, Ray took over. Used to the climate, with the eye of a marksman, he produced good footage almost from the start. Encouraged, Kleinschmidt showed the boy how to develop film by "feel" in a Steinmann tank, so that each evening they could check how that day's shooting had come out. And usually it was spectacular.[36]

They sailed for Siberia as soon as the ice broke early in May and had no trouble finding polar bears, sea lions, and great masses of walrus lounging on the ice floes. They photographed silver foxes, brown bears, a school of whales, and men at a whaling station cutting up the huge carcasses. There was a bit of hokum, too, where Ray and Kleinschmidt and Essie pretended they were lost on an ice floe and were forced to climb a giant iceberg. Actually, they filmed their "narrow escape" on the shore ice of the Nome beach, much to the amusement of the locals.

It proved a delightful summer. Bright and pleased to learn anything new, Wise proved a real asset to Kleinschmidt's little team, and the down-on-his-luck German—age fifty-one—grew increasingly charmed with the boy's good-natured innocence.

The show Kleinschmidt put together from the footage they shot would bring Ray Wise his first clips. True, he wasn't mentioned by name, but *Variety* gave *Captain Kleinschmidt's Adventures in the Far North* a good review. "The picture does not burden the audience with looking at one subject or scene too long," the writer began. "The titles are

BIG GAME HUNTER AND GUIDE FRANK KLEINSCHMIDT.
A successful boat captain during the Klondike and Nome gold rushes, Kleinschmidt later made his living guiding big game hunters and making movies of their hunts, which he exhibited during national lecture tours. About 1922, he hired Ray Wise out of Nome as a crewman and later taught him to run a movie camera. It was Kleinschmidt, too, who first recognized Wise's acting talents, starring him in an arctic drama titled *Primitive Love*.
Photo courtesy of Kleinschmidt descendant Peg MacGowan

cleverly handled with the caption reading that the incidents and scenes have been taken from a diary kept by Mrs. Kleinschmidt on the tour. It was a good idea and convincing."

Even their silliness on the Nome beach "icebergs" won praise. "[There was a] thrilling scene where Capt. Kleinschmidt, his wife, and a camera man are adrift on an ice floe and forced to seek refuge on the top of a giant iceberg," the reviewer enthused. "Other thrillers are the endeavor to capture a brown bear and a hunt for silver foxes. A battle between animals is also shown."[37]

Yet despite redeeming reviews for his latest work, Kleinschmidt was forced to rethink his approach to filmmaking that fall following the release of Robert Flaherty's *Nanook of the North*. An intimate look at the life of a primitive Greenland Eskimo family, the drama—considered by some to be the first feature-length documentary—became an overnight, international success. Anyone who knew anything about Eskimos and the Arctic could see that the footage was staged and often inaccurate. Flaherty's Eskimos were disarmingly simple, hunting with stone-age techniques, whereas, in reality, they had long been influenced by white men and used modern weapons. No lesser light than explorer Wilhjalmur Stefansson proclaimed the movie a fraud. But Flaherty, who had lived with the Greenlanders several years, did such a fine job in conveying their emotion-packed fight for survival against dire cold and ever-near starvation, he set the standard—inaccuracies and all—for Eskimo movies that followed. Nor did it seem he was that far off, when just two years after his film's release, his hero, Nanook, died of starvation while on a hunting trip.[38]

Flaherty's success created renewed interest in Kleinschmidt's work but also stiff competition. When President Warren G. Harding toured Alaska in the summer of 1923, most of the eighteen movie outfits that came north to cover him stayed on to make their own versions of *Nanook*.[39] Still, Kleinschmidt had the advantage of more than a decade in the Far North and owned miles of footage that he could reedit to produce "new" movies. "You wanted to know what my mission is this time," he wrote his niece, Minnie Louise Bismarck, while headed north on the SS *Nome* in April 1924. "Taking moving pictures of course and nothing else, that is no scientific Expedition although I am doing a little of it in spare moments. I am endeavoring to film three pictures: One: "The Life of an Eskimo" illustrating the adventures, joys, and sorrows of an Eskimo. Second: "The Life of Santa Claus". Santa lives up here the year around and I am taking his pictures of what the does. Third: "A Year with the Eskimos" by Mrs. Kleinschmidt. It illustrates what a woman sees and experiences up here in the north."[40]

This time he chartered a fifty-ton, two-masted schooner, *Notatak*, and headed once again for Siberia with his wife and Ray Wise in tow.[41] Results were so good that Kleinschmidt's still photos of their hunting exploits and of the Siberian Eskimos they encountered ran full page in the *New York Times*.[42] The impressive spread was headed by a picture of Essie in Eskimo regalia pouring tea for a group of Eskimo women decked out in traditional furs. It was supposed to have been taken in the sunlit interior of an Eskimo snow house, despite the fact that igloos were generally dark and that Siberian or Alaskan Eskimos never built them. Still, Greenland Inuit did build snow block shelters, and because they'd been featured in Flaherty's film, Kleinschmidt figured that his audiences would expect one. It did double duty as a set for *The Life of an Eskimo*, later renamed *Primitive Love*, which the moviemaker billed as "taken from the real life of an Eskimo family."[43]

They recruited Jimmie Ahkla as part of the cast. Wise, now nearly six feet tall and exotically handsome, played the lead. He also gamely donned a woman's parka to double as an Eskimo maiden who had to be rescued from an ice floe when the local girl engaged as his leading lady refused to take the risk. Once again, Kleinschmidt staged his drama on Nome beach shore ice, and this time the locals turned out in droves to watch. Wise looked so unladylike floating out to sea on a small, icy slab that Kleinschmidt had to shoot his rescue at considerable distance, nearly drowning his star in the process. Everyone, including the film crew, had a hilarious time. And Jimmie and Ray discovered they enjoyed entertaining them.[44]

After Wise wrapped up his assignment with Kleinschmidt, he reclaimed his old job on the *Silver Wave* which, finally released by the Soviets, was back on the mail run under the command of Captain John Hegness. The hardy Norwegian was famous for having won the first All-Alaska Sweepstakes sled dog race in 1908, but he was equally respected as a seaman, and Wise was pleased to have him as a boss.

Hegness was a close friend of famed Norwegian explorer Roald Amundsen, having taught him how to run dogs while they were neighbors in Nome,[45] and other international adventurers sought him out. In mid-August at Point Hope, Hegness picked up Knud Rasmussen, the short, boyish-looking Dane who was finishing his fifth Thule Expedition via dog team across arctic America without a photographer. The expedition's filmmaker, Leo Hanson, had gone off on the *Teddy Bear* with Captain Joe Bernard, who was attempting to rescue the crews of some ships about to be crushed in the ice pack off Barrow. Captain Hegness, who had once been Kleinschmidt's neighbor in Teller and knew of Ray's career as a cameraman for him, suggested Rasmussen hire the Eskimo to fill in. As expected, one of the ice-bound ships, the *Arctic*, was soon smashed to bits, but its crew escaped with the *Lady*

THE BEGINNINGS OF ALASKA'S SLED DOG RACING HERITAGE

From the time the last boat of the year left Nome in October until the arrival of the next season's first boat in June, pioneer residents were cut off from the world by nearly 1,000 miles of snow and ice, with only the telegraph and weekly mail delivery by government carriers driving dog teams for communication. Dog teams also provided the main form of private transportation, and drivers anxious to test their animals and make wagers delighted in holding races. To better organize and raise substantial cash prizes, race lovers formed the Nome Kennel Club in 1907 and one year later staged the first All-Alaska Sweepstakes, a 408-mile sled dog race from Nome to Candle and back.

John Hegness's winning time for the first event was 100 hours, 15 minutes. Two years later this was bested by John "Iron Man" Johnson, who made the run in 74 hours, 14 minutes. Amazingly, Johnson's record stood until 2008, when Mitch Seavey of Sterling covered the distance in 61 hours, 29 minutes.

OFF TO SIBERIA. Or maybe not. At the suggestion of Capt. Joseph Bernard (left), Danish explorer Knud Rasmussen hired Ray Wise as photographer for their brief voyage aboard the *Teddy Bear* to the Russian coast in 1924. Still in the throes of a revolution, officials there would not give the Dane permission to travel without a military escort and refused to let the rest of the party land. *Courtesy of Alaska and Polar Regions Collections, University of Alaska Fairbanks, from Joseph F. Bernard Collection*

Kindersly, which had been temporarily ice-bound. Luckily, the government boat that policed the Arctic, the revenue cutter *Boxer*, arrived in time to pick up the stranded sailors, so the *Teddy Bear* returned to Nome, where Rasmussen chartered it for a trip to Siberia.[46]

Always eager to work with professionals, Ray accepted Rasmussen's offer to stay on as Hanson's assistant for the Russian voyage and was pleased to learn that Earl Rossman, a famous big game hunter and travel photographer from New York, would also be aboard. Rossman, who was a friend of Stefansson's, had just spent the winter in Wainwright shooting the northern lights on 400 feet of a new kind of film that was in color. Glumly, he confided he had been unable to develop the footage before a small Eskimo lad opened all his film tins, ruining everything but eighty feet.[47] Nor did Rossman's luck improve. Unnerved by the heavy northwest gale the *Teddy Bear* had encountered off Sledge Island, he asked to be dropped off at Teller to catch a mail boat back to Nome. Crewmembers, who'd been aboard when Captain Bernard picked up the New Yorker at Wainwright a month earlier, suggested his desertion had more to do with Edna Claire Wallace than the weather. The pretty young woman, who Rossman introduced as his assistant cameraman and writer,[48] was actually a magazine writer who, they said, had lived off the generosity of a couple of wealthy arctic traders before attaching herself to the gullible Rossman.[49]

The Russian trip turned out to be a disappointment, delayed by horrible weather from which Captain Bernard had to seek shelter behind various islands. Rasmussen, exhausted from his long expedition and the wallowing of the little ship, slept much of the time. Then, when they finally did make it to Emmatown on Russia's East Cape, well-armed Soviet officials refused to let them land, insisting that the explorer must sail on to the town of Whalen[50] for official permission. There was no way Captain Bernard could buck the northerly wind off East Cape Peninsula to sail there, so Rasmussen hired a guide and made the journey overland to the next town. A day later he returned much disheartened because officials refused him permission to talk to any Eskimos unless a soldier accompanied him.

Captain Bernard, who knew many of the Siberians and had finally been allowed ashore, introduced the Dane to a few Emmatown Natives living near East Cape whom he was allowed to interview under the watchful surveillance of Russian soldiers. The Eskimos were delighted with their visitor whose language they could clearly understand. "This man has been with the Eskimo a long time and he must have been here before because he speaks as we do!" they marveled, not realizing that the famed Dane was part Inuit himself. But when the Soviets refused to allow Hanson and Wise to come ashore with cameras, Rasmussen finally gave up and they headed back to Nome.

The next morning, September 19, they encountered the same ice pack that had crushed the ship off Barrow, and their engine broke down. Captain Bernard tied the *Teddy Bear* to ground ice for the crew to repair it and went ashore to bring a few Eskimos back for Rasmussen to meet. Their meeting was brief. In a couple of hours, the engine was working again and the *Teddy Bear* headed across the Bering Strait. About ten miles out, they encountered four bull walrus snoozing on a cake of ice. Rasmussen wanted one for a specimen for a museum in Copenhagen, so Captain Bernard took the two Greenland Eskimos from the Danish party and paddled out to shoot all the animals. They also stopped at Little Diomede and King Islands,[51] which was nothing new to Wise, who had been there often with Kleinschmidt and the mail boat. About the only unusual thing Ray had to report when they arrived back in Nome two days later was that he had been arrested by the Soviets when they confiscated all the expedition's film.[52]

Rasmussen lingered in Nome for about a month, until the last boat arrived before freezeup and he had to choose between spending the winter and going home. Old-timers were fond of saying, "Even God leaves on the last boat,"[53]

and the town settled back to sleep through the long darkness.

There was a growing Eskimo community living in sod houses on the sand spit by the Snake River, but Ray found it more convenient to room in town because he'd taken back his water delivery route. Happily, he settled in for his weekly celluloid fix at the Dream Theatre, followed by occasional stops at the public library, the billiard parlor, and, on Saturday nights, the Eagle Dance Hall, where the orchestra consisted of a piano, a violin, and a drum. Men seriously outnumbered the women at this popular entertainment spot, so the dance master pinned patches on a number of coattails, signifying that those chosen were girls for a waltz or two, and everybody took turns. Gertrude Becker, who was now thirteen and getting more beautiful by the month, was not allowed to attend, but there were a number of Eskimo girls who found Ray charming, so he played the field.[54]

He also took occasional days off to go hunting with Jimmie Ahkla. His friend had married a beautiful girl from Golovin named Trixie, whose father, a wealthy white miner and fur farmer named James Berry, had also deserted the family. She was, however, well off because her grandfather, a cannery watchman and successful deer man, had given her a little herd. Trixie had been attending the fourth grade in Council when her teacher suggested that there was a nice young herder in Igloo whom she should get to know. Then Jimmie's neighbors, his former teacher, Harry Reese, and Harry's wife, Irena, began lobbying for him to meet a very bright little girl in Council. Trusting the Reeses, Jimmie hitched up his sled deer, made the trip, and was impressed. Trixie was as strong willed as she was bright, but she was also charming and accomplished. She spoke excellent English, played the

WISE AND KLEINSCHMIDT WITH SUSPICIOUS POLAR BEAR. Despite the fact that they worked closely for more than three years, this is the only surviving photo of Frank Kleinschmidt and his protégé Ray Wise together. One might guess there was a bit of danger involved in the job. *Photo courtesy of Kleinschmidt descendant Peg MacGowan*

piano beautifully, and sang with the clear soprano singing voice of an angel.[55]

It turned out to be a real love match. They had a little boy named Miles, whom Ray adored, and he came to think of them as his family. Jimmie was talking about moving where he could make more money, however, and Wise began to consider his own future. He didn't want to spend his life as a water boy. Sailing was seasonal, and he certainly couldn't depend on work as a photographer or an actor. It would take nothing short of a disaster, however, to provide direction.

In early January 1925, several Native youngsters came down with sore throats. Initially it didn't occur to Curtis Welch, Nome's only doctor, that the problem was anything but a common cold or maybe tonsillitis. Welch had never encountered a case of diphtheria and lacked a proper lab to detect the disease. So not until January 21, following the death of two Eskimo children down on the sand spit, did he report an epidemic. The city council immediately declared quarantine. School was canceled and so were all social activities, including shows at the Dream Theatre. The local paper advised frequent hand washing with a mild soap like Ivory, but what was really needed was an antitoxin. Although Dr. Welch had ordered some the previous summer, it had failed to arrive. Everything Welch had was outdated, and he didn't have very much of that. What he *did* have before the end of that month was twenty-two confirmed cases, fifty contacts, five deaths, and only telegraph communication with the outside world.[56]

The nearest antitoxin serum was in Anchorage, more that 600 miles distant, and a backup supply was en route from Seattle via a steamship headed for Seward. Flying the serum to Nome was considered, but many thought it impossible to equip men to endure aviation temperatures averaging 46 degrees below zero. The idea was abandoned completely when no suitable planes were available in Fairbanks.[57] Instead, the United States Signal Corps issued a call for dog team drivers to relay the serum from Nenana at the end of a rail link to Anchorage.[58]

Nenana musher Bill Shannon started the run the evening of January 27, battling temperatures as low as minus 62°Fahrenheit. His dogs' lungs began to bleed, but they managed to reach Tolovana before noon the next day, and Shannon handed the twenty-pound serum package over to the next driver. Leonard Seppalla, the main dog driver for a large Nome gold producer and the North's most famous dog racer, made the longest, roughest leg of the trip through fresh snow, gambling on a dangerous shortcut over the sea ice of Norton Sound.[59] But most of the glory went to Gunnar Kaasen, the last of twenty relay men, who stumbled into Nome behind his team in a blizzard carrying the antitoxin frozen but still usable, just seven days after the relay started. Exhausted, his eyes smarting from the bitter cold, Kaasen halted his sled at the door of the Miners & Merchants Bank at 5:30 a.m. February 2, lurched to his lead dog Balto, and collapsed muttering, "Damn fine dog."[60]

The mushers and their teams had beaten the existing record for covering the 675-mile trek by two full days, and Ray Wise was well aware through the local paper, the *Nome Nugget*, that the story had made international headlines.[61] Earlier, he had worked for Pathé newsman Merl LaVoy, who often covered Nome en route to climb mountains in Alaska's interior, and Wise correctly guessed that Pathé would be clamoring for newsreel footage. Borrowing a camera from a friend, he captured the harried Dr. Welch and a reenactment of the triumphant entry of Gunnar Kaasen and his team.[62] So when the wire and newsreel services hired Captain John Hegness, his former skipper from the *Silver Wave*, to mush to an ice-free port and then hand-carry the film on a southbound steamship, Wise's newsreel was included in the big sealed tin.

Hegness, who was not only a fine sea captain but had won the first Alaska Sweepstakes mushing from Nome to Candle in 1908, made good time to Seward, caught the first boat out, and then, three hundred miles north of Seattle, tossed the sealed tin to a small boat that met his steamship to deliver the film to a waiting seaplane. Five weeks from the day Hegness left Nome, photos of the epic venture hit the front page of the *Seattle Times* and made their way to movie theaters.[63] Wise got to see them, too, a few weeks later. "There was no holding me back after that," he later told a reporter. "The night I went down to the Dream Theatre to see the film, I made up my mind to reach Hollywood, under any circumstances. So I got a job on a steamer between Nome and a place called Kotzebue, to make enough money to get to California."[64]

Spring could not come soon enough for Ray Wise that year. ▪

Four

HOLLYWOOD

A t twenty, Merl LaVoy had attempted to climb Mount McKinley with two friends, hoping to prove that an earlier summit triumph claimed by some partying Alaskan sourdoughs was a hoax. It was LaVoy's third try, and his team was turned back by bad weather just a few hundred feet from the summit. A year later, the distinction of making the first successful ascent of Alaska's highest peak was officially awarded to Walter Harper, an Athabascan Indian guide who was first to the top. Hudson Stuck, Alaska's Episcopal archbishop, Harry Karstens, and Robert Tatum, had ascended the South Peak (the true summit) on June 7, 1913. But that didn't sour Wisconsin-born LaVoy on Alaska.[1] He was addicted, and his job producing movies for Pathé News gave him ample opportunity to travel the territory.

Exactly when he hired Ray Wise as an assistant cameraman is not known, for LaVoy was often in Nome. They came to know each other well, however, and the rugged newsman treated Ray not as a hired hand or apprentice but as a fellow professional.[2] Their relationship grew stronger after Ray sent his valuable footage of the diphtheria epidemic to Pathé, and he turned to LaVoy for career advice.

When Wise's edited film of the diphtheria toxin run finally arrived back in Nome, the understanding manager of the Dream Theatre had screened it just for him, again and again. "The focus was off, here and there; one of the sequences was badly overexposed and some of the others were panned too rapidly," Wise recalled with embarrassment. But the local audience loved it, and he'd done well enough to sell it to Pathé.[3] Certainly he could learn.

LaVoy, who was then helping arrange for Nome musher Gunnar Kaasen and his dogs to make a Hollywood movie, was encouraging. LaVoy himself had a part in Sol Lesser's *Balto's Race to Nome*, a movie that would be released in May 1925,[4] and he suggested to Ray that if he wanted to try Hollywood, he should go while the diphtheria run was still fresh in the public mind.[5] Meanwhile, Frank Kleinschmidt was heavily promoting his *Santa Claus* movie for release during the next Christmas season in hopes of earning enough

◀ **ONE OF THE RESIDUAL BENEFITS OF TINSELTOWN.** The young photographer took advantage of his new job to meet movie stars and starlets. This photo, which he sent home to his sister, Lorena, was made just after he filmed *Air Circus*. *Photo courtesy of Lorena Coats*

A HOLLYWOOD PROFESSIONAL AT LAST. By 1929, Ray had gained notice at Fox Studios for his work as an assistant cameraman, and studio manager Ben Jackson (left) decided some publicity shots would be in order. Ray's good looks and acting talents would continue to go unnoticed for several more years, however, even after amateur producer Frank Kleinschmidt engineered a modest publicity campaign for him as star of their Alaska venture *Primitive Love*.

Photo courtesy of Lorena Coats

cash to edit the footage in which Ray starred. With luck, *Primitive Love* would premiere in about eighteen months, and Wise wanted to be there.

Jimmie Ahkla and his family, which included a new baby named Billy, had just been hired by an Ohio businessman to travel the eastern United States in a theater act with a small herd of reindeer. Jimmie was to exhibit the deer and put them through their paces. Trixie would be playing the piano and singing simple, faith-based songs, some of them in Eskimo. Little Miles and even the new baby were to be part of the act, too, all dressed in traditional furs. And there would be an interpreter, although Trixie and Jimmie spoke excellent English. The idea was that if they appeared to know English too well, no one would take them for authentic Eskimos, Jimmie explained with a chuckle. If playing dumb was what it took to get into show business, see the States, and maybe visit their teachers, Irena and Harry Reese, who had recently moved to Pennsylvania, he and Trixie could do it.

The Ahklas were planning to leave on the last boat of the season, and Ray made up his mind to follow suit.[6] That summer he saved nearly everything he earned as a crewman on a power schooner that plied the route between Nome and Kotzebue and pursued odd jobs while on shore leave. By early fall, he'd amassed enough cash to make the trip, and he signed on as crew to work his passage south.

The problem was that Wise was a naïve traveler, and on the way—perhaps during the stopover in Seattle—he was mugged by two thugs who stole his savings along with his suitcase.[7] Then, arriving at the Port of Los Angeles without a dime in his pocket or a change of clothes, he discovered the port wasn't in Los Angeles at all, but about twenty-five miles south in a tough little town called San Pedro. Obtaining directions, he walked first to Los Angeles and then on to Hollywood, a trip which, had he not been terribly hungry, he might have enjoyed in the bright California sunshine, gawking at the grand hotels, stores, and night clubs in an exciting bustle of traffic. There were expensive automobiles everywhere, not just Model T Fords. The intersection at Wilshire and Western was said to be the busiest in the world, crossed by seven million cars a year.[8]

Topping a small mountain just behind the sprawling settlement was a sign that read HOLLYWOODLAND and was lit by 4,000 light bulbs after dark.[9] The temperature was so perfect no one wore a coat. Often the air smelled of orange blossoms. It was, indeed, the magic land Ray had dreamed of. And he wanted to stay.

Just in the nick of time he managed to locate Merl LaVoy, who fed him, loaned him 100 dollars, and also found him an entry-level job at Fox Movie Studios, where the photographer knew all the producers of Movietone Newsreels. "I started in digging ditches, then fed the incinerators on the sets. After that I was a stage sweeper," Wise recalled. Yet even the routine manual labor at Fox delighted him.[10]

The motion picture business had only recently moved from the East Coast to Hollywood, becoming the eleventh biggest industry in the nation, with earnings to spare.[11] The climate was magic, with about 320 perfect days a year. Twentieth Century Fox was not only the newest but the most wonderful of the Hollywood studios, settling first on cowboy star Tom Mix's old ranch and ending with 300 acres of parks and flower beds (later called Century City) and hundreds of gardeners to take care of them.[12] Even digging ditches and sweeping stages, Wise got to see some of the most famous people in the industry, like Louise Dresser, Tyrone Power, and director Howard Hawks. But the Alaskan didn't aspire to be a groupie or a stage sweeper, so after three months on the lot, making less money than he could have in Alaska doing the same work, he approached an

executive and asked for work on a camera crew. Merl LaVoy's recommendation was helpful and probably saved him from being fired his first day as an assistant cameraman, which proved a disaster. Less than an hour on the job, he dropped a heavy motion picture camera that cost $1,000 to repair.

"That was in 1926, and any betting man would quote very slim odds that Mala [a name Wise would later adopt as his own] would hold his job after that," a reporter for the film industry wrote in 1951.[13] But the assignment required focusing the camera manually by estimating the distance from subject to lens and moving the focal distance markings on the barrel. This had to be done *without looking through the viewfinder*, which was the domain of the head cameraman. Few possessed that skill, but LaVoy had claimed Wise was a natural, and the would-be hire quickly proved himself. In fact, Wise had already mastered the difficult "feather focus" which made distance shifts unnoticeable. He was as unobtrusive as he was efficient at placing marks on the floors of sets so actors would know where to stand. And he also did well as second cameraman, shooting negatives for the European market.[14]

What he didn't understand of the movie crew's jargon, he quickly figured out. He failed to panic, as did most novices, the first time he heard the head electrician, known as a "gaffer," yell, "Kill the baby and hit Mama Dietz." Watching quietly, he observed that the baby was a small light the cameraman used to reflect into actors' eyes, making them sparkle, while Mama Dietz was the big, broad light placed under the camera to illuminate the whole set. Later, he would learn that it was named after the wife of Ralph Dietz, who had invented much of the lighting equipment still used by the industry today.[15]

With LaVoy's help, Ray Wise was soon a card-carrying member of Hollywood's fledgling International Alliance of Theatrical Stage Employees, and none too soon. For the

A HOLLYWOOD PIONEER

Even if Ray had never stepped in front of a camera, he still would be remembered in Hollywood as a pioneer because he arrived at the dawn of movie-making's most exciting era.

Technicolor, introduced just a couple of years earlier, was still in the experimental stages and sound was crude at best. In 1926, Warner Brothers made *Don Juan*, the first movie with a pre-recorded score and synchronized sound system called Vitatone. Although reviews were good, the lions of the industry paid little attention until Warners topped that with *The Jazz Singer* in the fall of 1927, boasting the first human voice ever heard in a movie feature.

Other studios remained reluctant to invest in audio equipment, however, with the exception of Fox, which had already pioneered the use of Movietone sound in the production of a newsreel that showed Lindbergh taking off for the first successful plane solo across the Atlantic in May 1927, and later it was used again in filming a reception for the flyer given by President Calvin Coolidge and a speech by Italian dictator Benito Mussolini.

In 1928, Ray was assistant cameraman for *Air Circus*, a bold aviation film billed by Fox as "part talkie," and his studio's considerable investment in that medium thereafter is sometimes credited for its future success.

newsman went off on a long assignment in Samoa, leaving the Alaskan to fend for himself.

Filling the gap were Frank Kleinschmidt and his wife, Essie, who had moved from New York to a house just off Hollywood Boulevard on Carlos Avenue, in the hopes of getting a better footing in the movie business. Ray was sick much of the time, they observed with alarm. He suffered from frequent nose bleeds. He complained that his feet hurt, probably from walking too much pavement. He had a bout with rheumatic fever. A doctor warned that he had high blood pressure; that he should return to Alaska. Wise refused.[16] Concerned not only for his physical welfare but also worried about his moral fortitude in the Hollywood wilds, the Kleinschmidts found him a room with Elmer and Laura George just beyond Griffith Park on Edenhurst. Elmer was a civil engineer with the gas company and Laura was French Canadian like Essie, and a family friend. The Georges already had one lodger, Howell Stengel, who was four years older than Wise and also in the movie business. Mrs. George was over forty and the motherly sort, who occasionally voiced concern lest Ray fall in with fast women, but she had worked as a movie extra in her youth and was soon dedicated to helping him build his career. It was support Wise needed. He settled in happily in the accommodations, which were right on the streetcar route to the studio, and his health improved.[17]

During the movie season of 1926–1927, Warner Brothers had released nine films with musical sound tracks, and that fall there was Al Jolson's *Jazz Singer*, the first full-length movie with synchronized dialogue sequences.[18] Fox, which had purchased the rights to several sound systems, countered with Movietone talkies, producing both features and newsreels. Enter the "barney," a fitted cover that was put over cameras to cut out their noisy, whining grind in close quarters.[19] Cameramen were trying out color films, something Earl Rossman had mentioned to Wise some three years earlier. Everyone was experimenting with new shooting techniques and trying to photograph stories in original ways. Ray was delighted to be in the forefront of this technical revolution. But he was equally interested in screenplays.

No longer limited to once-a-week showings at Nome's Dream Theatre, he took in two or three movies each week at a choice of plush Hollywood theaters. Finally, he had gotten to see Robert Flaherty's *Nanook of the North*, a drama which was certainly as engrossing as its reviews had led him to believe. But watching Eskimo people portrayed as cave men and women, hunting with spears, and eating with their hands, bothered him. Earl Rossman's *Kivalina of the Ice Lands*, shot in Wainwright, provided more of the same, with ice igloos, spear hunting, and much eating of raw meat.[20] The northern lights footage that Rossman claimed was the first portrayal of the phenomenon on color film did impress Wise, but he grew angry all over again when he read the photographer's book *Black Sunlight*. "Eskimo intelligence is low in that it is incapable of sustained thought; nor is it original or creative," Rossman wrote. "Their forte lies in mimicry. Their language is one of prefixes and suffixes and is musical because of a heavy sprinkling of open vowels in it. Conversation is carried on in rather high pitch and with many inflections. Owing to their keen sense of mimicry, a word or two with gesticulation manages to convey the complete idea."[21] This in 1927, when Ray's uncle, John, made more money fur trapping in one week than Rossman probably did in a month. So much for mimicry.

The Alaska-Siberian travelogues of showmen Captain Jack Robertson, a former British war ace who had shot down nine enemy airplanes, and champion archer Arthur Young, were a refreshing change, in that they focused on wild game and the team's hunting skills, leaving the Eskimos in peace.[22]

MERL LAVOY AT HOME IN ALASKA. One of Pathé News photographer Merl LaVoy's favorite haunts was Alaska in the early 1920s, and he sometimes hired Ray Wise as his Nome assistant. Later LaVoy was responsible for getting the young Eskimo a job as an assistant cameraman at Fox Studios in Hollywood. This photo, taken in 1932, shows LaVoy having embarked on a rescue mission on Mount McKinley, which was probably his last trip to the Far North. *Courtesy of Alaska and Polar Regions Collections, University of Alaska Fairbanks, from the Francis P. Farquhar Papers*

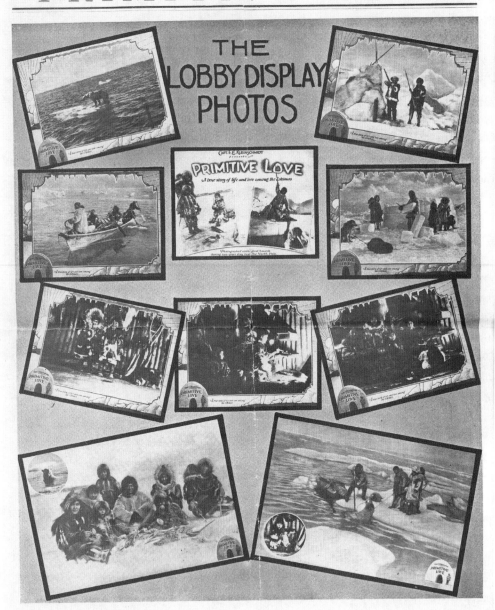

"PRIMITIVE LOVE"

THE LOBBY DISPLAY PHOTOS

◀ *PRIMITIVE LOVE* **LOBBY POSTERS**. Frank Kleinschmidt offered theater owners a wide variety of posters to promote his Nome-based epic. Note Ray Wise far left in the bottom picture. And, according to old timers who watched the filming, Ray is also seen bottom right dressed as a woman because the show's leading lady refused to hop from iceberg to iceberg. *Photos courtesy of Peg MacGowan, Kleinschmidt descendant*

On another front there was Columbia's *Justice of the Far North*, an epic about a noble, young Eskimo trying to reclaim his sweetheart, who lets herself be degraded by not one but *two* wicked white traders, while her pure little sister keeps her virtue. That the Eskimos in the show were portrayed with a bit more style and class than usual was easily explained by the fact that the entire cast was white. Critics gave them credit for "standout" performances, and Wise kept his opinions to himself.[23]

Then, in May 1927, it was his turn, for Kleinschmidt finally pulled together *Primitive Love* and got Mordaunt Hall, the famous *New York Times* writer, to review it. Which turned out to be a mistake. "An attempt to link romance with life in an igloo is made in Captain F. E. Kleinschmidt's Arctic production, 'Primitive Love,' now decorating the Cameo screen," the reviewer began. "The caption writer appears to have tried to jazz-up the frozen North in his valiant struggle to live up to the sense of the main title. There are in this subject a number of the passages that recall Robert J. Flaherty's memorable feature, 'Nanook of the North,' but except for these sequences depicting polar bears and walruses, this current attraction suffers by comparison with its predecessor."

The writer did concede that "on several occasions Kleinschmidt added an interesting note," and he also detailed the film's plot, which admittedly was as simplistic as it sounded. "Ok-Ba-Ok is described as a modern cave man: Sicca Bruna is his wife; Wanga is the flapper daughter, and Amutuk is the sensible daughter; Patunuk and Itak are rivals for the hand of Wanga, and Annok is Ok-Ba-Ok's grandmother," Hall reported.

"One of the sober titles sets forth that Annok feels that she must go forth to her death. She explains that her wrists are weak and her eyes are too dim to follow the needle. The old woman is supposed to be ready to crawl out onto the chilly wastes and stagger along until she perishes from exhaustion."

Hall's highest praise in this review went to footage from one of Kleinschmidt's previous movies of a mother polar bear and her cub. As for *Primitive Love*, Hall made it clear that the actors were upstaged by the filmmaker's fine wildlife scenes.[24]

Nor was the show business magazine *Variety* much kinder. "Elements of romance and drama are not well staged for effect," it read. "These need the aid of art and subterfuge. Here it is the titles that tell most of the drama, while the action by Native actors—the real thing, of course—are rather drab."[25]

Disheartened, Ray Wise purchased a typewriter to see if he could do better. His screen treatment, titled *Modern Eskimos*, is the straightforward tale of Tautuk, an orphaned young reindeer herder who has very little going for him except the love of a beautiful young woman whose parents insist she marry for wealth. The approved suitor illegally disqualifies Tautuk during a race at the annual reindeer fair, but Tautuk returns the next year to win both race and maiden. While the costumes, songs, and mores are traditional, Ray makes much of the fact that the couple "madly rub noses" and then go right back to work after their marriage service. There are no snow houses. No old ladies are set out on the ice to die; no feasting on raw meat. Nor are there any bears and walrus to upstage the actors.

The four-page summary, complete with dialogue and camera angles, was certainly as solid as many of the arctic films[26] he had suffered through, but Wise failed to sell it. Then, suddenly, his job at Fox became so promising that he put the project aside. The studio had purchased *Frozen Justice*, which was based on a meaty novel by Ejnar Mikkelsen about a beautiful Eskimo girl who abandons her Native husband to run off with a white sailor who has deserted his whaling ship.

The outsider debases and then deserts the young woman, leaving her to the bars of Candle, where she of course comes to no good. It was pretty much *Justice in the Far North* revisited, but that film had made money and Mikkelsen was thought to be a better draw because he focused more on the traditional Inupiat life.[27]

F. W. Murnau wanted to direct the picture. Famed for bringing *Dracula* to the screen, the handsome German was regarded by many as the best silent filmmaker of them all, and he wanted a dramatic entry into "talkies." He had just produced *Sunrise* for Fox with resounding acclaim, and the studio scrambled to keep him happy, assigning his assistant, thirty-year-old Ewing Scott, to join a special Alaska expedition to get preproduction footage of authentic Eskimo life.[28] Charles Clarke, twenty-eight, a veteran cameraman who had served in the army during World War I, was picked as expedition leader. In 1926, he had shot *Rocking Moon* for the studio in Sitka, Alaska, proving his management skills were as keen as his rare gift for shooting scenery.[29] When Scott suggested Wise, with whom he'd worked successfully on earlier films, Clarke readily agreed, not just because of the young Eskimo's shooting ability, but because he realized they would need an interpreter.

Ewing Scott had bailed out of the family fruit-packing business in 1920 to enter the movie trade as a technician, then moved up to become an assistant to Murnau in 1926 when the director was first lured to America. A jack-of-all-trades, including working behind the camera, Scott's specialty at the time was costuming and props. It would be his job to make certain that any Eskimos they photographed looked traditionally authentic, and also to protect Murnau's interests. "I guess it was he who fired me [up] with the idea of making unusual pictures," Scott told the press, adding that Murnau was a great fan of the documentary work of Robert Flaherty.[30]

Hoping to find Alaska's most primitive environment, Fox settled on the farthest north Eskimo village of Barrow, which had no electronic communications whatsoever with the outside world. Captain Jack Robertson, the British World War I ace who had just spent two years making movies in Alaska and Siberia, was hired for his skills with a relatively compact documentary camera called the "Akeley." Also assigned was Virgil Hart, who had many credits as an assistant director at Fox and was elected to hold the purse strings.[31]

The five men arrived in Fairbanks, last stop on the Alaska railroad system, early in May 1927, with 2,800 pounds of movie-making equipment, and hired Noel Wien to fly them to Barrow. The pilot's contract required two flights each for two aircraft: Wien with his roomy Stinson, and Russ Merrill, with whom he teamed, flying his open Travel Air biplane from Lockheed. Neither had ever flown to Barrow, but Wien had just pioneered the mail run to Nome, while Merrill, a former navy pilot, had a good record out of Anchorage. They left on May 13, a gorgeous day with no snow on the ground and scarcely a cloud in the sky, with Merrill ferrying Clarke and Robertson with the luggage, while Hart oversaw the camera equipment in Wien's Stinson. Wise and Scott were left to take care of business in Fairbanks but planned to follow on a second flight. They maintained radio contact until the pilots made it to Wiseman, their refueling stop about 200 miles north. Beyond that, they all knew there could be no contact, but good weather appeared to be holding. There was no snow on the south side of the Brooks Range, and the planes had only 315 miles to go.

Both pilots managed to maneuver their low-flying craft through the tricky mountain passes and out onto the arctic slope before weather closed in on them. Wien's map showed nothing beyond the mountains. The land was still covered with snow, and the Colville River they hoped to follow north soon disappeared in ground fog. Realizing their compasses couldn't be trusted in the region because of strong magnetic deviation, they decided to land and wait out the weather. This proved easy for Wien who had balloon tires, but Merrill's plane with its six-inch wheels was soon mired in snow. The next day being fair, they decided Wien and Hart would fly off to Barrow with some of the movie equipment and return with whatever it took to dig Merrill and his passengers out. It was a plan that probably would have worked if Wien had been able to relocate Merrill's plane. But on the return trip he just couldn't find it.

Blissfully unaware of this hitch, Russ Merrill and his two passengers settled into their cold encampment, taking turns sharing one sleeping bag in the Lockheed's cramped cockpit and camping in a frigid snow house they built for additional space. Clarke kept himself amused by reading the script for *Trader Horn*, a soon-to-be movie he thought he might like to work on, hoping to dream blissfully through the freezing nights about being in the Belgian Congo. Since neither Clarke's nor Robertson's digestive systems agreed with the chocolate that made up the bulk of Merrill's survival food, they limited themselves to half a cup of rice per man per day and the few flea-bitten squirrels they could catch.[32] Then, after a week with no rescue, Clark and Robertson decided to walk out, believing they were only 60 miles from the village when it was actually 115 miles distant. Merrill, who had hopes of eventually getting his plane off the ground, gave them his pocket compass and the bulk of his supplies, planning to follow them via air, but after his craft nosed over three days later, bending a propeller, he, too, set out for Barrow on foot.[33]

Meanwhile, back in Fairbanks, Scott and Wise were beside themselves. Scott, who had been promoted from costume director to "leader of the expedition" by local reporters *and*

ALASKA'S HIGH FLYER

Wisconsin-born barnstormer Noel Wien went on to become one of Alaska's most famous and long-lived pilots. Flying north in 1924 at age twenty-five, he established himself by becoming the first to fly from Fairbanks to Seattle, Fairbanks to Nome, beyond the Arctic Circle, across the Bering Strait, and round trip between Alaska and Asia. Later, with three brothers, he established Alaska's first airline.

Ray stayed in touch with the pilot following their aborted movie-making venture and the two men became lifelong friends. Wien died in Washington State in 1977, and the line he helped found was liquidated at a profit while on the verge of bankruptcy in 1985. At that time it was ranked the second oldest airline in the United States.

Fox Studios, had attempted to get a competing airline to fly a rescue mission without success, even after he got Fox to promise payment that was four times what Noel Wien had charged. The rival pilot taunted him with a rumor from Wiseman that none of the Fox crew could have survived. Ray Wise busied himself by interviewing anyone who arrived in town from the north in an attempt to track down the rumors and ran as much interference for the harried Scott as he could. Finally, Scott managed to get Anchorage pilot Matt Nieminen to fly to Barrow with a radio and a member of the U.S. Signal

JOHN HEGNESS ON A WINNING STREAK. As good at sailing as he was at winning sled dog championships, Hegness hired Ray Wise to help run his mail boat, the *Silver Wave*, sometime in the early 1920s. Later Hegness would mush from Nome to Seward and then take steamboat passage to Seattle to deliver pictures taken during the Nome diphtheria epidemic of 1925. The package Hegness carried included movie footage shot by Wise, which was sold to Pathé News. *Photo courtesy of Hans Olav Lokken, Hegness descendant living in Norway*

Corps to report what was happening. But Nieminen's radio malfunctioned. He was not heard from again, and the press reported excitedly that three planes were now missing.[34]

What Scott and Wise couldn't know was that Nieminen was still on the job. Making it safely to Barrow, he had discovered Noel Wien was flying daily, in even marginal weather, in an attempt to locate the missing plane. Teaming up, with Hart as a spotter, the two pilots flew a grid, finally locating the abandoned Lockheed and, with it, Merrill's diary explaining when they had started walking and the direction in which they were heading.

On the return trip, some fifty miles south of Barrow, Nieminen spotted two men, but overflew them when he saw one (Robertson) was wearing Eskimo garb he'd discovered in a studio prop box. Only when he glimpsed the second man, Clarke, giving the Masonic distress signal, did he decide to land.[35] The faces of the two lost cameramen were black, their lips swollen twice the normal size, cracked open and oozing blood. Their toes were frozen, and Clarke could no longer move his feet. He had lost forty pounds and Robertson had lost thirty, both near starvation. Nieminen first attempted to feed them, then, realizing it might be a dangerous thing to do, rushed them to the Presbyterian hospital in Barrow, where their lives were saved.[36]

Two days later, on June 1, Ray Wise's old mail boat skipper, John Hegness, was out hunting near Cape Halkett, where he'd moved to run a trading post, when he spotted what he thought was a polar bear. Approaching carefully, he finally realized it was a sleeping man, dead, he thought, for he never moved until Hegness turned him over and shook him. "You wouldn't be going to Barrow, would you, and could you give me a lift?" Russ Merrill asked.

Ever the jokester, the old skipper replied straight-faced, "Why, no! I've already got too big a load."

Without a word, the starved, snow-blind, black-faced pilot staggered to his feet and started reeling down the trail toward Barrow, still fifty miles distant, until Hegness, who realized the untimeless of his humor, captured him and sledded him to safety.[37]

On June 4, Wise and Scott finally got word from Nieminen that their party was safe,[38] and one week later he flew them to Barrow with the most powerful radio Scott could buy. Clarke had recovered enough to film Nullagatuk, the local whaling festival, and Captain Robertson was hoping to head for Wainwright, where walrus were reported. But their studio, which had racked up $45,000 in bills for the expedition to date, pointed out that the Eskimo whaling season was over for the year, and called Hart, Clarke, and Wise back to the States immediately. Captain Robertson was allowed to proceed to Wainwright with Scott, who was to make sure the Eskimo hunters were traditionally garbed and carrying primitive weapons for some walrus shots. But that, too, proved a disappointment. Because of the warmth of advancing summer, the Natives had traded their furs for calico outfits, and they much preferred modern weaponry to spears in any season.[39] Even before Robertson and Scott returned to Hollywood with the bad news, Murnau scrapped *Frozen Justice*.[40]

The closest Wise had gotten to his family was when pilot Matt Nieminen flew the Fox crew over Johnny Herbert's saloon in Candle en route to Fairbanks and the railroad connection to a southbound steamship.[41] The studio immediately put him to work on Howard Hawks's first aviation movie, *Air Circus*. It was an exciting assignment, with the challenge of shooting fast-flying planes and pretty Sue Carroll playing the girl aviatrix, but Wise would rather have stayed in Alaska. Captain Jack Robertson returned the following year on his own to make a wonderful film called *Break Up*, later rated one of the best documentaries of all time. Clarke was confined to a studio lot to shoot another arctic sleeper, *The Sin Sister*, about a vaudeville dancer stranded somewhere in Alaska who is attacked by a fur trader. When director Charles Vidor questioned the credibility of the script, reasoning some of its characters could not have survived being lost in arctic snows for a week, the cameraman was offered as proof to the contrary, but otherwise felt a letdown.[42] Virgil Hart was named assistant director for *FleetWing*, about a young Arab and a slave girl, and *Chicken à La King*, about a man who wants to marry a chorus girl, and would remain an assistant director for the rest of his twenty-year career.[43] Ewing Scott, who sought a similar job, was finally promoted to assistant director for *The Woman from Hell* with beautiful Mary Astor starring as a girl who works a beach concession,[44] but he wasn't happy either. His old boss, F. W. Murnau, who had just won several Academy Awards for *Sunrise*, was headed off to Bora Bora with Robert Flaherty to make *Tabu: A Story of the South Seas*, so Scott was missing a chance to work with two of the greatest names in his industry.[45] Even worse, Scott had become smitten with the Arctic and would remain so for the rest of his life.

The next year, Lenore Ulric, a big-name Broadway star who had signed an annual contract with Fox for $650,000, appropriated Ejnar Mikkelsen's *Frozen Justice* title and had a screenplay written for it about a half-breed Nome dance hall girl who goes astray. Wise auditioned but was turned down. Because Ulric looked nothing like an Eskimo, an all-white cast was chosen with her husband, Sidney Blackmer, as the Eskimo lead.[46] Few Americans had ever seen an Eskimo, producers reasoned, so who would know the difference? Wise realized he was well out of it. The writers portrayed the Inupiat as racially inferior, not too bright, and lacking in good moral fiber.[47] Wise could hardly bring himself to watch the film, and the whole experience left him keenly discouraged. ∎

Scott Arctic Expedition

Photo
Pilot Noel

Five
A BOTCHED CAREER

O n his return from the Arctic, Ray Wise lost thirty pounds.[1] Beside herself, his devoted landlady, Mrs. George, kept asking him what was wrong and trying to feed him ice cream, which she knew was one of his favorite foods. But he couldn't explain it. He wasn't sick. He had just lost his appetite.

The job at Fox was going well. He was assigned increasingly complicated shoots with increasingly competent cameramen and famous directors. The California weather still seemed like heaven to him, and he loved the excitement of fast-growing Hollywood, especially after spending two months in backwater northern outposts that lost more population every year.

He had an amusing girlfriend. Actually, a couple of them. Mrs. George was an overenthusiastic chaperone, but he enjoyed great nights on the town with some of the studio gang.[2] And, at last, he was in touch with his sisters, who were finally old enough to write him letters and figure out how to get them past their stepmother. He first heard from Lorena, now a teenager, just after he overflew Johnny's place in Candle on his way back to Hollywood following the *Frozen Justice* disaster. Figuring Hilda would intercept his reply, Ray sent an answer, complete with several photos of himself with stars on the set of *Air Circus* and *Heart of Salome*, directly to Johnny Herbert, who quietly passed it on to the girls. Encouraged, Wise wrote asking if Lorena could send him a photograph of their mother, and she smuggled out a treasure. Yellowed by time, creased and battered, it was still a clear picture of Casina as a young woman, fresh, lovely, in her early teens, gazing squarely at the camera as she had so often gazed at him. Not unlike the photos Lorena had sent of herself, he thought. Then, realizing from her letters that his sister was as bright as she was beautiful, he eventually mustered courage to ask the Herberts that he be allowed to send her to a California school. Hilda, who was undoubtedly

◀ **A THREE-MAN INDEPENDENT PRODUCTION.** In 1931, Ray (left), producer Ewing Scott (center), and cameraman Roy Klaffki headed for Barrow to film one of Hollywood's first independent productions, released a year later as *Igloo*. Although they worked on a shoestring budget and had to borrow money from Scott's father to get back to Hollywood, they eventually made money on the film. Ray, who starred with an all-Eskimo cast, garnered publicity that would later serve him well. *Photo by Noel Wien, Mala Family Collection* depending on the girl as a nanny for the two youngsters she had recently given to Herbert, absolutely refused. What parents in their right mind would let an innocent fourteen-year-old girl move to Hollywood under the protection of a twenty-three-year-old bachelor, she argued. And she did have a point. Frustrated, Wise sent his sisters lavish gifts, which Hilda insisted they share with their half sisters. She also demanded that Lorena and Harriet write replies discouraging their brother from contacting them again.[3]

Wise's real problem, though, was his lagging acting career, something he'd hoped *Frozen Justice* would kickstart so his family might respect him. Despite bad reviews, Kleinschmidt was promoting *Primitive Love* with some success, actually getting Wise an occasional newspaper interview. But weakness in the script, plus Kleinschmidt's inexperience in directing much except polar bears and walrus, would not gain Wise the attention he needed to win better parts.

The stock market crash of October 29, 1929, followed by the closure of 9,000 banks nationwide, looked like it might put an end to the most ambitious dreams, especially for those working for Fox. Earlier that year, wealthy owner William Fox had been horribly injured in an automobile accident that killed his chauffeur. Barely back on his feet, his finances—already stretched to the limit by his hostile attempt to take over the Loew's theater chain—were all but wiped out. A December 6, 1929 tabloid headline screamed "Stock Market Crash Traps Movie Czar in $91,000,000 Debt." It was followed one day later with a staid front page announcement by the *Los Angeles Times* that the movie mogul had relinquished all control of his studio. Yet, surprisingly, while surviving executives scrambled to keep things afloat, and Fox himself battled an investigation that would later send him to jail on charges of bribery and perjury, the studio kept producing movies.[4] Motion pictures,

so the theory went, helped the public forget breadlines and hard times, and the movie colony, now jokingly referred to as "Tinseltown," never looked back.

"Hollywood has more neon lights than Broadway, it knows how to build stars and gardens and cities overnight," a *New York Times* writer conceded in 1930. "It is gayer, newer, brighter, and younger than anything in the history of man." And, of course as everybody knew, it was also kinky. "Socially it is a conglomeration of experiments, a laboratory without rules or habits of procedure, where the natives of various states and countries come to live together in a climate that imposes neither closed doors nor shuttered windows," the *Times* reporter declared. "Here are experiments in race mixture, in religion, in the scope and power of government; experiments in ways of living and dressing, in house-furnishing, in the selling and buying of food, in the essentials of ordering existence; experiments in emotion and in loyalties, experiments in morality."[5]

Wise had been too busy trying to establish himself to experiment much with morality, but he had watched with fascination as the city quadrupled in size, and the Sunset Strip, a three-square-mile area that bordered Hollywood where he lived and Beverly Hills, became one of the most famous hot spots in America. Outside the jurisdiction of the City of Los Angles, it was patrolled by the Los Angeles County sheriff, who had his hands full with end-to-end hotels and restaurants, bookie joints, gambling establishments, openly gay bars with cross-dressing performers, conventional night clubs and many that were not.[6] There were also more than 200 movie writers, gossip columnists, and correspondents stationed in Hollywood,[7] and even nonwriters thought they had a chance at selling a screenplay. So, as the Depression increased the chances of Fox going under, Wise again peddled his *Modern Eskimo* movie treatment. Movie columnist Robbin

Coons, who wrote a few publicity pieces for *Primitive Love* on Kleinschmidt's behalf, actually titled one of them "Cameraman Tries Hand at Writing: Eskimo Boy Writing Story of Far North Between Crank Turns."[8] But there were no takers.

Still, Ray had his day job, when thousands could not get jobs, and Jimmie Ahkla and his family were stranded in Pennsylvania, completely broke because the man who had backed their reindeer show so successfully for the past two years had gone broke and failed to pay them. There they were, the owners of thousands of reindeer in the Arctic, without a penny to get home. Luckily, Irena and Harry Reese, Jimmie's former teachers at Igloo who now lived in Pennsylvania, had taken them in, pleased to have someone with whom their children could once again converse in Eskimo. Ahkla had written that it looked like the Territorial Bureau of Education might pay their way home, but it was a cliff-hanger.

So, suddenly, were things in Hollywood. Fox had just introduced a wide screen film process called Grandeur, which projected twice the width of standard films, and sound technology called Movietone. To make the most of them, the studio was producing a string of films with Jeanette MacDonald, a beautiful performer whose voice was golden. But all the other studios were making musicals, too, causing the bottom to fall out of that market, and in August there were no new productions scheduled.[9]

Ray, however, was working with Ewing Scott on a complicated western that had been started earlier that year. Although the two men had become close in Alaska, Wise had seen very little of his friend since because Scott's career was on the rise. Director A. F. Erickson was so impressed with his work on *The Woman From Hell*, he hired Scott to assist him with Zane Grey's *The Lone Star Ranger* with Sue Carol and George O'Brien, and for another western, *Rough Romance*, with O'Brien and Helen Chandler. Then, director Sidney Lanfield enticed Scott to his camp, along with a twenty-three-year-old movie extra Scott had been using as a prop man, for the musical *Cheer Up and Smile*. The extra, whose stage name was John Wayne, proved such a standout in an unaccredited bit part, he was chosen by director Raoul Walsh to star in a western titled *The Big Trail*, and Scott went with him as assistant director. Raoul was an industry legend, who had begun his career assisting D. W. Griffith in *Birth of a Nation* and had risen swiftly to the top.[10]

Scott now counted himself lucky that F. W. Murnau had left him behind on his South Seas venture. Robert Flaherty had walked off the set, never to return, and the show became a producer's nightmare.[11] But *The Big Trail* was no picnic either. Wayne had been ill so long with a bout of dysentery that Raoul almost replaced him, and rumor had it that the fiery-tempered director had come close to beating to death costar Tyrone Power Sr. for forcing himself on leading lady Marguerite Churchill.[12] Wayne survived to do a wonderful job, and Power, too, made a fair recovery. But the movie—an epic about a pioneer wagon train headed for Oregon—seemed to have a cast of thousands to manage and was shot in the most uncomfortable locations across the American West.

Finally, one day in the summer of 1930, working in the scorching heat of Death Valley, Scott and Wise took a break to wipe off the sweat and catch up. Scott, too, had been writing a screenplay about Alaska, he confided. In fact, he'd written the lead role just for Ray. Company gossip led him to believe that Fox might not survive, and even if it did, he had visions of being trapped in the job of assistant director as long as their friend Virgil Hart, who seemed to hold the record for nonpromotion, remained.[13] Scott was now thirty-three. The only real chance he had at getting back to the Arctic and at being recognized as a director, he figured, was to mount

TINSELTOWN'S SPARKLE PALES

The motion picture industry, which got its start in New York and New Jersey shortly after the turn of the century, soon moved to Los Angeles, Southern California's major city, to take advantage of its bright sunlight and nearly perfect climate. Then, with an eye to cost-cutting, filmmakers migrated to less pricey open country north of town, buying up old ranches and junglelike settings that would do double duty as movie sets. Thus the famous, forty-five-foot-tall HOLLYWOOD sign, planted on a vacant hillside by real estate promoters in 1923 just before Ray Wise arrived, became an internationally recognized landmark as the popularity of motion picture entertainment grew to a worldwide craze.

Of course Hollywood's magic was mostly a trick of celluloid and studio public relations departments, which is why some jokingly referred to it as "Tinsel Town" after a glittering but flimsy decorative foil that was virtually worthless.

By 1930, the joke had become a grim one. Studios, initially slow to accept talkies, were suddenly producing too many of them, mostly bouncy musicals of which audiences quickly tired. Many producers had gone into debt in making the audio transition and experimenting with color films, and no one was quite sure how the industry would survive as the Great Depression worsened.

his own production. Not only did he have Alaska experience, but the last four productions he had overseen had taught him how to really cut costs. Unsuccessful in finding financial backing for his project, Scott and his wife Jane had moved in with Scott's parents and started banking every dime they could save to form a company he'd named Arctic Productions.

Ray found himself in a similar position with his acting career. He was twenty-four, while John Wayne, their leading man, was a year younger. Plus, the Eskimo had an additional worry because the motion picture industry was in the process of adopting a code that, among other nonsense, forbad interracial love scenes. If Ray had any hopes of a major romantic role, it would have to be with another "exotic." White leading ladies would be off limits to him, and he'd seen few other options for advancement in Hollywood. How much longer would Eskimo films continue to be a draw?

Ewing mopped his brow and stared out on the baking sands. "Wouldn't you like to be up in Alaska right now, instead of this desert heat?" he asked.

"You bet I would," Ray replied enthusiastically. And they cut a deal, quite fittingly with Ray's "sweat equity."[14]

Mounting an independent production in competition with the major studios was a daring move, especially in the face of the Depression, but Scott was as determined as he was desperate to become a major player. He had saved $5,000, most of which would be eaten up by travel expenses, but they needed a professional cameraman who was as tough and willing to take chances as they were. Roy Klaffki filled the bill. Born in California and early in the trade, he was one of fourteen founding members of the American Society of Cinematographers and a master of his craft. Although nearing fifty with a wife and fifteen-year-old daughter, Klaffki was a born but prudent risk taker and strong as an ox.[15] Better yet, from Wise and Scott's point of view, he'd been recently screwed over by the movie industry. Twice!

Klaffki's first mistake was taking a shooting assignment with violent-tempered Erich von Stroheim, a brilliant but arrogant Austrian actor turned director. Three other cinematographers had quit Stroheim by the time Klaffki came to work on his ill-fated film *The Wedding March*. Their excuse was not only Stroheim's temper tantrums, but that he thought nothing of working them thirteen hours without a break. The initially expensive film was way over budget by the time Klaffki got the job. Worse yet, the director insisted on using soft focus throughout, making it appear that the cameraman wasn't paying attention.

Although the film boasted superstars ZaSu Pitts and Fay Wray and the studio had invested $1,125,000 in it, *Wedding March* was shelved after preview, leaving the frustrated Klaffki with nothing to show for nearly half a year's work.[16] Nor was his next venture, the multimillion dollar *Hell's Angels* with quirky director Howard Hughes, much more satisfying. Hughes crashed a plane and was injured while playing a World War I ace, holding up shooting which—even discounting the accident—took forever. The final indignity, though, came when *Hell's Angels* won Oscars for cameramen Tony Gaudio and Harry Perry, while Klaffki, listed under the "camera and electrical department," received no honors.[17]

Wise, Scott, and Klaffki left Hollywood on February 25, 1931, arriving in Fairbanks early in March with high hopes and 1,500 pounds of equipment. Scott told a local reporter that they intended to fly to Wainwright, where the movie, titled *Manna*, would be shot by the end of June. It would portray the struggle of the Eskimos for existence and would be filmed entirely in the Arctic, he said. The scenario called for a whale hunt and the killing of a polar bear.[18]

Unfortunately, the only planes available were old, and pilots wanted $3,000 to make the trip. Scott balked at the

▶ **FAMILY VISIT.** After shooting *Igloo* in Barrow in 1931, Ray finally got a chance to visit his sister, Lorena, who was still living in Candle, but his stepmother was as hostile as always, and he didn't stay long. *Photo Courtesy of Lorena Coats*

"TWO Girls Wanted!"—Janet Gaynor is one of them. Al Green, left, directed the production for Fox and the first prints are in New York. The two cinematographers on the right are Irving Rosenberg and Ray Wise. Wise (in sweater) is Hollywood's only Esquimo.

BEFRIENDED BY BIGWIGS. It did not take Ray long to find a place in the movie industry. He made a local newspaper in a photo with two prominent movie-makers on what must have been one of his first filming assignments in 1927. He would remain well-connected throughout his long filming career.

exorbitant price for nearly a month until he learned that the territorial governor was looking for a way to get diphtheria antitoxin to Barrow to fight an epidemic. Thinking they might engender goodwill, he changed the location of the film and hired pilot Joe Crosson to fly them up with the serum and their camera gear.[19] However Rev. Henry William Greist, the Presbyterian doctor who ran a nine-bed hospital in Barrow as well as a parish that covered

about 120,000 square miles, was not pleased to see them, and the enmity was mutual. Scott would later describe Greist as "a racketeering missionary-storekeeper, who resented shoe-string expeditions invading his little dictatorship."

But unfortunately Greist was the wrong man to cross, especially during whaling season, which was all-important in Scott's script. "We'd wait around all the week fretting and nary a whale in sight," the frustrated director recalled. "Then on the Sabbath, there would be a gorgeous run. But the missionary absolutely forbade the Natives to work on the Sabbath. He not only made them all go to church, but insisted upon us attending, too—otherwise, he hinted, there might be some pretty drastic 'non-co-operation.' Those darned whales were sure in league with the missionary."

When the Eskimos sullenly refused to do a song-ritual sequence on the grounds it was against tradition to have it photographed, Greist upheld them. Even after the Natives relented, suggesting they would do it for a dollar per day *each*, Greist was on their side.

Worse yet, when two important Eskimo cast members died because of a flu epidemic and everyone else got sick, the doctor refused to open his nine-bed hospital. According to Scott, he was mad at his nurse, who had dared to defy him and go to a neighboring village to see her daughter through her pregnancy. Luckily, the conscientious nurse returned in time to bring everyone through their sickness without pay. An unsung heroine, they decided.

Scott was kept busy rewriting his script to cover deaths and other shooting disasters. It was all too much for Klaffki, who, according to Scott, "hated Eskimo country and spent most of his time weeping with self pity."[20] But Ray's assignment turned out to be the toughest because, while they'd found several candidates beautiful enough to be his leading lady, not one would agree to work with them. "The women up there are wooden, just lumps," Scott complained. "They stare at one with expressionless faces. I'd take them one by one and work on them—striving to discover one with a half-way intelligent smile."

Unbeknownst to Scott, the problem might have been related in part to the one strong backer who had come to their aid, U.S. Deputy Marshall Richard "Bert" Merrill. The lawman, who stood six feet two and was part black and part Oklahoma Indian, had arrived in the territory twenty-four years earlier and had amassed more Eskimo wives and children than the film crew could keep track of. But Merrill found a warm place for the team to live at minimal rent. He presented them with an old stove left behind by explorer Roald Amundsen. When the village of ice igloos they had rebuilt for the third time blew flat in a blizzard, Merrill was there with condolences. Self-taught beyond the third grade, he was a voracious reader with many skills. He was their guide and mentor, patching up a hundred misunderstandings, and eventually finding an old, white whaling captain from Bert's home base of Point Hope, who helped them shoot wonderful whaling and wildlife sequences, just when they'd given up.[21]

To a man, the little crew would remember Bert Merrill as their precious friend, but two years later the lawman would be sentenced to a three-year term in McNeil Island Penitentiary for incest.[22] Since this was a charge rarely prosecuted in tight-knit arctic communities, rumors of Merrill's sexual appetites—whether real or trumped up through vicious gossip—most certainly would have been known among the locals. The film crew's close association with him would have made them suspect, especially to village women. Fortunately, Ray Wise's air of innocence that had so enchanted Kleinschmidt was genuine, and he really worked at getting to know the young Inupiat woman who showed the most potential.

"It was Chee-Ak's charms that finally won the glimmer of a tender smile out of one of them," conceded Scott, who had adopted the habit of using Ray's Eskimo name. "I seized upon her as though I had discovered a Garbo. How we worked on that girl! I was prepared for the worst, but to my amazement, she really did fairly well, all told."

Once the filming was over, Wise hitched a ride on a flight to Candle with writer Jean Potter, a researcher for *Fortune* magazine who was writing a book on bush pilots. Hilda, true to form, refused to speak to him. Johnny let him sleep at the bar but allowed only a brief chance to see his sisters. Wise left to stay with the Ahkla family until he could catch the boat south.[23]

His friends Jimmie and Trixie had finally made it back to Alaska, deciding to settle in Nome so the children could start school there. But little Billy had just died, either from smallpox or scarlet fever. He'd gotten sick in the States, but the doctor had not believed he had anything serious. "Well enough to appear in the pageant," Trixie recalled the medical man saying. It was the little family's last stage appearance after two very exciting tours. But the Ahklas had a new baby, James, who they called Billy to help them over the loss. Miles had grown into a sturdy little fellow with a singing voice as fine as his mother's. And they were looking to the future.

Although the Ahkla reindeer herd had grown to about 3,000 animals, Jimmie was finding it hard to hold herders. There wasn't a steady market for the meat, and poachers were driving them crazy. On the plus side, they had stopped at Dillingham on Bristol Bay on their way home, and they liked what they saw there. A hard-working man could support his family on the summer fishing season, Jimmie said. And they had been befriended by Anthony Dimond, a territorial legislator who, Jimmie predicted, would soon go the U.S. House of Representatives and help turn the economy around.

Jimmie had been offered work with linguist Melville Jacobs at the University of Washington and his mentor Franz Boas, who was known as the "Father of American Anthropology," but he turned down that full-time job in Seattle.[24] The Ahklas would be staying in Alaska, he said.[25]

While there, Wise also looked up Gertrude Becker, who had just lost her mother. Somehow the loss seemed to bring them closer together, and he found himself becoming really serious about her. She had grown into a lovely young woman and, reluctant to part with her, he promised he would write.[26]

On August 17, 1931, the *Los Angeles Times* ran a photo of Wise, Klaffki, and Scott with their camera in the Arctic, noting that they were safe after being rescued from a "trying ordeal." According to that account, the expedition, dispatched that February by producer Edward Small, had been lost to the world for thirty-two days while filming at Icy Cape but had finally returned to Hollywood with 100,000 feet of film.[27] In reality, their only rescue had come from Ewing Scott's father, who had mortgaged his West Adams Street home to pay for return travel, film editing, and recording of narration and music. Studio after studio turned down the finished product, until Small, a little known but prolific independent producer, came forward at the ninth hour with money to promote the show.[28]

Publicizing the film required several months of persistent hype via press releases and advertising that cost almost as much as the movie to produce. Klaffki did his bit by exhibiting his Eskimo pictures, flying the flag for Local 659 and the International Photographers of Motion Pictures Industries, which also prompted good publicity for *Manna*. "For the most part, the Eskimos proved a childish, naïve, religious people," he told the press. "They were easily swayed by oratory and any white man with significant ability could bring them to his views, no matter what their intrinsic worth. Should someone else convince them that they had been fooled, however, woe betide their deceiver if they ever laid hands on him."[29]

Scott was trying to fill in the gaps, finally agreeing to change the name of the film from *Manna* to *Igloo*, which Edward Small thought was more salable. It was showing under that title in a few local houses to fair reviews, but to go anywhere else would take the backing of a major studio. Finally, in late May, Scott talked Carl Laemmle, president of Universal, into distributing it.[30] Almost overnight, Wise found himself fielding *Time* magazine and then the *New York Times*, whose writer was pleased to note that the pure Eskimo had "learned to speak English like a good American." The paper had just reviewed the film as entertaining, "filled with dramatic incidents, and quite unlike the usual school fellows of the travelogue.

"But the story and the direction were handled by Ewing Scott, and the actors are all native Eskimos," the unnamed reviewer continued. "The lead of them, Chee-Ak, is a good looking young man who fills his role with a bland unconcern. The girl—for there is a love story, even in this sort of 'epic of the North'—is not so sure of herself. But Mr. Scott has known what to do with his actors, and there is a descriptive monologue that tells what his camera might have missed."[31]

Universal began placing one-column ads, featuring Ray Wise, or Chee-Ak, as a romantic lead:

IGLOO
Presenting
A NEW HERO
In MOVIE-LAND
CHEE-AK

Then, declaring Wise as "The Sheik of the North," they summed up the plot in six and a half terse lines:

> CHE-AK, a great leader and hunter, loves the daughter of a chief. But famine is abroad and game has disappeared. CHEE-AK, after a most exciting hunt for polar bear and walrus, wins the approval of the gods and demands his dusky sweetheart.

Reviewers, however, were far more interested in the curious and bizarre. "You see twin infants, divided in famine, one to die, with dogs fighting over its grave," reviewer W. E. Oliver wrote breathlessly. "You see the old abandoned, according to the law of tooth and fang. . . . Actual scenes of the killing of bear and walrus are shown. The impact of a spear into the bear's body sends a gasp through the theater. The drinking of the animal's blood is also shown."[32]

Columnist Robbin Coons credited Scott with casting "half savage" Natives, and also noted the movie revealed a "stone age folk."[33]

Meanwhile, Ray as Chee-Ak, the "pure Eskimo," gave endless interviews as honestly as he could without dealing with the inaccuracies of the picture's snow houses or its atypical, spear hunting Inupiats, starving in Native costume.

Instead he talked about his early years of living by subsistence, exposure to a Quaker missionary school, and the death of his Eskimo grandmother. He explained that whale blubber tasted something like pickled pigs' feet, and that it was a poor Eskimo boy indeed that didn't own at least two Eskimo canines to race. He said that a family in White Mountain, Alaska, 150 miles out of Nome, could live in solid and substantial comfort on $300 per year. And, yes, their women did wear ermine coats.[34]

KYAKING IN THE ARCTIC OCEAN. *Igloo*, shot in Barrow and Point Hope, boasted authentic Eskimo trappings and an all-Inupiat cast. *Mala Family Collection*

New Movie Magazine writer Ted Le Berthon could barely suppress his astonishment when Ray showed up for their interview in an Oxford gray suit with peak lapels and a solid yellow cravat that blended well with his brown skin. "Ah! Hiawatha gone Hollywood," he decided. But he gave Wise a three-page spread.

When they discussed religion, Le Berthon quoted Wise as saying that Eskimos had no word in their language for God, as they had no word for time—or even the hereafter. "They like Christ, because He seems more like the Eskimos, the 'real people,' than the white man!" Le Berthon quoted Wise as saying, adding that the Inupiat was also quite conversant on current films.[35]

Columnist Harry Steinfeld reported a favorable reaction from Captain Earl F. Hammond, who had based at Point Barrow with explorer George Wilkins in 1926, and was then in Oregon on a national lecture tour. Steinfeld explained that Hammond was "known the length and

A VERY PRIVATE VALUE SYSTEM

In the 1880s, after Presbyterian minister Sheldon Jackson discovered the United States had little desire to invest in the education of Alaska Natives, he called a meeting of all the church organizations interested in the territory (with the exception of the Russian Orthodox, who were already entrenched), giving each a monopoly on a specific region and allowing them to proselytize as part of their educational program.

Ray's region fell to the Quakers, who took religious and moral training just as seriously as they did the teaching of geography and math. However, the youth spent equal time working at his stepfather's saloon and hotel, and with his Inupiat grandmother, who greatly valued their Native heritage.

As a result, Ray emerged with a healthy appreciation for all religions, including that of the Russian Orthodox Church, in which his wife had been reared, and the solid Jewish faith of his father. However, he apparently never chose to officially adopt any faith and championed only one lifestyle, that of his Eskimo people.

breadth of Alaska as an explorer, archeologist and navigator." Wise, who'd never heard of him, pasted the review in his scrapbook with a notation that read, "Is he a quack?"[36] But he was grateful for the plug, as he was for all of them, even when Universal dubbed him "The Eskimo Clark Gable."[37]

There was one sour note. Columnist Harrison Carroll interrupted the fantasy by reporting that Wise was a card-carrying member of the Hollywood cameraman's union and was part Jewish. The latter was countered by a stout denial from Ewing Scott, who insisted his star was "pure Eskimo." Chee-Ak had simply chosen the last name of Wise "out of admiration for Bill Wise, a San Francisco real estate man," the producer explained.[38]

Ray, it turned out, had managed to locate his father, who owned two of the Bay City's finest hotels. But uncertain of the reception he would receive, the actor was determined not to look the old man up until he was assured of stardom. Much to his relief, Carroll's column appeared to go unnoticed by Bill Wise, and other reporters failed to pick up on the negative publicity. One reviewer observed that while "a thin thread of a story had been woven to supply that seemingly necessary romance, there are few artificial adventures shown in 'Igloo,' " and that the leading actor was definitely an Eskimo. Another gave Scott credit for writing and directing a story that "goes deeper into the primitive than any other camera-explorer I have seen," and pronounced Chee-Ak "a grand photographic subject and a good actor."[39]

Igloo played to full houses throughout the hot summer of 1932 and made a solid profit. At one point, reviewers judged it the best picture of the month along with *Rebecca of Sunnybrook Farm*,[40] and Ewing Scott had good reason to feel that Arctic Productions had served him well. He had returned from the North to learn that F. W. Murnau had been killed in a car crash with his fourteen-year-old Filipino valet, leaving some unsavory rumors about what the pair had been doing while driving.[41] But with the accolades Scott had been getting, he no longer needed the help of his old mentor. Soon after Universal purchased *Igloo*, making him again solvent, he landed the plum assignment as director of *Into Little America*, a carefully crafted "documentary" on Admiral Richard Byrd's second Antarctic Expedition (1934).[42] In the excitement of heading off, he neglected to pay Ray's *Igloo* proceeds, forcing his friend to sue for back wages.[43] But there were no hard feelings. Scott had come to see the Arctic as his destiny, and nothing would stand in the way of that adventure.

Although cinematographer Klaffki received little mention for *Igloo*, he was as relieved to be out of the Arctic as Scott was to return to it. Gratefully, he went back to work as usual in Metro's Camera and Electric Department, never again receiving credit as chief cameraman.[44]

Wise returned to his old job at Fox, convinced his big chance would come soon. It was Mrs. George who first brought him the happy news that Metro-Golden-Mayer was considering a movie titled *Eskimo*, by Danish adventurer Peter Freuchen. As usual, his landlady proved to be an excellent source of Hollywood gossip. As she had predicted, he was perfect for the part of a primitive young Eskimo who murders the trader responsible for the death of his wife and then has to deal with the government police. Wise had regained the thirty pounds he'd lost on his last bad run in Hollywood and was in top physical shape from seven months of roughing it in the Arctic. Universal was continuing its publicity blitz for *Igloo*, so his name was often in the papers with good reviews. He spoke fluent Inupiat, which would be used by the film's Eskimo cast, and his voice, while soft, was pleasing. When Hunt Stromberg, one of MGM's "big four," complimented him on his screen test, he assumed the part was his. But he hadn't counted on the film's director, W. S.

"Woody" Van Dyke, who absolutely refused to consider Wise.

Known as "One-Take Woody," because he seldom had to reshoot a scene and usually brought in his movies on or under budget, Van Dyke had deeply endeared himself to the studio when he was assigned to assist Robert Flaherty in 1927 on *White Shadows of the South Seas*, filmed in Tahiti. Flaherty, arrogant from his success with *Nanook of the North*, had little understanding of how the studio system worked and paid no attention to Van Dyke, most recently the director of Class B movies, who could have helped him. Used to working alone, the documentary maker also had little idea how to manage the huge crew MGM had provided him and dallied for months without sending any rushes back to the studio. Finally realizing he was over his head, Flaherty resigned, and head cameraman Clyde De Vinna, who was much respected by studio executives, talked them into letting Van Dyke direct. Accustomed to working together, and having had many months to consider what was wrong with the shoot, Van Dyke and the cameraman not only saved *White Shadows*, but won an Oscar for De Vinna's spectacular shooting.[45] Then they teamed successfully on *The Pagan*, shot in Tahiti, French Polynesia, and Papeete, and *Trader Horn*, made in Africa, using indigenous amateurs for the bulk of each cast.

Their most recent triumph was *Tarzan the Ape Man*, shot in a phony Hollywood jungle, featuring Olympic swimmer Johnny Weissmuller instead of aborigines. However *Eskimo* would mark a return to the wild, so Van Dyke insisted on a 100 percent Native cast.[46] Studio executives pointed out that the female principals he'd chosen were Oriental. That was a necessity, Van Dyke countered, because everyone knew Eskimo women couldn't act. But it was a definite "no" on the Jewish boy. Van Dyke had made up his mind, and no one at MGM cared to buck him. ∎

Six
SUCCESS, OR MAYBE NOT

ay Wise thought of himself as many things. First, he was Eskimo, for that was the language of his mother's people and his early years. He thought the way Inupiats thought. He shared their value system.

Second, he was a loner. Since the death of his mother, there was no one with whom he came first. He had many good friends and valuable mentors, too, but they all had someone of their own . . . a mother, a wife, children, siblings. He did not.

He thought of himself as Alaskan. Cold and bleak though the Far North might seem to others, he would always count it as home, no matter how long he stayed away. Yet he also thought of himself as a member of the Hollywood movie colony. He was a cameraman, which is how he thought of himself most often when he wasn't thinking about acting. But *never* had Ray Wise thought of himself as *Jewish*. He didn't know any Jewish people well, and he had little idea of what being Jewish meant.

What it did mean to him, though, in the spring of 1932, was that he couldn't have the job for which he was probably the best qualified human under the sun. Nor was there one single thing he could do about it. He couldn't bring himself to cut his hair, which he had grown long for the screen test. Yet, resigned, he went back to work with the Fox camera crew and tried to distance himself from the disaster. Losing another thirty pounds certainly wasn't the answer. Nor was feeling sorry for himself.

The toughest thing to deal with was newspapers, something he'd really enjoyed since Universal started publicizing *Igloo*. His movie was still in the news, but so was Woody Van Dyke and all the usual preproduction hype about *Eskimo*, which hurt to read. He read the articles, of course, and was startled to learn that his former boss, Captain John Hegness, was in town to help MGM find the right boat for the film. Hegness picked an old arctic fur trading schooner called the *Nanuk*,[1] perfect for the job, Wise knew from his days as a deckhand. How he'd love to be headed north on her.

RAY AND BARROW CO-STAR. At this writing, the name of the brave young woman, who Ray and Ewing Scott finally talked into starring in his Barrow film, remains unknown, but the independent producers considered themselves lucky to have her, for most Native women in that village wanted nothing to do with their movie making. *Photo courtesy of Anna Jobson*

ESKIMO SURVIVAL PHILOSOPHY

Because there was little margin for error in a migratory lifestyle based on subsistence hunting and fishing in a land where brutal winters made up the majority of each year, Eskimo philosophy allowed for little frivolity but was more tolerant than most in dealing with human foibles. Of necessity, families and small tribal groups lived for long periods of time in isolation, needing to share and work together to survive. Therefore, harsh criticism and finger pointing were avoided. Talk was considered cheap and actions spoke louder than words.

Even today, if you understand Inupiat, you'll sometimes hear elders marveling that their Caucasian brethren think *saying* "thank you" is enough. A traditional Eskimo may never say it at all but will wait a decade or more if necessary to find a way to *show* thanks in a gesture so spectacular, the person to whom he is indebted will not be able to top it.

In mid-June of 1932, Van Dyke and company flew to Nome, boarded the *Nanuk*, which had just arrived from Seattle, and sailed to Grantley Harbor off Teller, Alaska. Fighting drift ice, crews off-loaded fifty tons of equipment they had brought up from Hollywood.[2] The "camp" they established included a movie theater, library, steam baths, billiard parlor, two wireless stations, individual "bungalows" for the white crew and Oriental actresses, a staff of housekeepers and waiters, a canteen, dining room, and kitchen overseen by a famous Swiss chef, two assistants, and a baker.[3] Through the Lomen Commercial Company, which controlled most of the region's reindeer operations and pretty much had a monopoly on trade, Van Dyke had recruited about 150 Eskimo men from Kotzebue to Cape Prince of Wales and off islands. As requested, they arrived in traditional skin boats—fifteen umiaks—dressed in Native garb, to screen test for the part of Mala. Robert Mayo, an apparently "pure" Eskimo from Wales, got the job, and the rest stayed on as extras.

However, Jack I. Andersen, the young manager Lomen Commercial had assigned to assist the movie crew, balked when Van Dyke instructed him to feed them Native foods. "I'm not coming up here to spoil these people," Van Dyke insisted. "They're going to get their Native food."

"But Mr. Van Dyke, you don't understand," Andersen argued. "These fellows may be dressed in Native costume, and are real Eskimos, but they are accustomed to white man's food, and you'll lose all your Eskimos unless you feed them what they are accustomed to eating."

Even then, there was trouble holding them. MGM paid every Eskimo—man, woman and child—five dollars per day for appearing in the picture, but as soon as they acquired a bankroll, they wanted to go back to Nome to spend it while there were still fresh summer supplies. Arguing that it would seem strange to moviegoers if one Eskimo family suddenly changed to another in the middle of the film, Van Dyke offered more money, suggesting that the Natives might save it. Stoically the Alaskans refused. If they had more money, they'd just waste it on liquor and useless purchases, they reasoned.[4]

The exasperated director and Peter Freuchen, author of two books on which *Eskimo* was based, were equally surprised to learn that the Alaskans, unlike their Greenland counterparts in Freuchen's fiction, had no idea how to build snow igloos or sew skin tents. Worried lest the Eskimos fear the movie camera, assuming they'd never seen one before, Van Dyke did all the early shooting on the grounds that he knew best how to deal with aboriginal people.[5] His cast, with typical Inupiat politeness, never mentioned that most had worked in a similar capacity for Ray Wise, Ewing Scott, and other Hollywood types.

The Oriental actresses assigned the female leads annoyed the crew by demanding star treatment. However, Freuchen found the women diligent in learning Inupiat, which it was his job to teach them, even if "as every American, they missed the tone of the language and had a hard time pronouncing many of the words."[6]

And so it went, with Van Dyke quite pleased with himself for staying on course. By mid-July they had pretty much wrapped up summer shooting, as planned. But off shore, the crew of the *Nanuk* was playing hide-and-seek with the captain of a Soviet icebreaker bent on arresting them, while assistant director Eddie Hearn tried to shoot whaling scenes with Robert Mayo. It was a frightening game of cat and mouse, particularly for chief engineer George Hunter, who had recently spent four years in a Russian jail after revolutionaries seized his Siberian trading post. Also unnerved was Hearn, forty-four, who had enjoyed a long acting career but was new at directing.

Captain Louis Lane, who'd taken command of the *Nanuk* at Nome, deftly managed to escape the Russians by sacrificing a whale they'd just caught for a butchering scene.[7] The worst was yet to come, however, for Robert Mayo suddenly announced to Hearn in English, "Work no more!"

Figuring Mayo's resignation had little to do with the Soviet threat, but convinced that the Eskimo was serious, Hearn called Van Dyke on the shortwave radio and was ordered immediately back to Teller. The director, known for his rotten temper, kept his distance from Mayo, who was left aboard the *Nanuk* until they could find out why he wanted to desert. No one seemed to know. Those who did were not anxious to break the news that some men in camp had made advances to Mayo's wife. Completely frustrated, Van Dyke dispatched Jack Andersen, the Lomen manager, to reason with his star, but that, too, failed. Robert Mayo was anything but convincing when he explained that his mother-in-law was going to have an operation and that he and his wife must be with her. Van Dyke gave him twenty-four hours to change his mind, and when the Eskimo refused, handed him a check for back wages he had readied in advance, fearing the worst.

"Get out of here and if you or your wife or child ever set foot in this area again, I'll have you thrown overboard," the furious director roared.

For the first time in his life, One-Take Woody was way over budget and no longer on schedule, but he was still thinking ahead. Well before his final meeting with Mayo, he had contacted MGM's Hunt Stromberg, who immediately telegraphed Ray Wise at the Fox lot.[8] The message, dated July 22, 1932, read:

PRACTICALLY DECIDED YOU WILL PLAY MALA. KEEP IN TRAINING AND ON SPECIAL DIET ALL THE WAY UP AND BEGIN TO THOROUGHLY ABSORB CHARACTER SO YOU WILL GIVE GREAT PERFORMANCE. MAKE VAN DYKE FEEL YOU ARE PARTICULARY GRATEFUL TO HIM OVER HIS WILLINGNESS TO USE YOU AND ALSO MAKE HIM FEEL HE CAN CALL ON YOU FOR ANYTHING DARING OR THRILLING HE WANTS TO GET. WITHIN YOUR POWER AND COURAGE IS NOW THE CHANCE TO OBTAIN SENSATIONALISM AND GREATNESS.[9]

One week later, Wise arrived in Anchorage with character actor Ed Dearing, who had been hired to play the part of Constable Balk, and stopped only long enough to talk to a local reporter and buy a newspaper. Merl LaVoy, and someone named Andrew Taylor, were in the process of climbing Mount McKinley to recover the body of Theodore Koven, a mountaineer from an earlier expedition, at the behest of the climber's mother, Wise learned.

"At this time of year the mountain is particularly dangerous," LaVoy was quoted as saying. "At the section where Koven is, it is heavily crevassed and bridged with snow spans that easily give way."

LaVoy had to be pushing fifty and was only recently back from the South Seas, which would make the cold climb tougher yet. Taylor appeared to be a friend of the Koven family, and who knew if he had climbing skills? Still, Wise guessed correctly that his friend would complete the mission. He hoped his own luck would hold as well.[10] It

seemed a good sign that the pilot assigned to fly them to Nome was Matt Nieminen, who had helped rescue Fox's *Frozen Justice* crew in 1928.[11] Yet there was no getting around the fact that Wise would be working for a man who never wanted to hire him.

It was the beginning of August when Assistant Director Ed Hearn, wondering how to fill the gaps in Van Dyke's new shooting schedule, was startled to see a small floatplane landing in the lagoon off their Teller camp.

"There comes your Mala," the director called out. Puzzled, Hearn recognized Ed Dearing, then, looking beyond him, was relieved to see someone who was also familiar despite his shoulder length dark hair. Hearn had worked with Ray Wise earlier and found him a pleasure to deal with.[12]

Knowing Hearn helped take the awkwardness out of Ray's introduction to Van Dyke, who was gruffly cordial. The director was tall and lean with close-cropped, wiry hair, and steel blue eyes that could look right through you.[13] Rumor had it he'd been a soldier of fortune, a gold miner, and a lumberjack before embarking on a movie career with D. W. Griffith, and he looked like a tough man to cross.[14]

Fortunately, the whole crew was hurrying to complete summer retakes and move to winter camp before snows fell. There was little time for social niceties, and it appeared they might be bypassed entirely when Van Dyke and Hearn found themselves at odds. Putting Hearn in charge of the tug and the barges deployed to move the camp, the director had specifically warned him not to move more than one barge at a time, but because the seas were calm, the assistant director doubled up. Angered that Hearn had ignored orders, Van Dyke accused him of risking all their gear. Hearn, who had made the move on the sound advice of Lomen manager Jack

TELLER LOCATION. Much of *Eskimo* was shot at Teller, where filmmakers kept an anxious eye to neighboring mountains, hoping they would turn white with snow. Here, Ray prepares for a scene with Eebrulik Rock (right), a Point Hope Inupiat. *Mala Family Collection*

Andersen in attempt to save the company money, was furious. Tension mounted in the camp when the two refused to speak to each other for three days, and Hearn asked to be taken off the picture. Yet when Van Dyke finally patched things up quietly, Ray realized Woody wasn't quite as gruff as he seemed.[15]

Nor did Wise have any problems with Peter Freuchen, forty-six, who had explored Greenland with Knud Rasmussen, but believed *Eskimo* to be the turning point in his long, adventurous career.[16] Freuchen had lost one leg and nearly his life during a winter's trek from his Greenland trading post to Pond's Inlet on Baffin Island to catch a boat home to Denmark. He credited his survival to a young Eskimo boy named Mala, and Ray had feared the writer might be overcritical of anyone who played his role.[17] Instead, Freuchen buried himself in the job he'd been hired for, "sort of an Eskimoic expert or arctic guide or something else," he wrote a friend.[18]

The Dane was huge, almost a foot taller than Wise,[19] who wondered how the outgoing explorer had ever partnered with quiet, diminutive Rasmussen. It helped when Freuchen learned that Wise had sailed with his old friend, and that Wise, too, was willing to do everything it took for *Eskimo* to succeed.

Freuchen's main complaint was the actresses, with whom he warred to the point that Van Dyke made him apologize. Ray found no friends among them, either, but he was always polite and let Freuchen deal with it.

Lotus Long, twenty-three, the gorgeous product of a Hawaiian mother and Japanese father, had so impressed Robert Flaherty and F. W. Murnau in *Peacock Fan*, they had considered her to star in their South Seas production, *Tabu*, until Anne Chevalier, a native of Bora-Bora, edged her out.[20] Born in New Jersey as Lotus Pearl Shibata, she was married to assistant cameraman William James Knott, a Canadian who was also working the Alaskan shoot.[21] Her part as Iva, the wife with whom Mala finally escapes lawmen after murdering the wicked trader, was key and she insisted on preferential treatment.

Iris Yamaoka had been born in Seattle of recently immigrated Japanese parents who eventually settled with five of their adult children in Los Angeles. While most of her family made a living selling produce, Iris's older brother worked as a salesman for a costume company,[22] and it was perhaps with his help that she landed a small part in a 1929 film called *China Slaver*. Just twenty-one, fluent in both Japanese and English, and a charmer, Yamaoka played one of Mala's more amusing, if slightly dim, wives. Unfortunately, the girl fainted the first time the cast killed a walrus and, despite Freuchen's ridicule, made no secret of her squeamishness.[23] She was, however, being courted by cameramen Clyde De Vinna and Josiah "Bob" Roberts,[24] assuring her some excellent footage.

Least experienced, but by far the most mature of the trio, was Lulu Wong, thirty, older sister of international star Anna May Wong. Freuchen observed that she was the prettier of the two, "and intelligent as a pocketknife,"[25] but that didn't make her easy to work with. Her only experience had been as an extra in a few mob scenes until Van Dyke spotted her on the MGM lot. Her part as Aba, Mala's first wife, required her to evolve on screen from a traditional Eskimo girl to the drunken toy of a ruthless trader, a role she approached with considerable skill. Vanity got in the way, however, when she appeared on the set one morning with glamorous makeup and an elaborate hairdo. Freuchen, who played the part of the evil trader as well being an "Eskimoic" expert, insisted that Wong take down her hair, and when she refused he did it for her.

"Help!" she screamed. "Help! Freuchen is attacking me!"

Van Dyke engineered a compromise. The actress could appear glamorous half the time if she would leave her hair uncombed for the rest. Privately he explained to Freuchen and Wise that there would be no film in the camera for the glamour shots,[26] an arrangement that pleased Wise because it provided a chance to rehearse his part.[27] The director's judgment was sound. Wong was turning in a fine performance and looked so good on film she would soon be dubbed "the Eskimo Gretta Garbo." But she was a tradition-oriented Chinese woman, who, after working in her father's laundry, had spent four months with her sister enjoying some of Europe's finest hotels and meeting famous people.[28] She hadn't anticipated on the isolation of the Alaska assignment or its length and was fast discovering she didn't want to be a movie star.[29]

What pulled them all together was Van Dyke's careful directing, in which Ray Wise quickly put his faith and trust. Ewing Scott had been better than Kleinschmidt, but it didn't take long to see why Woody was an acknowledged genius. He knew instinctively what would play. He would wait with incredible patience for just the right weather and light to stage, a perfect setting. He had no qualms about working with inexperienced actors if they could take direction.[30] A born arbitrator, and well aware of the social problems involved in an isolated shoot, he often indulged his people.

When the three actresses, who were served by a sweet half-Eskimo maid, demanded they each have separate maids, Freuchen told them that if they couldn't pull up their own stockings, he'd do it for them, adding that they could go to the devil. Van Dyke managed to negotiate a truce without hiring extra maids. Later, when the women discovered there were no fresh grapefruit left in Teller, he appeared to buy their story that they were suffering from vitamin deficiency, if not scurvy, giving them several days off until a plane could make the run from Seattle with fresh fruit.[31]

He was fierce, though, when it came to the safety of his film crew. The lecture on the mortal dangers of Alaska he gave the newcomers on arrival at Nome was so frightening that Freuchen told Ray, tongue in cheek, he had considered bowing out, despite the fact he'd survived twenty-six years worth of arctic expeditions.[32]

Van Dyke had come by his fears honestly. Two years earlier, while on location in Africa, he'd lost one crewman who fell into a river and was eaten by a crocodile and a Native boy who was killed by a charging rhino (a catastrophe which was captured on film and used in the movie). Van Dyke himself had contracted malaria along with most of his crew, and beautiful Edwina Booth, who played the White Goddess, was still bedridden as a result of the shoot.[33]

Enjoying the warmth of the midnight sun and the relative safety of their main base "Camp Hollywood," few took Van Dyke's cautions seriously until August 18 when two of the crew became lost on the tundra for six days in an unexpected blizzard.[34] Others nearly perished on hunting trips, charged by angry walrus or adrift on breaking ice without food or water. Entries in the log of the *Nanuk*

SNOW HOUSE HASSLES

The fickle climate of the western Arctic, which sometimes produces winds called "Chinooks" that suddenly raise temperatures from 50 to 68 degrees in the dead of winter, made Greenland-styled igloos impractical, and there is better building material available.

After selecting a dry base and excavating a foot or two for a floor, Alaskan Eskimos traditionally lashed together dome-shaped frames of driftwood or whale bones and covered them with large, brick-shaped blocks of tundra. An animal gut skylight was added for illumination and a long entryway engineered to trap the cold.

Sod houses, like the one in which Ray Wise was born, proved far warmer than the "civilized" wooden dwellings insulated with newspapers that were favored by white residents of his era.

showed that winter temperatures sometimes dropped as low as minus 50° Fahrenheit. "If it hadn't been for men like Freuchen, who know the Arctic inside out, and Ray Wise (Mala) who was part Eskimo himself, they would have been stumped more than once," Van Dyke conceded.

On October 18, the *Nanuk*, supposedly frozen fast in the ice, had to be rescued from drifting out of Grantley Harbor. The following month, beleaguered chief engineer George Hunter was severely burned from the explosion of a blowtorch and had to be flown to Nome for treatment. The crew had been divided into several units, working in various locations which were hard to keep track of. Finally Van Dyke instituted a system where every member had to check out with headquarters and back in again on return.[35]

An even bigger problem was boredom, for Van Dyke had made it clear that Native women were off limits. "I explained this situation to my crew the day we arrived in Nome," he later told the press. "I told them bluntly that if they violated the law as it applied to Native women, they would not look to me for help. I threatened to leave behind any man who acquired a Native squaw.

"As a rule they are indescribably homely and utterly filthy of person," he added for good measure. "The only vaguely attractive ones are half-breeds and they are none too cleanly. A white man must stay longer in the North than did our troupe to overcome revulsion to such squalor."[36]

Freuchen, who had two children by a Greenland Eskimo wife he had loved deeply and buried, did not comment. Just to be safe, the white crew decided to make their camp "at least four miles away from the Eskimos" for they feared the "smell," while Freuchen moved to the Eskimo camp, ostensibly to protect the cameras which were stored on a nearby set. But that, too, had its drawbacks. When the Alaskans staged wild drinking parties, the Dane became doubly alarmed because he discovered they were drinking wood alcohol which, he lectured, would blind or kill them.

"Only for foolish Americans who had no knowledge of chemistry," they insisted, filtering some of the stuff through coffee grounds and a handkerchief, and bolting it down with seemingly no ill effects. [37]

As for the Alaskan women, Freuchen, whose second marriage was an open one, decided to stay clear. "The Natives are not as pleasant as in Greenland," he explained to artist Kent Rockwell, with whom he corresponded frankly. "The girls are either religious or have gonorrhea. Of course there is not much difference, but I do keep out."[38]

Instead, he took his frustrations out by writing fictitious press releases. Young *Nanuk* crewman Mike Phillips, who had fallen into freezing water, was saved at the last minute by strong, fast swimming-director Van Dyke.[39] Leading man Ray Wise had taken a boat to Seattle but was too timid to purchase a railroad ticket, so he walked from there all the way to Hollywood to get his leading role.[40] The bombastic Dane's best work, though, was how cameraman Clyde De Vinna, who was also an amateur radio operator, had been overcome by carbon monoxide poisoning while transmitting from his tiny shack, but saved from death by a fellow ham in New Zealand. That story sounded so good that eventually De Vinna came to believe it and actually developed a cough.[41]

As for Wise, he spent his spare time with old friends: Metta Muller, their Eskimo cook from Teller; John Hegness, who worked as a scout for the film crew; and big Bert Merrill, who had gotten a job with the outfit on the strength of his film experience with Ray and Ewing Scott in Barrow. But Wise was kept busy with his acting plus a number of unofficial assignments like survival expert, hunter, and deckhand after the company moved aboard the overcrowded *Nanuk*. Sleep became a precious commodity.

"Thirty-five men, cooped up in the narrow quarters of a whaling schooner that was hotel, laboratory, machine shop, and everything else that goes with the making of a picture, a literal studio in the midst of a white sea of ice," Van Dyke later complained. "I won't lie. I hated every minute up there, frozen in the *Nanuk* in the middle of an ocean of ice."[42]

During the worst of it, Jack Andersen and his wife Loretta threw a party for the entire crew at their home in

Teller, about three and a half miles from the MGM base. Although Wise was often kidded because his conversations in the company dining room were generally limited to "Pass the bread,"[43] he attended with the rest, but remained his usual quiet self. However, after the crowd departed, the Andersens—startled by loud snoring—discovered the actor had fallen asleep while waiting for everyone to hit the road, camped on the floor in back of an overstuffed chair, fully clothed in fur parka, mittens, and mukluks. Before they could figure out how to get him home, Van Dyke had dispatched a search party, which was pleased to report back to the worried director that his Mala replacement was safe.[44]

Freuchen was getting tired of building snow villages, but none of the Alaskans could do it and he was beginning to understand why. His first effort, which took three days to construct in February, melted in an unexpected thaw. A second proved to be in the wrong location when snowmelt bared mountains in the background. Finally, he located a good setting near Nome, marred only by a house which MGM bought and moved, promising to return it for free in the spring.[45]

The whole company, long cooped on the *Nanuk* and nearby base camps, was delighted to move to town, and Ray Wise was happier than most. Since he was in only a few of the scenes to be staged there, he finally had some down time which he invested almost immediately in the Eagle Dance Hall.

Gertrude Becker had a date that night with her steady beau, a Norwegian, but for some reason, he didn't show. She was ambivalent about running into Wise, for she'd heard the movie company was in town, but she had a new dress and she let her sister talk her into showing up.

MALA TRIES TO RESCUE HIS WIFE IN *ESKIMO*. Lulu Wong, sister of Hollywood star Anna May Wong, had no acting experience but played the part of an Eskimo wife gone astray with style. In this scene, Peter Freuchen toys with her, as Ray, playing her husband, looks on. *Mala Family Collection*

When Ray asked her to dance, she refused. He had promised to write, she reminded him, but he hadn't. She bet he had a girl back in Hollywood, or one of those beautiful actresses that she'd seen around town. Wise made no comment on actresses. He had been going with someone in Hollywood, he said, but it wasn't serious. He told her she looked great because she did look great. She told him she had a good job at the Miners and Merchants Bank. Then, somehow, they were talking about more personal things,

THE WEDDING OF THE YEAR FOR NOME. Homegrown movie star Ray Wise wed Gertrude Becker, a local girl, just as an MGM movie crew finished filming *Eskimo* in February 1932. In this official photo, Director Woody Van Dyke, who stood in for the father of the groom, congratulates the happy couple. *Mala Family Collection*

right back where they'd started. They danced until the hall closed and all the MGM crew had to go back to base. Ray said he'd return, and this time he did.

The move of the film crew to Nome, headlined in the *Nome Nugget* February 4, provided wonderful social opportunities for townsfolk who, up to that point, had little opportunity to meet them. The MGM men challenged a Nome team to a baseball game and won it

with Van Dyke playing left field and Ray Wise among the missing.[46] There was a Valentine's Day party and a local stage production at the Eagle Hall billed as "Follies Nouvelle" in which both locals and MGM performers took part. Singled out for special review was Miss Gertrude Becker and her sister Margaret, who—made up as Negros—"touched many hearts" with the sentimental ballad *My Drowsy Babe*. "The audience liked the song so well, they were forced to sing it several times before the curtain rang down on their act," the reviewer noted.[47]

The wedding of Gertrude Becker to Ray Wise on February 16, 1932, caught nearly everyone by surprise including the groom. Colleagues, who failed to talk him out of the match, assumed the bride had told him she was pregnant. A larger truth was that Ray Wise had spent a lonesome ten months in the Arctic, working on a mind-numbing assignment without a break and, in fact, he'd been lonesome almost as far back as he could remember. Gertrude was as amusing as she was beautiful and up-to-date. A mixed breed with class. He was twenty-six years old, and she would soon be twenty. Ray Wise had more in common with Gertrude Becker than any woman he had ever met. He'd left her twice but never felt good about it. She hated the thought of parting again. So they decided to make it legal.

Grant Jackson, Gertrude's boss at the bank, and his wife hosted the wedding in their elegant home. One of Gertrude's sisters, Mrs. Margaret Yenney, was her matron of honor. Ed Hearn agreed to be Ray's best man, although he'd worked in Hollywood long enough to insist it was the dumbest career move the actor could make. And what about Van Dyke's threat to abandon any crew member who acquired an Eskimo squaw?

Alaska territory did have some stiff legal penalties for white men who abused Native women, Wise conceded. But he wasn't planning to abuse Gertrude. If he did, she'd probably whack him. Instead, he was marrying her with John Becker's full consent and Father Ed Budde, the local Jesuit priest, officiating. Besides, according to the publicity clippings he'd recently received from his Hollywood landlady, Van Dyke was already promoting him as a "full-blooded Eskimo," which meant he'd be in trouble only if he tried to wed a white woman.

Slightly bemused, the two men purchased Filson suits, neatly tailored wool work outfits so popular in the territory that they were referred to as "Alaskan tuxedos," at the local department store. Van Dyke, who volunteered to fill in as father of the groom, bought one too. As there were no bridal shops in Nome, Gertrude settled for a long white evening dress and they had fresh flowers flown up from Seattle.

It was, by all accounts, a small but lovely wedding, followed by a delightful buffet supper. A large group of the *Eskimo* crew and cast crashed the party to discover their Mala could be quite social on occasion. The *Nome Nugget* followed up with congratulations. "Bon voyage, to both of them!" the editor concluded.[48]

Van Dyke wrapped up the shooting a week later and sent all but a skeleton crew south via small planes to catch a boat out of Seward. Freuchen later reported his party, which included Iris, Lulu, and the Swiss cook, actually survived two plane crashes en route, and at one point had to walk through neck-deep snow to find shelter in the Yukon village of Nulato. He and the cook enjoyed the disasters, he said, because they ganged up on the once-pampered "stars" and made them do the cooking while they awaited rescue.[49]

Arriving in Seward, March 12, they received a cable that there had been a terrible earthquake in Hollywood, Long Beach, and most of Southern California. It was rumored that all the studios were in ruins and the death toll was tremendous. Ray, who had enjoyed an otherwise uneventful trip, went ballistic because he had no idea where Gertrude was. He knew she was traveling to Hollywood with the Jacksons, who were escorting three

Eskimo families to appear in studio scenes for postproduction, but no arrangements had been made when he left. Arriving in Seattle a few days later, he learned the death toll was smaller than originally thought, but he was forced to board the train for California still wondering if his bride's name was on the list.

A hero's welcome awaited the company in Glendale, complete with brass bands, reporters, and photographers. The three Asian actresses were whisked off to keep up the pretense of an all-Native cast, while the few real Eskimos they had brought with them, quite miserable in the arctic furs, were mobbed. So was Ray, who was wearing a tie and button down shirt but still had shoulder length hair. It was great publicity. Freuchen spun a few yarns about how he had managed to kill a polar bear with his pocket knife, and praised Mala's natural prowess as a hunter. The mayor of Los Angles gave them his personal welcome to the grind of newsreel cameras and the pop of flash bulbs. But Wise just wanted it over. Families kept rushing up to crew members, welcoming them home. Freuchen's wife, Magda (who turned out to be white) was there to greet him, too.[50] Where the hell was Gertrude?

The missing Mrs. Wise had so enjoyed her first visit to Seattle, she didn't write her husband and it never occurred to her to call. Mrs. Jackson took her trousseau shopping in some huge department stores, and up in an elevator, the first she'd ever seen, to the top of the Smith Tower, then Seattle's tallest building. She caught cold, of course. Alaskans usually did when they traveled to strange places because they had no immunities, Mrs. Jackson explained. So she kept pretty much to herself on the long train trip south. In Pasadena, there were studio people to meet the Eskimo families, but no one seemed to be expecting her. After waiting an hour, she finally took a cab right through Hollywood to the address Ray had given her, 4048 Edenhurst, the home of Elmer and Laura George.

Ray was so relieved to see her he almost cried, but he was also furious. Why hadn't she written or called? Finally, he calmed down enough to introduce her to Mrs. George, who had a French-Canadian accent, as did Gertrude's father. That was the only thing Gertrude had in common with the forty-seven-year-old housewife. They hated each other on sight. The house was nice, though, and the couple had a big, well-furnished room to themselves. When Gertrude showed Ray the new outfits Mrs. Jackson had helped her pick out, her groom was very pleased. He knew a lot about fashion, and happily predicted she would be a standout.[51]

Her first chance to find out came in early April when Woody Van Dyke held one of his famous cast parties in his fabulous Hollywood mansion. Gertrude had barely recovered from the white-on-white interiors, the servants, and all the stuffed African animals when she found herself meeting Anna May Wong, who came with Lulu, and Jean Harlow, who seemed even more beautiful in real life. Johnny Weissmuller, whom Van Dyke had starred as Tarzan, was there too. The highpoint of the evening, though, was a chat with Grace Kingsley, one of Hollywood's longest established gossip columnists, who interviewed the newlyweds right on the spot. Ray was delighted, for Kingsley, who had a national following, headlined them a couple of days later with a little feature about Gertrude's first trip to the big city.

▶ **NEW FAVORITE WIFE.** Having lost one wife to the evil trader, Mala makes Lotus Long the object of his affections, a trust that is not misplaced. *Mala Family Collection*

PICTURE SHOW Congratulates

The four Marx Brothers on possessing such an abundance of U.S. currency—even if it is only for "Duck Soup," their newest film.

These two delightful Aberdeen pups on having an even more delightful mistress, Joan Crawford, who is adding them to her present cannine family of three grown-up Scotties and a St. Bernard.

Metro-Goldwyn on putting Mala and Aba, these two charming Eskimo lovers, on the screen in "Eskimo."

Gary Cooper and George Raft on their evident enjoyment of an after-luncheon story.

"And though she is a highly cultured young lady, she has never seen a play on stage! Mr. Van Dyke advised 'Dinner at Eight,' at the Belasco," Kingsley reported. [52]

Much relieved that Gertrude had done well at Van Dyke's and anxious to show off his bride, Wise introduced her to the Kleinschmidts, who found her charming. Their house, too, was full of stuffed animals, Gertrude discovered: glass case after glass case, but at least they were from Alaska. She found the walrus head in the living room distracting and was at first uneasy over Frank's stiff military bearing and German accent. But Essie, who was also French Canadian, was welcoming and motherly, and the filmmaker wasn't as off-putting as he looked. It was the first of many delightful visits.

Frank had been touring America, lecturing, booking *Primitive Love*, and selling his *Santa Claus* movie to department stores for special promotions. [53] It proved lucrative, but always being on the road was hard duty, he said. Which was why he was excited about the job offer as a technical advisor he'd just gotten from RKO. The studio had purchased Ainsworth Morgan's hilarious book *Man of Two Worlds* about an Eskimo's first unfortunate brush with civilization. [54]

Cast with Eskimos, Ray wondered? No, Kleinschmidt lamented. It would be introducing the famous Czech star Francis Lederer to American audiences as the bewildered Eskimo. Blonde Elissa Landi, an Italian stage actress, who had starred in many American movies, would play the white lead. But they hadn't filled the other parts yet. Would Gertrude be interested, Kleinschmidt wondered? [55]

Soon Gertrude was awarded a small uncredited role and also the lead in another column by booster Grace Kingsley. "In Alaska, the men make love to the girls, but I see that in Hollywood the girls make love to the men!" she began by quoting Gertrude.

The actress's name was Kalgutaluk, which meant "White Gull" in Eskimo, Kingsley explained. The girl was "otherwise known as Mrs. Ray Wise, wife of the actor who, under the name of Mala, is playing the lead in M.-G.-M.'s 'The Alaskan' [then the working title of the film]." Describing her as tall, dark and handsome with "flashing eyes," Kingsley went on to announce that Kalgutaluk had just won a part in *Man of Two Worlds*, and was "showing great talent."

"I arrived in Hollywood a bride of two weeks," she quoted Gertrude as saying, "and it had scarcely been that long when my Eskimo husband left me. I could not understand, even when I heard that he had gone to Hollywood. Gradually I understood what was meant. Such things do not happen among Eskimos."

Gertrude had, of course, not been at all surprised when her bridegroom took off for Hollywood, but it was not unusual for columnists to make up whole interviews, Ray told her. Kingsley also quoted the girl at length about her first 800-mile airplane ride to Fairbanks, her terror at the "puffing, rushing monster" (a train), and her first voyage on an "*omiak-puk-puk*, as we Eskimos call steamboats." But the columnist's real focus was romance.

"The women of Hollywood seemed beautiful to me, and the men were handsome, though, being much in love with my husband, I haven't eyes for them," she quoted

---

◄ **PUBLICIZED IN GOOD COMPANY.** Ray was delighted to find himself and Lotus Long pictured with George Raft, Gary Cooper, Joan Crawford, and the Marx Brothers in a movie magazine spread. *Photo courtesy of Ted Mala Jr.*

the new Mrs. Wise as saying. "I had never heard of a gigolo until I came to Hollywood. Such men would not prosper long among the Eskimos. There, a man to win admiration of women must be a great hunter of polar bear and the walrus, rather than of women."[56]

Idiotic as the column was, Ray was delighted with the plug. It was too embarrassing for Gertrude to send home, and the reviewer had never mentioned her real first name, but Ray explained that was pretty much standard in Tinseltown and, silly as it sounded, it all helped sell movies, which was their goal.

While Ray was busy at MGM filming additional scenes for *Eskimo*, Gertrude found herself on the RKO set, mostly as a fascinated bystander and passing the time with Kleinschmidt, as she had only a few lines to say.

Then MGM decided press coverage was needed for the Eskimos who had been sent south for studio work to advertise the authenticity of Van Dyke's film.[57] Publicist John Jobson, who had spent time in Alaska, enlisted the Wises to take the visitors to Santa Monica beach, which proved the beginning of a long, close friendship. Almost as tall as Freuchen, looking like a young Hemingway, Jobson had spent his early summers working on ranches near the Dakota Sioux reservation where he often hunted with the Indians. Although slightly younger than Gertrude, he had already traveled the whole United States and part of Central America as road manager for Captain Earl Hammond, who lectured and exhibited wild animals following his Alaskan expedition with George Wilkens. In fact, Jobson told them proudly, it was he who got Captain Hammond to endorse Ray's film *Igloo*, which came out while he was lecturing in Oregon. Wise remembered the

clipping, for it was the one he'd questioned as a fraud. But in promoting *Eskimo* he worked daily with Jobson, who soon became his best friend.[58]

Wise found another ally in Johnny Weissmuller. Although the actor was already rich and famous when he hit Hollywood, having become an Olympic swimming champ and then signed a contract to promote BVD underwear for $500 a week,[59] both men had been brought up in a family-owned bar and deserted by their fathers. They were the same weight and height, had the same coloring, and were nearly the same age. Both had broken into the bigtime under the careful direction of Woody Van Dyke, and both were caught up in an exhausting and often frustrating studio publicity mill in which neither the truth nor their personal lives mattered much.

Discovering that Wise had been a deckhand, Weissmuller invited him and Gertrude for a sail to Catalina Island on his thirty-foot schooner *Santa Guadalupe*. Gertrude declined. Ray got the feeling she didn't much care for Weissmuller, although she never said so. But, enjoying Weissmuller's company and wanting to learn more about the industry, Ray went along. The boat was sluggish and had to be manhandled, but Catalina wasn't far and they had a good chance to talk after they anchored up to swim.

Wise hesitantly mentioned that the studio did not seem pleased with his wife, although many others, including himself, found her charming.

"Join the club," the Olympic champ said, and proceeded to enlighten the newcomer. Just before MGM took interest in him, Weissmuller had wed Ziegfeld showgirl and club singer Bobbe Arnst, a pixyish brunette. It was his first marriage, and he was very much in love. But when he appeared to sign his MGM contract, he was told there was one minor condition he should be aware of.

"You have to get rid of your wife," studio executives informed him.

Weissmuller thought they were kidding. When they made it clear they were not, he refused to sign. Eventually the studio bosses wanted him badly enough so they backed down, but they didn't give up. Thinking the matter closed, Weissmuller went to New York for the premiere of *Tarzan the Ape Man*, leaving Bobbe in Hollywood. By the time he returned a month later, she was considering divorce a reasonable option because the studio had offered her ten thousand dollars to quit.

"I'll go visit mother . . . and I've still got my voice, and . . . ten thousand dollars is a lot of money, Johnny," he recalled her saying. Feeling ashamed of himself, he agreed. It was April 1932, and two months later he was again a bachelor.[60]

Now it was Ray's turn. What the studio couldn't do to enable his career, Mrs. George quickly accomplished, badgering Gertrude, prying, and giving unsolicited advice. After Gertrude finished filming of *Man from Two Worlds*, Ray was gone most of the time and Mrs. George nearly drove the girl crazy. Did Gertrude know Ray had a serious heart problem? Mrs. George seemed delighted to break that news, suggesting that the couple should limit making love to once a month, as she did with her husband. An amateur spiritualist, she said she had contacted Ray's mother on numerous occasions. He found it comforting, Mrs. George added. Perhaps she should get in touch with Gertrude's long dead mother, too.

Gertrude doubted that her mother, although not so long dead, would have much advice on the problems she was having in Hollywood, which was mainly Mrs. George.

To escape, the girl started going to the movies—double features when possible—returning one evening to find her husband angrily pacing the floor. She'd forgotten they had been invited to the Sam Goldwyns for dinner. When they arrived late, Goldwyn was cool and would remain so.

Finally, Gertrude told Ray that if he didn't find another place to live, she would. He rented half of a nice duplex but that didn't go well either. Ray wanted her to start entertaining studio people, something that would forward his career. Having never thrown a party or even entertained guests for dinner, she declined.

"You're kinda keeping me back in my career," he countered. "I have a chance to date actresses." Gertrude's response was to throw her wedding ring over a bridge in Pasadena and pay a private visit to Essie Kleinschmidt. Realizing Ray was like a son to Frank, Gertrude tried to be fair. Ray had offered to pay her way home, she said, but she couldn't bear the humiliation of going back, any more than she could stay with him. And she didn't know how she would support herself.

Essie was incensed. Gertrude must start by taking Ray Wise for everything he had, she insisted. "At least make him pay your way to beauty school." Heartbroken and confused, trying to hold back the tears, Gertrude gazed around the Kleinschmidts' spacious living room, full of glass cases of artifices, stuffed birds, and eggs. "She was the only one alive," she would later remember.

Nor was she free of Mrs. George, who came to visit when she heard Ray had moved out, worried now that he might *not* move back in. If he returned and wanted to sleep with her, Gertrude should cooperate, her former landlady insisted. She didn't want Ray going off with strange women from whom he might catch something, Mrs. George warned darkly.[61]

As the Kleinschmidts suggested, Wise paid Gertrude's way to beauty school and tried not to worry about her. John Becker had arranged for Jesuit fathers in the area to keep an eye on the girl, and she remained close to Frank and Essie, who had distanced themselves from Ray.

Ray missed them and he certainly missed Gertrude, but he moved back in with the Georges and began to feel better as the all-important New York premiere for *Eskimo* neared. With last-minute takes and studio arrangements to worry about, there wasn't time for much else. Even on the train trip across country, there were reporters and last-minute details to deal with. Then he found New York City so exciting, he forgot about everything else.

Back in California, just before the film's official opening, the Alexander Theater in Glendale ran out of review cards for its sneak preview, "so heavy was the demand from spectators," the local paper reported. "Many of them having no cards, wrote letters, sending a total of 900 pieces of mail, according to Hunt Stromberg, producer of the picture."[62]

The film's official, standing-room-only opening at the Astor Theater and the good New York reviews that followed were everything Wise had dreamed of. After which, of course, there was an awful letdown. And Ray was not pleased when he learned that Gertrude was dating his friend John Jobson. But it was Woody Van Dyke who provided the biggest dose of reality.

Asked if he thought Ray Wise would get ahead in the movie industry because of the fine performance he had given as Mala, Van Dyke expressed regrets. "I don't think so. It's really too bad," he said. "He's a type, and in the movies that's bad. Mala not only will be established in the minds of the people as an Eskimo—he actually is part Eskimo. Even if a professional actor does exceedingly well in a character study, the audience wants to see him in that kind of role from then on."[63]

Wise tried to shrug off the comment. Gossip columnists were saying that Irving Thalberg, one of the truly great producers, was seriously considering him for the lead in Pearl Buck's best seller, *Good Earth*.[64] It was a part he was sure he could handle, and he was certain it would be an award-winning movie. The prediction proved correct. Luise Rainer, the female lead picked for the film, won an Academy Award for the role as did Karl Freud, the head cameraman. However, Rainer was not Oriental but a German Jew, while the lead Wise hoped to get went to Paul Muni, who had been born in Austria-Hungary.[65] ■

▶ **MALA CAPTIVE.** The hero of *Eskimo* does not realize the Northwest Mounted Police intend to see him hang. Here a fellow Inupiat suggests Mala attempt an impossible escape in the dead of winter. *Mala Family Collection*

Seven

TINSELTOWN BACHELOR

Melbourne Spurr was hard of hearing, which was just fine with Ray Wise.[1] That meant Spurr didn't expect any small talk, at which Ray was not particularly adept, and the photographer would be totally focused on his work. Which was why he was Hollywood's most famous photographer. With Mary Pickford's enthusiastic backing, Spurr had made it to the top. His clients included everyone important from Ramon Novarro, John Barrymore, and Fanny Brice to Greta Garbo. All it took to deal with him was a wheelbarrow full of money and Spurr would make you look just like you wanted to look which, in Ray's case, was like anyone but an Eskimo. Spurr's resulting portfolio showed the Alaskan as a creditable Arabian sheik, matador, cowboy, stateside Indian, South Sea Islander complete with well-tailored loincloth, and an American businessman. There were none of Wise as a rabbi, but the collection was so darned diverse he thought for one wicked moment of sending it to Woody Van Dyke.

Instead, Wise turned his back on his old job as a Fox cameraman, determined to wait out what he passionately hoped would be a temporary slump in leading roles. Two years earlier, while he and Ewing Scott had been going their independent way, movie revenues had fallen from $80 million to $70 million and Warner Brothers had lost $8 million. Then Paramount took a record dive of $21 million,[2] with Fox tottering on the brink. Fox's brightest star, Will Rogers, was still going strong, but Shirley Temple, another longtime moneymaker for the studio, was outgrowing her childish box office appeal, and the studio had little new to offer.

There was still a good market for movies, however, especially after the industry discovered that double features were a Depression draw, and no major studio had gone under. Twentieth Century Pictures, an aggressive production company recently formed by Joseph Schenck, Darryl Zanuck, and William Goetz, had no studio or distribution network of its own and was poised to rescue Fox, which would add Tyrone Power, Alice Faye, Don Ameche, Sonja Hennie, and Linda Darnell to its lineup.[3] Film attendance had risen from

◄ **AUTOGRAPH, PLEASE**. Ray enjoyed his fans and treated them well. This photo appears to have come from a series taken by MGM publicist John Jobson, who became Ray's close friend. *Mala Family Collection*

HOLLYWOOD KAYAKING LESSONS. As one of his publicity gimmicks, Ray gave kayaking lessons to a bevy of Hollywood beauties on Santa Monica beach. But it was more than a stunt, because the Eskimo had learned to navigate on the Arctic Ocean at an early age, so male kayaking fans signed up, too.
Mala Family Collection

60 million in 1933 to 70 million that year, and was still going up.[4] With all the good reviews from *Eskimo*, Wise was certain another major role would soon come his way.

Meanwhile, with the help of MGM's publicity machine, Ray worked at being a movie star. The studio had arranged for him to escort Florine McKinney, a lithe, blonde starlet, to a fabulous dinner given by writer Edgar Allan Woolf, a gourmet chef whose weekend Hollywood parties were legend. Ray had felt a bit silly arriving in his bird skin parka, but the studio insisted it would be a hit,[5] and Florine, who had managed to snare nine tiny parts in her twenty-four-month career, was delighted with the attention. Some of her girlfriends, all want-to-be starlets, suggested that they might accompany the exotic Eskimo to other events, and soon Ray was arriving at parties with a bevy of beauties, looking like a real ladies' man.[6] "I

have grown to like the slim beauty of American women, although to an Eskimo they are much too thin," he admitted to *Los Angeles Times* reporter Barrett Keisling in a well-illustrated article that ran full page. "An Eskimo woman must be sturdy to carry burdens, to trudge long, weary miles."

Then, perhaps mindful of what the folks back home might think of that confession, not to mention his chances of getting other Eskimo roles, he moved to temper the statement. "I can't say that I have been happier than I was in the North," he added. "There is a call to the Arctic that is very strong. Very few Eskimos ever stay long away from their frozen land. I, too, will go back."[7]

During this period, Wise enjoyed a close friendship with Johnny Weissmuller. Happily, the swimming champ had invited him to join the squash team of the Beverly Hills Club, which led to many novel publicity stunts. Soon Ray was teaching kayaking in the club pool and down at Santa Monica beach with appropriately clad bathing beauties. His antics were reported at length by sports writer Maxwell Stiles, and also he remained a favorite of columnist Grace Kingsley.[8]

Weissmuller usually traveled with a group of friends—sort of an early Hollywood rat pack—which included Errol Flynn, Humphrey Bogart, John Wayne, and director Raoul Welsh. Highly successful in the industry, they all prided themselves on having the best of everything and could afford to spend considerable time partying.[9] Their private yachts gave them some much needed privacy to drink and do some serious poker playing, and Ray was welcomed. He really enjoyed poker, but he wasn't much of a drinker, and he noticed that Weissmuller was becoming involved with Lupe Vélez, a high-maintenance, tantrum-prone Mexican actress who many people thought was crazy. Fun though the crowd was, Wise began to feel increasingly uncomfortable as its only unemployed member, and he was still at loose ends emotionally.

It hit home one afternoon when he spotted his ex-wife Gertrude on the pier where they had docked. There with a group of friends to watch the boats, she was as pleased to see him as he was to see her. He'd forgotten how beautiful she was and how tall. He invited her out for coffee, promising to drop her off at her apartment afterward in the cute little convertible he seemed so proud to show off. It was a used car he'd managed to acquire in trade for two fox skins, he told her.[10]

Ray knew the movie in which Kleinschmidt had gotten Gertrude a part, *Man of Two Worlds*, had received bad reviews. Czech star Francis Lederer was hilarious as the civilization-wary Eskimo lead and soon became a star in America, but Elissa Landi had been woefully miscast as his love interest, and the film had lost $220,000 at the the box office.[11] Still, Gertrude didn't seem in the least discouraged. She'd managed to find work in the industry as a hand model, filling in with close-up shots for a number of leading ladies who had hands like a gorilla's. She also had a good job in a beauty shop, she said, and was happy in her new life. Maybe she would eventually go back to Nome, but she was having too much fun at the moment to consider it.[12]

While neither wanted to rekindle their romance, their meeting was so pleasant it reminded Ray of how he much he missed having a family. Although soured on marriage, he decided to chance contacting his father.

William "Bill" Mandel Wise, ensconced in his elegant, ten-story, two-wing Granada Hotel at 1000 Sutter Street in San Francisco, was astonished but pleased to make the acquaintance of a famous son he did not know existed. Nor did he question the lad's parentage. At forty-eight, the senior Wise was still handsome—a bit beefy, but charming in an outgoing hail-fellow-well-met way that Ray could not have duplicated for all his acting skills. But the two men moved alike and even a stranger could notice a

resemblance.[13] Having sired no other children, legally or illegally as far as he knew, Bill wondered whether he'd enjoy being a father. Neither was sure where to start, so they settled on a game of squash, a sport in which they both excelled, and slowly caught up on family history.[14]

Bill Wise had finally made his million around 1909 in the gold fields of Iditarod about 200 miles south of Candle, and had returned to San Francisco immediately, only to discover that his mother had disappeared in the San Francisco Earthquake. After a considerable search, he found her living in terrible poverty in Hermosa Beach.[15] After rescuing her, he purchased two of San Francisco's most expensive hotels: the Granada and the Normandie.

Unfortunately, he also aspired to high society. In 1915, he wed comely, wide-eyed Etta Steinberg Churchill, blonde daughter of Sigmund Steinberg, a wealthy lumberman, in a lavish ceremony at the Normandie attended by 300 of San Francisco's finest. Serving as his best man was Sylvan Kasper, wealthy member of a prominent Jewish family. Also on hand for the elaborate affair were his mother, his two sisters (now Mrs. Theresa Simpson and Mrs. Nettie Dunn), plus his adored but long-missing father, Mendel Wise. The bride, for whom this was a second marriage, met her groom in a bower of yellow chrysanthemums and ferns, wearing a gown of yellow taffeta and tulle and carrying a shower of lilies of the valley. Wise's sister, Nettie, served as matron of honor in a cream brocade satin dress trimmed with duchesse lace and roses in an apricot shade, while sister Theresa, a bridesmaid, wore a coral panne dress trimmed in spangled cream lace.[16] Mr. and Mrs. Sigmund Steinberg were also in attendance.

Yet despite its splendor and family backing, the marriage lasted little longer than the wedding celebration, for while motoring south for their honeymoon, the groom discovered his bride was a total bore. According to litigation

FAMILY AT LAST. Ray waited until *Eskimo* was featured on billboards across America before contacting his father, Bill Wise. In this early family photo, he poses happily with Bill and his wife, May, but the father and son relationship would become rocky. Discovering his father had used their mutual last name to empty the actor's bank account, Ray legally became Ray Mala, remaining in touch with his father, but he did not trust him. *Mala Family Collection*

that followed, being forthright in nature, Wise declared immediately he had "made a mistake in getting married, as any man is better off single." In addition, Etta quoted him as saying that "his family hated her, and always would hate her," and that on several occasions he had spoken to her in a harsh and humiliating manner in the presence of friends. When she filed for divorce a scant two months following the wedding, Wise assured the press he would not contest. "My wife is a splendid girl, but I am not the man for her," he explained diplomatically. "We are both young, and there is no reason why we should blight our futures by remaining together."[17]

During divorce proceedings, however, Etta testified that Wise had "told her she was not sufficiently educated and refined to be introduced to his friends, that he made a big mistake when he married her, and wished there was some way of getting rid of her." Obligingly she provided a way by leaving him, taking the Normandie Hotel with her as a settlement.[18] "It's the first time in my life I have ever worked, but I find the work interesting," she told reporters when she assumed the job as Normandie manager following ten weeks of married life. "And it keeps my mind off my troubles."[19]

Once free, Wise turned his attentions to one of San Francisco's most famous madams[20] and managed to stay out of the news until the spring of 1920 when he was sued for failing to keep up payments on an $800 fur coat. Miss Virginia Dohrman had filed the action, alleging that about a year earlier Wise had accompanied her when the purchase was made, guaranteeing, but failing, to make payment. [21] But Wise assured his son that he had since cleaned up his act. His fiancée, May, was an elegant fashion buyer for Bullock's Department Store chain, and was Australian by birth. Ray liked her immediately and felt even more comfortable with her daughter Maxine and her husband, Bob Shean, who was a banker. It was obvious, however, that the rest of his new family would not be easy to crack.

While Bill's mother, Dena, made annual headlines by swimming in San Francisco Bay each New Year's Day, she was otherwise reclusive and suspicious of strangers. Bill's father and sister Theresa had died, and Ray saw very little of brother Abraham, who traveled as a concert violinist. Sister Nettie, who lived with Dena, proved as distrustful of him as her mother. Maxine Shean confided that both women were so paranoid they were always hiding diamonds, jewelry, and money in their house, apparently still haunted by their narrow escape from Russia and from poverty.[22] It would take time to win them over, Ray decided. After all, they had been raised as Russian royalty and still favored the language. No doubt they were shocked to have an Eskimo bastard in the family.

On the other hand, Bill Wise soon grew so welcoming it felt like they'd known each other for years. Relieved that he at last had someone to turn to, Ray began confiding in the older man, especially when it came to finances. Mrs. George, still his landlady, had insisted the actor set up a savings account, something he still carefully maintained. Although he had dipped into it to cover tuition for Gertrude's beauty school and occasional card playing losses, he'd amassed a formidable balance, which he realized he should be investing. He had been hesitant because he knew nothing about the world of finance or whom to trust. So when he discovered his father was planning to sell his hotel to invest at Pismo Beach, a pretty, unincorporated little town just south of William Randolph Hearst's grand estate at San Luis Obispo, he decided to join him.

High profile in the area was Floyd Calvert, once a successful Hollywood developer who had lost everything in the Depression except forty acres of Pismo beach and pea fields that he had found difficult to sell. Calvert was finally managing to peddle some of his lots at five dollars a month,[23] but Bill Wise claimed he had a better idea. Knowing a group of Spanish American War veterans who had money and needed housing, Bill was planning a development just for them, but with room for private investors and family members, too. If you had money and knew what you were doing, the Depression was a great time to make more money, he maintained.

BOX OFFICE BONANZA

Contemporary sources have reported that *Eskimo* was a box office failure. Actually, international returns on the rechristened film were more than gratifying, especially in Scandinavian countries, France, and Germany, where Danish author Peter Freuchen accompanied it and rallied interest of the press.

In his biography *Vagrant Viking*, Freuchen enthusiastically reported his successful promotion schemes, also noting that studio head Louis B. Mayer had congratulated him and promised him a "fabulous career" in the movie business. Sadly, MGM later reneged, failing to renew Freuchen's contract just as it had that of Ray Wise.

Together father and son drove 200 plus miles south from San Francisco to view the property and were charmed. Although the town was about 160 miles north of Hollywood, they knew many stars drove even farther than that each weekend to visit the Hearst estate, so they bought. Soon columnists were referring to the star of *Eskimo* as a businessman with acreage at Pismo Beach between Hollywood and San Francisco, which he planned to subdivide. Ray was growing enthusiastic about his financial future.[24]

There was less cause for optimism, though, over his acting career. Although *Eskimo* had won much critical acclaim, plus the first Oscar ever awarded for best editing, its Alaska filming alone had cost $1,300,000,[25] and it was not doing as well as expected at the American box office.[26] The studio turned things around by adding some steamy sex scenes and renaming it *Mala the Magnificent* for the European market, but to the surprise of many in the industry, MGM failed to renew Ray's contract. Finally, after an agonizing wait, independent producer Phil Goldstone signed him up, and Ray returned to MGM.[27]

"Despite the fact that M-G-M was reported to be completely off long-distance expeditions for pictures, preparations are being made for the filming of 'Jungle Red Man' on a grand scale," the *Los Angeles Times* reported April 14, 1934. "Technical staff is already on the way to the Amazon country in South America, which is the locale of the picture.

"George B. Seltz, the director of the picture, is en route, too, and what's more, I hear there is a good chance that our old friend Mala (Ray Wise) will play the lead. He was the hero of 'Eskimo,' and it is understood that despite the fact that this picture was a bit fluttery at the box office, they have hopes of making Mala a bright star."[28]

Goldstone had made money a year earlier when he produced *The Vampire Bat*, starring Fay Wray, who would soon become famous in *King Kong*. MGM apparently took the producer seriously, but when *Red Man* was canceled for reasons never explained, he and Wise were out in the cold. Taken with Peter Freuchen's financial success as an author, Wise busied himself writing a 48,000-word autobiographical novel titled *Far North*, then an even longer fictionalized story, *Snow Man*, with no takers.[29]

Meanwhile, Goldstone went back to the drawing board, and a year later sold the studio on letting him produce Herman Melville's book *Typee* in Tahiti, with Ray Wise in the lead, Lotus Long as his leading lady, and Clyde De Vinna as cinematographer. It was to be called *The Last of the Pagans*. It was to be the largest overseas expedition in film history, justified because MGM was combining *Typee*'s filming with that of *Mutiny on the Bounty* with Clark Gable, Charles Laughton, Hawaiian native Mamo Clark, and cameraman Charles Clarke, who had led Wise's *Frozen Justice* expedition. The two companies, which included sixty technicians and all the principal players, were shipped with more than 100 tons of equipment to the South Seas from San Francisco on the SS *Maunganui* in February 1935. En route, they mustered separately to work on production plans, but joined forces daily to attend Tahitian language school under the tutorage of Clyde De Vinna's adopted daugher, Toni Bambridge, a Tahitian islander and the company's interpreter.[30]

Also dispatched south was the schooner *Nanuk* on which Wise had camped while filming *Eskimo*, but now it was rigged as the British ship HMS *Pandora* for the *Bounty* filming. In its stead, Ray was to live in a grass hut on what the studio described as a "coral island, untouched by civilization," and he loved it. He was not pleased with the Native diet—raw fish with coconut milk, or daily raw bananas, boiled and fried. Nor was he happy when the Native cast, recruited in Papeete, laughed so hard at his version of the hula that tears came to their eyes. Yet, living quite comfortably on mangoes, he spent all his off-camera time boating with the Tahitian islanders and came to love the South Seas.

"One has to learn a lot about nature there—in self-defense," he said. "I was early initiated in how to stand off a

▶ **MORE EVIL TRADERS OUT TO SPOIL THE NATIVES.** Originally written from Herman Melville's classic, *Typee*, the *Pagans* script was changed so that the original storyline was almost unrecognizable. The movie screened to lukewarm reviews, but everyone agreed the cinematography was simply grand. *Mala Family Collection*

wild boar with a spear—how to fight a shark in case of attack—how to avoid the poisonous black fish that our director used to refer to as an 'underseas black widow,' and a lot of things like that."

He was also grateful for history lessons learned. "I visited Point Venus, where Captain Cook landed, and also the lighthouse which is his tomb and monument," he recalled. "I saw the boat *Cimba*, which sailed around the world. We made a special trip to Fapaua Falls, which were filmed by the late F. W. Murnau."

But for reasons he never quite explained, the experience was far more personal than the usual tourist jaunt. "It was the only place that ever made me cry when I left," he would confess to a reporter years later. "The white moon, the big fires for the dances, swimming in the surf—it was wonderful." [31]

Pagans' director Richard Thorpe was highly regarded by the studio, because he stuck to budget and usually brought his pictures in early, but he was not as sensitive as Woody Van Dyke had been and did not manage Ray's acting talent well. Thorpe would later be fired from *Wizard of Oz* for trying to make Judy Garland into a teenage vamp, complete with blonde wig, instead of a lost young girl from Kansas. [32] In Thorpe's defense, however, the script they were handed had so little resemblance to Melville's classic, and, in the words of a modern-day reviewer, redesigned for "those who like travelogues with a touch of romance."

Wise's role was that of "the male chauvinist pig who steals beautiful Lotus Long from her native village and claims her as his own," wrote John Seal in an apt comment for *The Internet Movie Database*. "*Last of the Pagans* is a relentless parade of cultural imperialism and clichés about primitive people and noble savages, but it looks absolutely gorgeous. You're best advised to turn the sound down, ignore the subtitles, and soak up De Vinna's superb camera work." [33]

Ray returned to California five months later to more grief than lukewarm reviews, for his Pismo Beach development was folding, and Bill Wise had traded on the family name to run up mammoth bills on Ray's accounts. Exasperated, but with no wish to alienate his father, whom he'd grown to love, Ray officially changed his last name to Mala, which provided needed financial distance from the former millionaire.[34] When Bill Wise wed May late in 1936, his son was on hand to see the couple off on the honeymoon, which he suspected his father could not afford, via cruise ship to New York.[35] But when the old man returned eager to promote new real estate deals, Mala quietly declined to back him.[36]

In December, MGM unleashed a promotion for *Last of the Pagans*, which included a review from *Daily Variety* that began, "Here is fascinating eavesdropping on the love-life of an unspoiled people in the South Pacific Eden."[37] However, the most used publicity by newspapers around the country was a photo that showed Mala pinning Lotus Long to the ground after kidnapping her in a raid on a rival tribe for "brides." Headlines like "Where Caveman Methods Still Work!"[38] generally went with the art.

A MAN OF MANY PARTS. Although he got good reviews for his work in *Eskimo*, Ray was not offered another good part by MGM. Thinking it was better to be typecast as an "exotic" than an Eskimo, he added diversity to his portfolio. Photos from the left to right:

◄◄◄◄◄ **A thoroughly modern Eskimo.** Ray trusted famous Hollywood photographer Max Munn Autrey to shoot photos for his portfolio that distanced him from the Eskimo stereotype. Here he posed in a tuxedo.

◄◄◄◄ **Putting aside his suit.** Ray bared his chest to show his fine physique.

◄◄◄ **Maybe a jungle jaunt.** Ray posed for Max Munn Autrey as near naked as decorum would allow in hopes of winning the part of a South Sea islander.

◄◄ **The Eskimo as a businessman.** Melbourne Spurr, another Hollywood pro, was hired to add variety to Ray's photo collection. In this profile, the young Eskimo shows himself well suited for the occasion.

◄ **Spanish heritage.** Ray even posed in a matador costume, to exploit his "exotic" looks.

Mala Family Collection

Advertising slogans recommended by the studio included such bland enticements as "Romance of a vanishing race!" and "A THUNDERING WAVE OF HUMAN EMOTIONS . . . SET TO THE HEARTBEATS OF A PAGAN PEOPLE." But theater owners needed stronger stuff: "Love-Thrills!—As the bride hunters capture their mates."[39]

Although the *Pagans'* plot eventually turned Mala's dubious character into a hero with whom his captive bride falls in love, the promotional campaign provided him with a whole new image as a swashbuckling rapist. Shortly thereafter, he signed on for a supporting part in *Jungle Princess,* which Paramount was producing to showcase Dorothy Lamour as Ulah, a beautiful young woman abandoned in the jungle to be raised by animals. Ray was to play the bad guy, Melan, a Native who disliked the princess, her furry family, and her come-along-lately British hunter-sweetheart.

No one had to tell Ray that the demotion from star to supporting player was a bad career move, but he had come to realize that as an "exotic," no movie company was going to give him a long-term contact with continued star buildup. He'd watched Anna May Wong, famous sister of Lulu Wong, bounce from studio to studio in minor roles, despite her unique beauty and the fact that she'd upstaged Marlene Dietrich in *Shanghai Express.* Forbidden by the recently enacted Hayes Code from playing romantic roles with non-Asian actors, Wong had finally solved the problem by working in Europe. Multilingual and an excellent dancer, she appeared on stage and in nightclubs as well as in foreign films,[40] but the Alaskan had no such options. The only languages he spoke were Inupiat, English, and Tahitian, and his Eskimo dancing and hula efforts lacked popular appeal.

If nothing else, doing *Jungle Princess* proved a great way to stay in shape. Unable to ship the cast to Malaysia, which was the movie's setting, Paramount opted for a remote spot called Brent's Crags in the San Fernando Valley, where it set up a tent town, complete with mess hall. However, the vegetation was so dense, it was impossible to drive through it, so getting to the set each day required a tough, forty-five-minute march for cast and crew carrying props and cameras.[41]

Leading lady Lamour was a slim but well-endowed, luminescent beauty, who been kicking around Hollywood for a while, taking occasional bit parts.[42] Uncomplaining, she hiked with the best of them and gave her all in the hard sixteen- to eighteen-hour days the job required, but remained aloof from cast and crew. While most decided she was a snob, Ray wondered if, like himself, Lamour was just awkward at small talk, especially when focused on acting. She was married and not his romantic type, but hiking along beside her on their daily commutes, he occasionally hazarded a wry observation that would make her laugh, and they became good friends. [43]

Male lead Reginald Truscott-Jones, renamed Ray Milland, had been discovered while on his way to interview for the job as a filling station attendant, and proved a delight on the set. Director Wilhelm Thiele, however, was hard to understand and given to shouting in a thick German accent to vent his explosive temper. Milland, who nicknamed him "Attila the Hun," also referred to him behind his back as the "Pomeranian Pimp," for Thiele appeared to care little for the comfort and safety of his people.[44] Dorothy's role, that of a singing, sarong-clad jungle girl, provided her with a tiger cub, leopard, and a chimpanzee named Gogo as companions. She got along well with her four-legged costars but, during an unguarded lapse Thiele should have covered, the chimp scratched one workman's back to ribbons and threw another down a forty-foot waterfall, ultimately causing his death.[45]

Mala, like the rest of the cast, sighed with relief when the shoot ended, only to discover the job that followed was far more dangerous. *Robinson Crusoe of Clipper Island* was to be a twelve-part serial, the movie version of a soap opera to be shown in weekly episodes. It was to be shot in three weeks, and Ray's contract required him to share star billing with a horse and a dog. On the other hand, the money was good . . . $5,000 for twenty-one days of work, which would tie him with Hoot Gibson, Sammy Baugh, and Ralph Byrd as Republic Studio's highest single-serial salaried performer.[46] The picture, which began in September 1936, was a spy-thriller. Instead of the usual embarrassing racial stereotype, Ray got to play a federal intelligence agent (billed as Agent Ray Mala), actually wearing a business suit, at least before the plot went "island" and he reverted to a loincloth. There were the scenes with hostile, spear-throwing Natives, tribal ceremonies and dances, dangerous crocodiles and sharks, and beautiful Princess Melani who required rescuing, but script writers had also programmed in plenty of mechanical toys—planes, dirigibles, cars, motorboats (real and miniatures shot as real) plus complex spy equipment.[47] Melani, in real life Mamo Clark, a Hawaiian girl Ray had met during Tahitian lessons on the SS *Maunganui*, had showed herself to be a fine actress in the role of Clark Gable's wife in *Mutiny on the Bounty*.

Actually a princess in her own right, Mamo had been raised traditionally in Hawaii, but with an eye to the future. Her adopted mother, May Kaaolani, was a member of the Hawaiian royal family, and had attended Mills College in California at a time when higher education for women was unusual.[48] Returning to the islands, she married a commoner, a handsome, well-heeled chicken farmer who believed their daughter should also have the best possible education. They enrolled her at the University of Southern California and,

REX THE WONDER HORSE STANDS READY. Ready to trample any male actor who crossed his path. For that reason, Ray rode his stand-in, Brownie, but nearly broke his back in a resulting fall. *Mala Family Collection*

after talent scouts tapped the girl for a major part in the *Bounty* film, they moved to Hollywood to be with her.

Recently shaken by her mother's death from cancer, determined to keep her private life private, and gifted with a strong academic bent, Mamo had little in common with her quiet costar except the fact they were both trapped in a Class B movie. In Clark's case, she believed she had ended up in the low-budget serial due to the malice of a studio executive or fellow actor from MGM, where she, like Ray, was on the contract roster. However, she was a thorough professional and as easy to work with as she was to look at.[49]

Rounding out their spy-chasing team were John Ward, an experienced actor from New York,[50] who played Agent Mala's bumbling sidekick with a broad English accent; William Newell, dedicated to an amazing career as a character player and was Mala's beach-combing aide;[51] and Buck, a gentle, intelligent, nondrooling Saint Bernard, who had recently been featured as "King" in *Call of the Wild* with Clark Gable.[52]

Then there was stuntman Loren Riebe, a trapeze artist and a great tumbler and acrobat, who was to serve as Mala's double. In a preshoot for the production on one of the Santa Cruz Islands off California, Riebe had dived into the surf from a 150-foot cliff, a stunt so spectacular it was used for the serial's opening.[53]

With so many professionals, Mala wasn't worried until veteran crewmembers warned him about Rex the Wonder Horse, who was also prominently featured. A beautiful Morgan found running wild in Arizona, Rex had been abused by his first trainer and was given to running down male actors. Women and dogs didn't bother him, just men.

On one of his last assignments for Fox, Ray had been sent to Arizona with Daniel Clark, a famous photographer of animals who had just been promoted to director, to shoot rodeo footage of Rex for a movie titled *King of the Wild Horses*. John Wayne, who was to star, knew little about riding, so they located a pretty lady in Flagstaff to give him some quick pointers and assigned him a gentle horse for practice. Meanwhile, Clark spent so much money staging the rodeo that the studio canceled the film before they got to work with the Wonder Horse, which was probably just as well.[54] Recently Rex had crashed a Republic set to terrorize Ernie Adams, a small but athletic young western star who scrambled under a Buick touring car with the horse in hot pursuit, still trying to bite him. Rex photographed beautifully for wild horse sequences and had a great following of fans, but no actor in his right mind would willingly work with him, old-timers said.[55]

The four-footed terror had been written into the script as sort of Robinson Crusoe's man Friday, with Agent Mala treating the animal as his best friend, giving him comradely pats and riding him often, usually bareback. The Eskimo, who had only occasionally ridden his stepfather's work horses, was enormously relieved when the studio decided to use enough stock footage of Rex to make his star billing legal, while substituting his gentle stand-in, Brownie, for the actual shooting. Despite the horse trade, however, Agent Mala was still headed for trouble.

Ray Taylor, who codirected the serial with Mack V. Wright, was given to drinking his lunch, a preference that sometimes clouded his judgment.[56] This might have been the case in the final week of shooting, when Taylor allowed Mala to throw himself on the fast-moving horse for an escape scene. Assistant director William Witney pointedly suggested that Taylor use the actor's double, but when Taylor, who was always in a hurry, seemed hesitant, Mala said he could handle it. Brownie, with stuntman Loren as his rider, came in at a full gallop. Loren reached down with his right hand and caught Mala as he made the leap, but the momentum of the horse failed to throw the actor aboard. Instead, Ray nearly broke his back falling on rocks. Though hospitalized only briefly, he could barely walk for the rest of the picture.

Then, the day before shooting finished, cameramen set up two open arc lights without their usual protective lenses, and shoveled up lots of explosive flash powder to replicate a volcanic eruption. The results were spectacular, but Mala's leg was burned by the flash powder,[57] and John Piccori, a British player nicknamed "Sir Piccori," sunburned his eyes so badly from the arcs that he had to keep poultices on them when not delivering his lines as the evil high priest.[58]

The studio's carelessness was noted with concern by Johnny Weissmuller and his card-playing friends, when Ray came limping in for their weekly game of poker. Humphrey Bogart suggested that Agent Mala consider joining the recently formed Screen Actors Guild so they could give him a decent funeral tribute, and he wasn't exactly kidding. Membership was expensive, not too popular with studio executives, and also hard to obtain, but Bogart, who served on the board, promised to submit Mala's name. And he made it happen. Early that October, Mala was one of only eight Class A candidates accepted, including John Barrymore, Barbara Stanwyck, and Claire Trevor.[59]

Membership proved immediately useful, for *Robinson Crusoe* came in over budget. Since theaters paid by the episode, Republic decided to add two more to the series requiring two extra days of shooting. Mala's contract stipulated "21 days consecutive employment" but was muddy on whether it was "consecutive calendar days" or "work days." Represented by Guild member Edward Arnold, who would later become the organization's president, the actor asked for $1,200 additional salary, but failed again to luck out during arbitration.[60]

Tired and battered, for once Ray Wise Mala was thankful he had no new film scheduled.

The three movies he'd made in the past twenty-two months had been almost back to back, with five of those months having been spent out of the country. He had taken time out to escort visiting Alaska pilot Noel Wien and his wife, Ada, to the glamorous premiere of Charlie Chaplin's *Modern Times* in February of that year.[61] And, he also frequented ice-skating rinks which looked especially good after his return from Tahiti.[62] Now he took advantage of the break to spend time with May and his father, who threw wonderful parties

THE ROYAL DOWNSIDE

While Ray Wise's paternal grandmother, Dena Weisbleeth, was apparently a member of the Russian royal family, as was Galina's father Colonel Kropotkin, they seem to have been on opposing sides of the Russian Revolution that so altered their lives.

While little is known about why the Weisbleeth family was forced to flee to the United States, it seems certain their expulsion was engineered by Tsar Alexander III following the assassination of his father, Tsar Alexander II in 1881, which many historians feel was the beginning of the revolution. Also, after Dena's husband, Mendel Weisbleeth, became an American citizen, he disappeared from all American records for several years, so one might guess he returned to Europe to join some revolutionist group.

In contrast, Galina's family was enjoying the life of Russian aristocracy when revolutionists killed the royal family in 1918, forcing them to flee. Which might explain in part why Galina's mother was opposed to her marriage to Ray Wise. Later, however, the in-laws appear to have engineered a peaceful coexistence to the satisfaction of their children.

in San Francisco. In addition, he joined friends in Palm Springs and renewed his membership in the Beverly Hills Country Club, and enjoyed what was left of the beach property he was stuck with at Pismo.

Somewhere during this period, he also attended a social at Hollywood's Studio Club, where he met resident Galina Liss, a seemingly fragile blonde Russian who was barely five feet three but was an excellent dancer. The club where she was living had been commissioned by the YMCA with Mrs. Cecil B. DeMille as its chairman, after young Virginia Rappe, the fresh-faced cover girl on the sheet music for *Let Me Call You Sweetheart*, died under X-rated circumstances at a drunken party thrown by her overweight date, Roscoe "Fatty" Arbuckle.[63] Studio Club girls were chaperoned, but many became famous movie stars anyway.

Liss appeared to be a strong candidate to capture the actor's attention. She was, Ray decided, the most beautiful woman he'd ever seen. She had appeared in a couple of Spanish films, was working as a double for Claire Trevor, and dating Ramon Novarro, a romantic leading man from *Ben Hur* and *Mata Hari*. Novarro's most recent film, *The Sheik Steps Out*, had garnered only lukewarm reviews, but his career was still viable and he was as rich as he was handsome. Mala was encouraged by insider information that Navarro was gay, until he learned Galina was also dating one of Novarro's younger brothers who was not. Then he discovered she was actually a Russian princess, college educated as well, and fluent in French, Russian, and English. Her aunt, Princess Alexandra Kropotkin, was a popular lecturer and magazine writer, always in the headlines. Galina's late father had been Colonel Feodor Lissivetz Kropotkin, Alexandra's brother, who had served under the tsar.[64] Liss was, in fact, so firmly entrenched in Hollywood's exotic community of deposed royalty that, had Mala not

been utterly taken with her, he might have given up his suit. However he kept inviting her out to movies, the theater, and concerts, as well as for hamburgers and to the beach. To his astonishment, she kept accepting, and finally he came to realize that her early life, despite its seeming glamour, had been even more traumatic than his own. Galina Liss felt comfortable with him.

Galina's mother, Maria, had married Feodor when he was an engineer for the Moscow-Petersburg Railroad. Maria's parents, Stanislaus and Antonia Bilkevich, were close relatives of Tsar Nicholas II. Galina, also known as Princess Kropotkin, was only ten when the Russian ruler was murdered with his family by the Red Army in 1918 and her own family was targeted. Feodor dispatched his wife and daughter to relatives in France, before narrowly escaping himself to Constantinople, Turkey. On March 6, 1923, he made his way to Ellis Island,[65] filing intent to become a naturalized U.S. citizen and making it official in 1926 as Theodor Liss, a resident of California.[66] Meanwhile, Galina completed high school in France. Not until January 26, 1929, did she arrive in New York via the SS *America* with her mother. The ship's manifest listed the mother, age forty, as an English-speaking housewife, which was stretching it, and Galina, twenty, as a French-speaking student.[67]

Maria's brother Eugeny, six years her senior, had made it to the States earlier via Harbin and Shanghai, landing in Seattle, July 6, 1923, and then settled on a chicken farm in Petaluma, California, north of San Francisco.[68] But they never saw any of the rest of their large family again.

Maria changed her name to Mary Liss, and got a job in the San Francisco garment district, making enough as an accomplished seamstress to support her dying husband, and to enroll their daughter at the University of California Berkeley.[69] An education major, Galina also showed skill as a dancer, and on graduation decided to try her luck in

MALA ASPIRES TO CAPTURE JUNGLE PRINCESS. Ray befriended Dorothy Lamour, appearing with her in her first major movie, but as with all his leading ladies, they were just friends. Mala kept his private life separate from his movie career. *Mala Family Collection*

Hollywood.[70] Mala soon discovered, however, that she was not as independent as she seemed. The death of her father had shaken her, and she had grown unusually close to her mother. So Mary Liss still indulged her daughter, now on record as age twenty-four, while also maintaining tight-fisted control over her.

Still, Mary Liss was living in San Francisco, which gave Ray an edge. It became obvious that Galina favored the determined yet soft-spoken actor over richer and more famous Hollywood men she had been dating. She seemed ready to settle down, but Ray feared she would never defy her mother to marry him. And there was also a legal problem. Even if Mother Liss decided to allow her daughter to marry an unemployed actor she had known only a few months, and accepted the fact he was part Eskimo and part Jewish, California outlawed interracial marriage.[71]

Galina Liss had come to trust her mother's judgment long before the canny Russian woman managed their escape from the conquering Red Army. Her mother did not favor Ray Mala. Friends described the girl as timid, despite her excellent performance skills as a dancer and an actress. Yet in late May 1937, Galina Liss traveled boldly over the border to Tijuana, Mexico, to wed Ray Wise Mala,[72] for better or for worse. He would never underestimate her again. ∎

Eight

A FAMILY OF HIS OWN

Mary Liss was not pleased to learn of Galina's elopement, but her daughter was so obviously in love, it was difficult to stay angry for long. Ray, well used to Russian expatriates from his dealings with Bill Wise's sister and mother, quietly moved to fill the breach. To Mary's surprise, he made no attempt to interfere with the girl's unusual dependence on her. Instead, both honest and childishly open, he confided that since the age of twelve he longed for a mother of his own and hoped she would accept him as her son. Six months after the wedding, they were enough of a family so that Ray presented Mary Liss with a Melbourne Spurr portrait showing him as himself and signed "To my dear mother," while Galina, who also sat for the famous photographer, signed hers lovingly in Russian.[1]

The couple took up residence in a small but pleasant apartment at 6163 Glen Alder in the hills just north of Hollywood, about four miles from Laura and Elmer George. Ray had been the Georges' boarder for a full decade, discounting the month he moved out at Gertrude Becker Wise's insistence. They had watched him grow up and would miss him, they said. But, this time they believed he had made a good marriage.[2] Ray's father, his wife May, and Bob and Maxine Shean were similarly impressed with the solidarity of the handsome couple, as was Galina's uncle Eugeny, whom they drove out to visit on his chicken farm at Petaluma.

Newspaper columnists took interest, too. "Ray Mala's Russian bride got rid of a swarm of pesky bees with a vacuum cleaner after they settled on the ceiling of a vacation cottage they rented at Pismo Beach," *Los Angeles Times* writer Read Kendall noted in his "Odd and Interesting," column, July 18, 1937. Two months later, there was a note that the couple had promised to bring home "bushels of the huge and famous Pismo clams for their friends."[3] Mala was delighted to discover that Galina, unlike his first wife, enjoyed entertaining. She had volunteered to give up her job as Claire Trevor's stand-in[4] when she married him, and they spent much of their time entertaining each other's friends.

◄ **TRYING HER LUCK IN HOLLYWOOD.** In January 1936, Galina moved to live at Hollywood's popular Studio Club for young, professional women. This photo was shot of new arrivals on the club's patio with Galina holding the cat. It was there she met Ray at a well-chaperoned social. *Photo courtesy of Ted Mala Jr.*

TRAPPED IN THE STAR SYSTEM

Johnny Weissmuller's story offers a prime example of the damage Hollywood's studio-controlled "star system" could do to the life of anyone caught in its grasp. Not only did MGM destroy what might have been a lasting marriage for Weissmuller with his first wife, but when his role as Tarzan proved to be a sensation, studio executives relentlessly typecast him, even refusing his request to take acting lessons.

Too well paid to buck the system, Weissmuller settled in to become a playboy, a lifestyle that Ray soon tired of because his hopes were focused on family and his acting career. Weissmuller went on to marry three more times and sired three children with whom he had scant contact. Ironically, just about the time his star was fading along with his finances, Ray's acting career was showing promise and he had established a close-knit family with whom to share it.

One of their crowd was Johnny Weissmuller, whose marriage to the tempestuous Lupe Vélez was not going smoothly, but who was pleased to have Ray's company as an "old married man." Together they teamed to give life-saving demonstrations on a local beach in a kayak Ray had designed for rescue operations.[5] Also, a regular was comedian Stan Laurel, who was dating Countess Vera Ivanova Shuvalova, a brassy blonde singer with Russian movie credits who was a childhood friend of Galina's.[6] Stan and Vera were wed January 1, 1938, in Yuma, Arizona, with Countess Sonia Belikovich and Galina's dance instructor, Roy Randolph, in attendance. The next day Laurel's former wife, Virginia Ruth Rogers, flew in to explain her divorce from Laurel wasn't final, so the wedding was scheduled for a second run in March, same time, same station.[7]

Shortly thereafter, Johnny Weissmuller came home from a working trip to New York to discover Lupe had poisoned his dog. He responded by wringing the neck of her pet parrot, a highly vocal bird that had constantly screamed for her former lover, Gary Cooper. Lupe's statement to the press: "Marriage? Eeet steenks!"[8] Their divorce left Johnny so embittered he consigned himself to the world of men. "To hell with women," became his mantra. Joining the Lakeside Golf Club, he spent most of his spare time on the links, where Ray sometimes joined him for a round or two with Bob Hope, Bing Crosby, and Jack Oakie,[9] another comedian who was successfully freelancing his talents following the expiration of his contract at Paramount.[10]

The couple also saw a lot of John Jobson, who was still doing studio publicity but was also trying to help Ray sell his autobiography. Ewing Scott was around, too, hobbling with a broken leg from an auto accident earlier that year but thoroughly engrossed in directing four pictures for RKO.[11] Divorced from his wife, Jane,[12] he was rumored to be seeing Phyllis Loughton, a well-known talent coach at MGM who had better connections than all of them combined. A year earlier, she had married screenwriter George Seaton, so when a gossip columnist reported that she and Scott had vacationed in Alaska and were secretly wed, the news caused a scandal Scott did not care to discuss.[13]

With so many friends in the film industry, Ray figured it wouldn't be long until work came his way, but nothing materialized for months after his marriage. In September, Paramount tested him for a Chinese, role but he didn't make the cut.[14] Finally, just before the end of 1937, he picked up an uncredited walk-on in Rex Beach's *The Barrier*, made mostly on Washington's Mount Baker by Harry Sherman Studios, which produced Hopalong Cassidy westerns.[15]

Then Republic came through with *Call of the Yukon*, a film about a plucky female reporter, actress Beverly Roberts, who winters over in the fictional Inupiat village of Topek, enjoying great rapport with the local wildlife. The story came from a best-selling book by James Olive Curwoods, who focused on a parallel between a domesticated female dog who runs off with the leader of a wolf pack, and the overrefined reporter who takes up with its human equivalent. Ray's character, Olee John, was a traditional, fur-clad Eskimo leader of a tribe where other important members favored Tlingit Indian regalia—certainly an oversight (among many) by the wardrobe department— and all the aborigines spoke painful pigeon English.

However Mala was happily reunited with Buck, the good-natured Saint Bernard from *Robinson Crusoe*, and first-time director Jack Coyle, who had worked on the earlier film in special effects. Teamed with them was veteran director B. Reeves Eason, with a list of credits an arm long, plus producer Arnold Schaefer, who was even deafer than photographer Melbourne Spurr except when you said something you didn't want him to overhear.[16] A *New York Times* writer pronounced the film "saccharine," offering rave reviews for a couple of bear cub extras, while ignoring the human cast.[17] Still, the movie, released in April 1938, kick-started Mala's career as a second-string regular.

On the heels of *Call of the Yukon* came an offer from Mack V. Wright, the saner of Ray's former Republic directors, who was making a serial for Columbia. The Alaskan's assigned role, Little Elk in *The Great Adventures of Wild Bill Hickok*, was small but credited, and was Mala's first chance to play an American Indian. The plot of the fifteen-episode cowboy romp dragged whenever a crew of juvenile actors joined the marshal to take on the phantom rustlers, but leading man Gordon Elliott was impressive. Born in a small Missouri town, Elliott had grown up around horses and was a natural for what was his first starring role in a western. Also, a plus was Monte Blue. A former football hero, the rugged actor had starred with beauties like Lillian Gish, Clara Bow, and Gloria Swanson in silent films, then deftly restructured his career to play character parts when age caught up with him.[18] Despite the studio's low budget and slapdash approach to shooting, no one was surprised when the *New York Times* declared *The Great Adventures* "the best serial Columbia Pictures ever made." [19]

Following this success, Republic awarded Mala his meatiest role of the year as Kias, a deaf boy saved from the jaws of a tiger by Bruce Bennett playing the Tarzan-like hero Kioga, in another serial titled *Hawk of the Wilderness*. Directing were John English, who had cut his teeth on *The Lone Ranger*, and William Witney, who had worked as an assistant on *Robinson Crusoe*. Monte Blue was recruited, too, this time as an evil witchdoctor named Yellow Weasel.

The serial featured all the usual plot ploys: fuming volcanoes, ferocious wild animals, another Wonder Dog (this time an Australian sheep dog named Tuffie), a cache of valuable gem stones, and a party of rescuing whites in which Bennett plays his own father. Set on a semitropical island "above the Arctic Circle," the movie was actually shot at Mammoth Lakes, California,[20] and the hero was actually Herman Brix, a champion Olympic shotputter, originally chosen as MGM's Tarzan. Injured while scrimmaging in a football movie, Brix lost the part to Johnny Weissmuller but later starred in a competing film backed by Edgar Rice Burroughs, the book's author. Although he had to fight for survival in the Guatemalan jungle, doing his own stunts, Brix received much critical acclaim for his role, but practically no salary because the production company went broke. Worse yet, he found himself hopelessly typecast and had just changed his name legally to Bruce Bennett in an attempt to break the curse.[21] The big man's acting talent was obvious, even in a hokey series like *Hawk of the Wilderness*, which was eventually recognized as one of the best serials Republic ever released.[22]

Johnny Weissmuller, now starring in his fourth Tarzan film for MGM, was more than interested in Herman Brix's career move for, despite the high salary Weissmuller commanded from MGM, he was beginning to wonder just how lucky he had been in winning the part. At first he chuckled over the simplistic dialogue he was given to work with—idiot fare such as "Umgawa," "Tarzan eat now!" "Cheeta come!" and "Me, Tarzan. You, Jane." "I sure as hell don't have to stay up nights memorizing my lines for the following day," he told Mala, when the Alaskan declined a social invitation because of his next day shooting schedule. Now, after filming four jungle epics, the former Olympic champ hoped to move on to a bigger challenge. Yet when the studio turned down his request to take acting lessons, he resigned himself to enjoying his swimming scenes and playing with the animals.

Weissmuller was finally dating again, this time an elegant socialite he met at a golf tournament at Pebble Beach.[23] Still, Ray and Galina were worried about him. A nondrinker, Johnny had begun hitting the bottle during his

hellish marriage to Lupe and showed no signs of stopping once free of her.[24]

The Malas also concerned themselves over the increasingly stormy relationship between Stan Laurel and Vera Shuvalova. Following their wedding the couple had been stalked by Stan's second wife, Virginia Ruth Rogers, who made it clear she wanted the comedian back. For starters, she sent a fire truck to Vera's home in Beverly Hills and then followed up by dispatching an undertaker. To escape her, the Laurels moved to North Hollywood, not far from Galina and Ray, where they soon took to fighting among themselves. There was a gulf between their ages: Stan was forty-two while Vera claimed twenty-eight. Both quick tempered, they were known to chase each other around the kitchen with butcher knives. Vera was arrested for drunken driving after hitting two cars on Beverly Drive and crashing into a tree. Laurel, arrested at a later date on the same charge, was discovered to be wearing only socks and boxer shorts. He claimed Vera threw sand in his eyes while he was driving. She said he tried to hit her with a five-foot shovel, threatening to bury her in the yard. The Malas tried to mediate but found it a relief when Vera fled east, leaving Laurel to move back in with Virginia Ruth.[25]

Also in peril was Ewing Scott, whose reported romance with MGM studio executive Phyllis Loughton had become a career killer. Fired from MGM, Loughton stayed with her husband, George Seaton, who had just scored his first major screen credit writing a Marx Brothers comedy titled *Day at the Races*, and was being hailed as a rising star. Scott, meanwhile, had lost his RKO contract and suspected he was being blackballed by Seaton's friends in the industry.[26]

In contrast, Ray's freelance career picked up, with four offers in 1939, all of which he accepted. The most impressive picture for publicity was Cecil B. DeMille's *Union Pacific* with the usual cast of thousands. Lost in the credits were Mala, Monte Blue, and Italian Iron Eyes Cody, all cast as thieving "redskins." Ray's big moment was confrontation with a cigar store Indian he discovered while looting a train. Heavies Joel McCrea, Robert Preston, and Barbara Stanwyck oversaw construction of the pioneering railroad with the help of Lon Chaney Jr. and Anthony Quinn, who had become a family friend.[27]

Ray also played an Eskimo dog team driver, in a Columbia movie titled *Coast Guard* with Frances Dee, Randolph Scott, and Ralph Bellamy, enmeshed in a love triangle that involved a mission to the Frozen North. There was *Desperate Trails*, in which Ray appeared uncredited as part of a western comedy series for Universal, with a veteran comic who went by the name of Fuzzy Night. And, finally, a major Universal venture titled *Mutiny on the Blackhawk*, where, as Wani, a Native slave leader, Mala was billed near the top with Richard Arlen and Andy Devine. Mamo Clark, who had snared only supporting roles and walk-on parts since her appearance as Ray's leading lady in *Robinson Crusoe*, agreed to lesser billing, as "a Native," with an eye to paying tuition at UCLA. Directing was Christy Cabanne, who had started his career with D. W. Griffith and ran his own studio with considerable success. But Cabanne was also accused of being "the dullest director in silent films"[28] and, although the Universal venture was a talkie with a great publicity buildup, it proved no exception. To the defense of Cabanne and his cast, the script started off with a mutiny at sea and ended with a cavalry rescue. So badly did the writers wander that a *New York Times'* reviewer suggested mutiny by the audience." 'We've got a long haul ahead of us,' said Guinn Williams, the First Mate, at the onset of the voyage. And he was just referring to the first half of the picture," the *Times* man noted wearily.[29]

GIRL FROM GOD'S COUNTRY. Ray appeared as Joe, a local Native, with Jane Wyatt as the damsel in distress. Mamo Clark, with whom Ray had starred in *Robinson Crusoe*, played a bit part with no credit. *Photo courtesy of Ted Mala Jr.*

The year that followed, 1940, would be Mala's most prolific as an actor, although he began it with a small role in *Green Hell*, which was even a bigger bomb than *Blackhawk*. Englishman James Whale had made a name for himself directing Boris Karloff in *Frankenstein* in 1931 and followed up with an impressive list of horror films. When that genre lost favor, he'd scored a financial success with *Man in the Iron Mask*, but studios were beginning to avoid him because he flaunted the fact that he was a homosexual in an era when most stayed in the closet.

When Universal offered to gamble on him, Whale picked a high-profile cast. Included were Douglas Fairbanks Jr., Joan Bennett, George Sanders, and Vincent Price, with Mala and Iron Eyes Cody engaged as Indians. Their problem was an extremely weak script. Cranked out by overprolific screenwriter Frances Marion, who was also suffering a career lapse, *Green Hell* was lustily promoted as the story of "seven men and a woman, pitted against Nature and at times against themselves." It was the film's dialogue, however, that turned out to be their real enemy. Actor Price later expressed relief that his character, one of the exploring anthropologists, was picked off by poison darts early in the show. The movie was one of the most unintentionally funny films ever made, he added.[30]

"Oh, the monotony of it!" a reviewer from the *New York Times* gleefully quoted an actor as saying in a scene where his character was driven to hysteria by the deadly jungle. "What a word for the best worst picture of the year."[31]

For once, Ray Mala could be thankful that he didn't have a larger part. However, he did impress Universal with his willingness to work hard at small roles and was quickly provided three more. There was hardly any need to change costumes to play a Native in *Zanzibar*, yet another jungle tale involving a white expedition. Then, there was a two-episode appearance in the serial *Flash Gordon Conquers the Universe*, which, like the Alex Raymond cartoon that inspired it, had become wildly popular. Granted, as Prince of the Rock People, the Alaskan was required to do most of his acting with a stonelike bag over his head to guarantee protection from the giant lizards that prowled his realm. His dialogue, mainly calling to Flash Gordon for rescue from a magnetic beam, was played backward on the sound track to sound appropriately foreign. But it was interesting to work with Buster Crabbe, 1932 Olympic 400-meter freestyle swimming champion, who had gotten awful

reviews in the lead of Universal's Tarzan series, but redeemed himself as a space hero.[32]

Finally, Mala found himself working again with director Christy Cabanne, as a South Sea islander named Talamu in *The Devil's Pipeline*. Buoyed by good-natured Andy Devine and leading man Richard Arlen, this adventure proved a better credit than Ray's earlier film with the occasionally sluggish director, but it ended his run at Universal, which had no more films to offer him.[33]

Unfazed, Mala tested for the part of a Malayan in *The Letter*, a vehicle for Bette Davis at Warner Brothers[34] and, that failing, returned to Edward Small Jr. (the producer who had rescued *Igloo*), for *South of Pago Pago*, in which he played a Native diver. Next, Republic cast him and Mamo Clark as Eskimos in *Girl from God's Country*. Mala played Joe, assistant to a white doctor hiding from civilization, while Mamo appeared as pregnant Mrs. Bearfat Tillicoot. Both were awarded screen credits and speaking parts, although the dialogue has been described as a "Hollywood patois resembling pig-Latin Esperanto," and their job was mainly to prop up the white man's love triangle involving Jane Wyatt, Chester Morris, and Charles Bickford.[35]

Capping the year, Mala landed another DeMille spectacular, *North West Mounted Police*, which also managed to feature a Texas Ranger. Starring were Gary Cooper, Lon Chaney Jr., and Paulette Goddard. As usual, Ray appeared as an uncredited Indian along with Monte Blue, Chief Thunderbird, Chief Yowlache, and a Portuguese actor named Nestor Paiva. The only one missing from their aboriginal fraternity was the Italian, Iron Eyes Cody.

Inspired by improved finances, Ray teamed with Galina to entertain friends from Alaska. They traveled to Northern California, where they helped Mary Liss celebrate her acquisition of American citizenship, and took in a few of the many parties thrown by Bill and May Wise. They also camped with May's daughter, Maxine, and her husband, Bob, and enjoyed the company of Alaska bush pilot Noel Wien and his wife, Ada, who moved temporarily to southern California to improve their health.[36]

They saw less of Johnny Weissmuller, who had wed golfing socialite Beryl Scott and produced a new baby, Johnny Junior.[37] There were hopes that fatherhood would settle him down, although he had begun to fight quite publically with Beryl as he had with Lupe. Even the two daughters that followed could not save the marriage, and Weissmuller's career was also showing signs of stress.

Not that the Malas' future seemed much more secure. Since no children had come their way naturally, they considered adopting, but finances were again tight. Nor did it help that Galina's girlhood friend, the Countess Vera Ivanova Shuvalova, was under observation in Belleview Mental Hospital. Having fled to the East Coast after her divorce from Stan Laurel, Vera had happily announced her engagement to James Long, a seaman who was a brother of the late Louisiana governor Huey Long. Shortly thereafter, though, she tried to jump out the window of the high-rise office of her theatrical agent Eugene Fouvan.

"She just keeps singing," Fouvan told the police that he had summoned for assistance.

"That's a lie," the distraught Shuvalova said. Then burst into "When Irish Eyes Are Smiling."[38]

The Malas needed a change. So did their friend Ewing Scott, who had remarried. He had earned no new Hollywood credits since his RKO contract died in 1937, but he hadn't been idle. In late 1940, he asked Ray to consider a script

GALINA LISS AS A STAR STAND-IN. Galina Liss dropped out as an education major at the University of California Berkeley to become a double for Claire Trevor when family finances grew slim. The petite dancer was well on her way to star status of her own when she eloped with Ray.
Mala Family Collection

he'd written titled *Son of Nanook*, to be shot at Barrow with a Native cast. Taking his cue from Mala's early screenplay, Scott had based his story on the Eskimo reindeer industry, and had gotten tentative approval from Republic Studios to take camera and sound crews north.[39] Flying to Seattle with their wives, the two friends stopped just long enough to announce their new film to the press before taking the steamship *Baranof* to Seward.

STILL A BIT NAÏVE

Friends recalled that Ray Wise Mala remained a bit too trusting as an adult and was sometimes taken in by investment schemes that lacked real grounding. His plan to team with Raymond Cannon may have been a result of this, but Cannon was still connected to Hollywood even though his fabulous directing career, which included making *Intolerance* with D. W. Griffith and *Joy Street* on his own, had cooled. At the time he was living with his "secretary," beautiful Carla Laemmle, who was also the niece of Universal Studio founder Carle Laemmle. In addition, he was still on the payroll at Universal, though simply as a writer of comedy shorts.

Following his failed venture with Mala, Cannon's *Mongolian Emperor* morphed into *Samurai*, a Japanese spy story rife with propaganda, which was released in 1945, with little recognition, through Cavalcade Pictures, a little known studio. Then, with no other movie deals pending, Cannon relocated to become a fishing expert on the Sea of Cortez.

"In 'Son of Nanook,' the story of the introduction of reindeer into Alaska, my role is the sort I like best to play," the *Seattle Post Intelligencer* quoted Mala as saying. "I feel it will be my very best characterization."

The world premiere would be held in Seattle, Scott added.[40] But, for reasons never explained, the venture failed to materialize. The Malas returned to California in time for Ray to pick up only two acting jobs in 1941: uncredited parts in *Hold Back the Dawn* with Charles Boyer, Olivia de Havilland, and Paulette Goddard, and *Honolulu Lu* with Lupe Vélez.

With America's sudden entrance into World War II, the future of the movie industry was uncertain at best. Both Ray and Johnny Weissmuller were disqualified from service because of well-documented heart problems. Weissmuller went back to making *Tarzan* movies, four of them in three years, plus one happy appearance as himself in a wonderful movie, *Stage Door Canteen*.[41] Ray landed four fairly substantial parts, all credited. Republic cast him as an islander in the swashbuckling *Son of Fury: The Story of Benjamin Blake*. Universal provided a similar role in *The Mad Doctor of Market Street*, which was also set in southern isles. He got to play an Eskimo in Republic's gold rush melodrama *Girl From Alaska*, and rounded out the year with *The Tuttles of Tahiti*, a money-losing RKO film comedy in which Charles Laughton managed to earn bad reviews.

Then, suddenly, there appeared to be no parts in sight. Raymond Cannon, a famous director in the '20s, whose career had languished with the advent of talking pictures, offered to help. Cannon had started with D. W. Griffith, traveling to China to research *Broken Blossoms* for him, and later studied Asian religions for six months in a Buddhist monastery there. Mala had met him when Cannon was in his prime at Fox, writing and directing *Joy Street* and *Imagine My Embarrassment*, while developing twin dissolve cameras and a waltzing dolly, which produce special effects still favored by cinematographers.[42] Then, Cannon suffered what appeared to be a nervous breakdown; he emerged in 1935 to author six successful movies, and disappeared again.[43] Now he was offering Mala a script titled *The Mongolian Emperor*.

SHADOW OF A DOUBT. Ray's stock in trade as a cinematographer had risen to a point that famed director Alfred Hitchcock hired him for this mystery thriller, which they filmed in the fall of 1943. Stars Joseph Cotton and Teresa Wright stand ready for directions from Hitchcock, center. Mala can be seen far right, ready to take orders. Hitchcock later said the film was his personal favorite. *Mala Family Collection*

As with Ewing Scott, Mala traveled with Cannon to hold a press conference in Seattle announcing the film. The difference was that this time, Alaska was not involved. Mala had just come from studying Chinese acting methods in San Francisco, he said. And he wouldn't be returning to the land of his birth any time soon. "Mala stood at a Seattle cigar stand today and shook dice for his cigarettes," a reporter noted. "His tan shoes were well shined. His double-breasted gray suit was striped in red and chalk white. There was a definite Hollywood flair to the set of his hat."[44]

Would he like to go back to Alaska? someone asked.

"No. Not to live," the actor replied with a shiver. "It's too cold there. I've been down south too long."[45]

The Seattle press conference would mark Mala's final try at backing an independent production, for nothing came of *The Mongolian Emperor* and he had grown tired of the uncertainty of an acting career. The next news he generated was an article headed "Mala in New Job that Pays," in which the reporter concisely summed up the Alaskan's career challenge for a decade to come: "When the Eskimo picture cycle came to a full stop, Mala became a Polynesian and cavorted on palm-studded beaches with maids who wore sarongs. An Eskimo in South Seas pictures is an oddity in itself—and Mala is really an Eskimo," the reporter explained.

"Then the war knocked out Polynesian pictures. Hollywood isn't ready to resume the Eskimo theme. So Mala got himself a paying job. He's now assistant cameraman at Universal and is working behind the cameras in *Nightmare*."[46]

Ray stayed with Universal through 1943, ending his tenure behind the camera there with *Shadow of a Doubt* under Alfred Hitchcock when he was rehired by Fox. His old studio's merger with Twentieth Century Pictures had not only saved it from going under, but had provided the status of an industry giant, attracting the best and the brightest. Among them was Joe LaShelle, who had gotten his camera training from Charles Clarke, the man Fox had appointed to head Ray's ill-fated *Frozen Justice* expedition to Alaska.

LaShelle had been supervising the printing department of Paramount's film lab in 1926 when Clarke took LaShelle as an assistant to make *Rocking Moon* in Sitka, where Joe developed a bias for Alaskans.[47] Later LaShelle became assistant to Arthur C. Miller of *Perils of Pauline* fame, moving with his boss to Fox in 1932.[48] LaShelle was as innovative as he was meticulous, and he quickly discovered Ray Mala was of like mind. When he was promoted to chief cameraman early in 1943, LaShelle purposely remained aloof from his crews, but he made an exception with the quiet Eskimo. Later that year they were assigned *Laura*, originally slated as a Class B movie, but LaShelle managed to win an Oscar for cinematography with their unique craftsmanship.[49]

Then the studio dispatched Ray to assist Charles Clarke, an unsuccessful Oscar nominee for the past two years, with whom he hadn't worked since their aborted trip to Alaska in 1928. Their film, *Son of Flicker*, starring Roddy McDowell, Preston Foster, Rita Johnson, and a big white horse, has been described as awesome, but from that point on he worked mainly with LaShelle.[50] Impressed with the smoothness of their teamwork, Joe insisted that Mala be assigned to all his films, and it wasn't just Ray's camera skills that impressed him. During down time on a San Francisco shoot, Mala had invited his boss to meet his friends, Richard and Alfred Livingston Gump, who owned a fabulous store for millionaires there. "He knew everybody, and not just in the industry," LaShelle marveled. "The Gumps were so pleased to see him, they opened the vaults and brought everything out: art, jewelry, stones. Everything! He was so quiet, but they were really friends."[51]

As part of LaShelle's crew, Mala's life and finances became more predictable, and things went better with Galina, who had grown restless with her lonesome housewifely routine, because as a couple they now had more time for family and friends. Ray's sisters and their stepsisters, grown now and with husbands of their own, were back in touch, joining a welcome stream of Alaskan visitors who enjoyed the Malas' California hospitality. Dorothy Lamour, Bob Hope, and Hope's wife, Delores, became close friends. Stan Laurel, now in the process of divorcing Virginia Ruth Rogers for the second time, was seeing Ida Kitaeva, a widowed Russian opera singer whom Galina had befriended.

Surer of their finances, the Malas decided to move, first to a larger apartment on South Orange Grove near Wilshire Boulevard and Hancock Park, and then to Fountain Avenue in West Hollywood between Hollywood and Santa Monica Boulevard,[52] right next door to Allen and Jane

Handler, who were old friends from Ray's squash-playing days. Allen, a wealthy real estate developer and writer, had been an early investor in the prestigious and lucrative Racquet Club of Palm Springs. Jane, who had divorced a famous millionaire to marry him, sometimes worked as an actress to amuse herself but had plenty of time to keep Galina company when Ray was on location.[53]

Much of the work Ray and Joe LaShelle did was for Otto Preminger,[54] the ill-tempered Viennese director whom many regarded as a tyrant. Although humorless, stubborn, and given to bullying actors,[55] Preminger was also a perfectionist, which the cameramen appreciated. They saw a lot of him on the set of *Doll Face* in late 1945, but not because he was directing as usual. The film had been adapted from an autobiographical play titled *The Naked Genius* by stripper Gypsy Rose Lee, who was Preminger's mistress. Preminger, who enjoyed an open marriage, didn't want to leave anything to chance with Gypsy's first movie script. Luckily, director Lewis Seiler, a veteran of the silent era and a string of Tom Mix westerns, was a careful troubleshooter.[56] Ray was fully focused on working with him and the lively cast of *Doll Face*, which included Vivian Blaine, Dennis O'Keefe, popular singer Perry Como, and samba dancing Carmen Miranda, when his world turned delightfully upside down.

After nine years of marriage, Galina was pregnant. The Malas were ecstatic. They just couldn't believe their luck. It would be a blonde little girl, they assumed, as did family and friends.[57] But on February 3, 1946, Mr. and Mrs. Ray Wise Mala were pleased to announce the birth of Ray Theodore Mala. Jane and Allen Handler, who'd just moved to a house at Malibu, immediately returned to inspect the new addition and were astonished. "He was a beautiful Eskimo baby, and he weighed seven and a half pounds!" Jane recalled. ∎

BEYOND THE SARONG. Ray looked quite respectable in the ice cream suit the costume designer favored for island travel, but soon abandoned it to "go Native" as an undercover agent on Clipper Island. *Mala Family Collection*

Ray Mala

MOVIE POSTERS

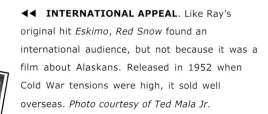

◄◄ **INTERNATIONAL APPEAL.** Like Ray's original hit *Eskimo*, *Red Snow* found an international audience, but not because it was a film about Alaskans. Released in 1952 when Cold War tensions were high, it sold well overseas. *Photo courtesy of Ted Mala Jr.*

◄ **GRIM *ESKIMO* POSTER.** Woody Van Dyke's graphic film pitted Ray Wise, playing Mala, against Danish explorer-writer Peter Freuchen, playing the lecherous trader. The movie got good reviews and today it is considered a classic, but some early viewers found it too graphically grim. *Photo courtesy of Ted Mala Jr.*

ROMANTIC *ESKIMO* LOBBY CARD. Ray took on several wives in *Eskimo*, and the romantic angle of the film played well. This poster features him with Lotus Long, who was part Hawaiian and part Japanese. *Photo courtesy of Ted Mala Jr.*

◄ **KLEINSCHMIDT PROMOTES**. Frank Kleinschmidt booked a nationwide tour and printed up lively promotional material to go with his selling of *Primitive Love* in 1927. Unfortunately, the *New York Times* reviewer gave the film's wild animals more praise than Ray and the rest of the human cast. *Illustration courtesy of Peg MacGowan, Kleinschmidt descendant*

LOCAL CARTOONIST INCLUDES MALA. Feg Murray, a sports cartoonist for the *Los Angeles Times*, included Ray's *Eskimo* character of Mala in a column along with Gary Cooper and Ann Rutherford. *Photo courtesy of Ted Mala Jr.*

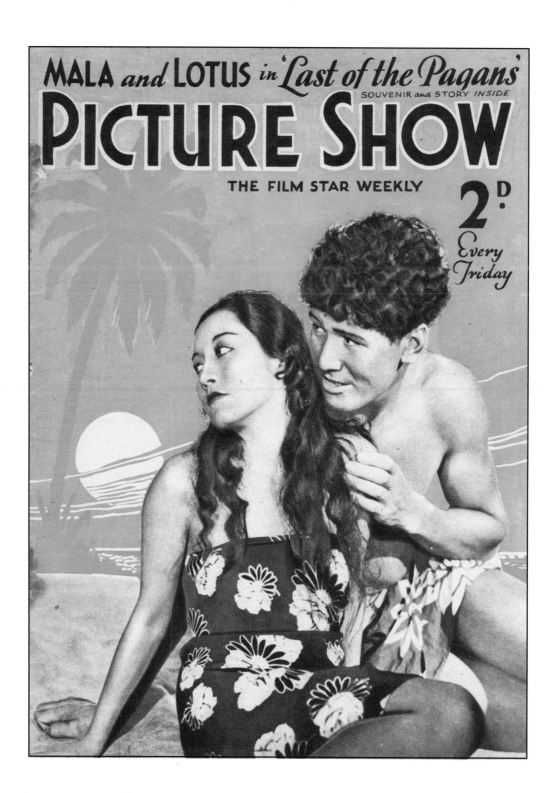

MALA and LOTUS in 'Last of the Pagans'

SOUVENIR and STORY INSIDE

PICTURE SHOW

THE FILM STAR WEEKLY

2D. Every Friday

ONE STEP BACKWARD. Unable to find another major role, Ray took a supporting part as a crafty Native in *Jungle Princess* starring Ray Milland. Newcomer Dorothy Lamour, cast as a beautiful princess brought up in the wild, kept mostly to herself, but Mala befriended her during the grueling jungle hikes they had to make daily to get to their overgrown California location. *Photo courtesy of Ted Mala Jr.*

◄ **THE COVER STORY.** Ray began appearing on magazine covers, many of them foreign. Here he is featured with Lotus Long from *Last of the Pagans. Mala Family Collection*

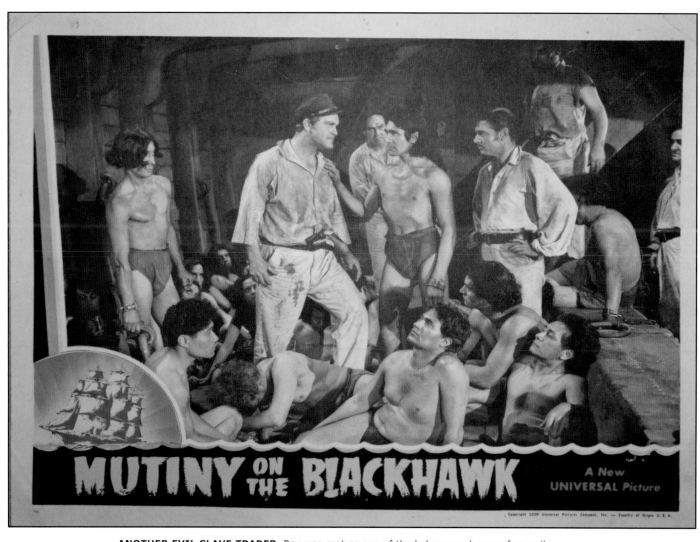

ANOTHER EVIL SLAVE TRADER. Ray was cast as one of the beleaguered crew of an evil captain in 1939 in *Mutiny on the Blackhawk*. Photo courtesy of Ted Mala Jr.

BACK TO BEING INDIGENOUS. In 1938, Ray was cast as a Native in *Call of the Yukon*. The film also reunited him with Buck the Saint Bernard with whom he'd shared billing in *Robinson Crusoe of Clipper Island*. *Photo courtesy of Ted Mala Jr.*

AN ALL-STAR MOVIE WITH HORRIBLE REVIEWS. *Green Hell*, filmed late in 1939, featured
Douglas Fairbanks Jr., Joan Bennett, John Howard, George Sanders, and Vincent Price, all
famous stars, as was English director John Whale. Unfortunately, the script was so horrible
Ray might well have been relieved that he had just a small part as a jungle Native.
Photo courtesy of Ted Mala Jr.

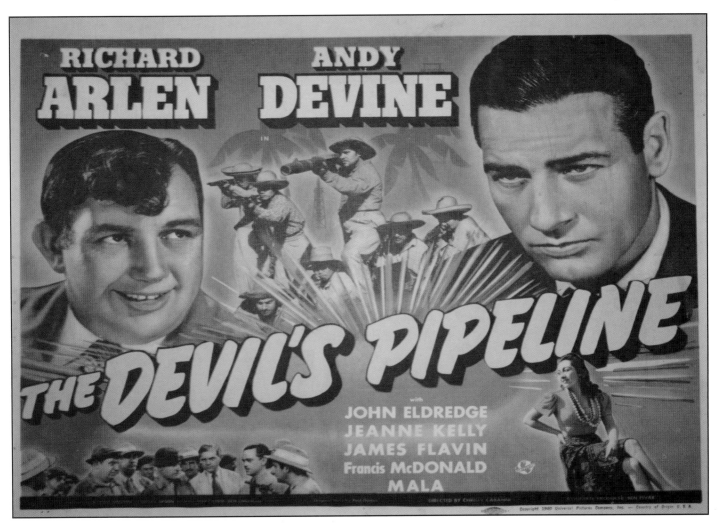

ISLE OF MISSING MEN. Ray was cast as a South Seas Native in *Devil's Pipeline*, a cliff-hanger with Richard Arlen, Andy Devine, and Francis McDonald. *Photo courtesy of Ted Mala Jr.*

THE TUTTLES OF TAHITI. This film gave Ray a chance to appear with one of the biggest stars of his day, Charles Laughton. According to many reports, the British actor was not much fun to work with, but Ray didn't complain. *Photo courtesy of Ted Mala Jr.*

FAVORITE POSTER. This advertisement for *Red Snow* is a family favorite. Ray was cast as an Eskimo scout serving as a member of the U.S. Air Force. *Photo courtesy of Ted Mala Jr.*

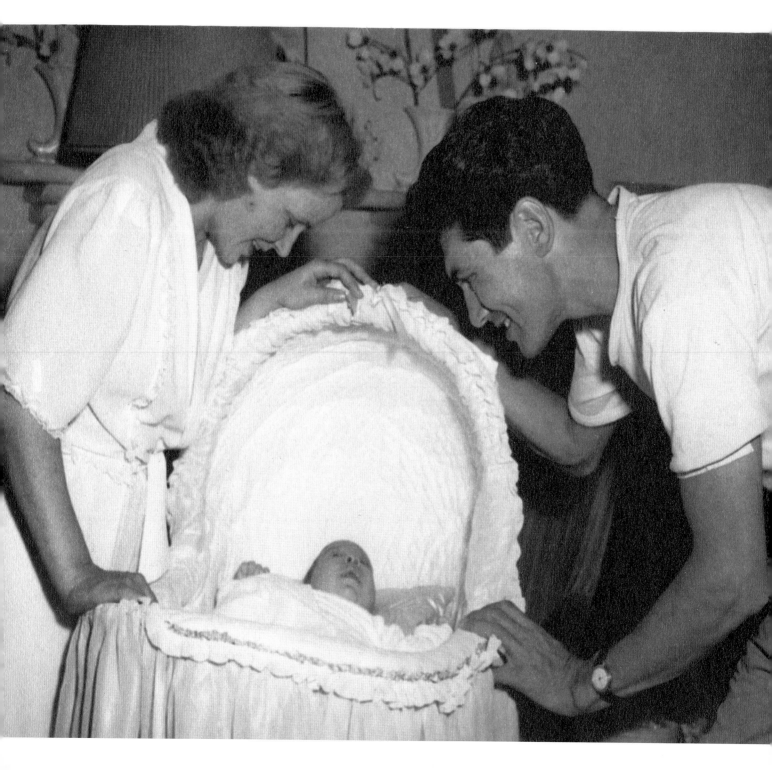

Nine

ALMOST A HOLLYWOOD ENDING

The christening of "Little Fedya", as they called their new baby in Russian,[1] was an event to remember. For starters, a godfather was required, and the Malas' first choice had the flu. Would Allen Handler substitute?

Handler was more than willing, but he'd never been to a Russian Orthodox service before and found it daunting. The priest, "a real Russian" and a bear of a man with a bushy black beard, was dressed in long black robes. Someone had accidentally filled the christening basin with water so hot it would have boiled the newborn, had steam not been detected. And the good baby was painted with little crosses all over him, a fascinating thing to see.

His adoring Russian grandparents, Bill Wise and Mary Liss, did not appear to be on good terms but put their differences aside for the occasion. Galina was obviously nervous, for she had very little experience with babies and was worried sick that she might do something wrong. Her baby was unquestionably a gift from God. So, when the priest placed his huge hands under Fedya's little arms and shoved the child underwater, his mother screamed, certain the boy was drowning.[2] Luckily, he was not, and she clutched him with relief at the end of the long service.

In contrast, Ray Mala, who utterly adored his son, had a good grasp of childcare because he'd helped bring up his little sisters as long as he'd been allowed to stay with them. So Galina followed Ray's lead and, when he was working, sought advice from her mother, Bill Wise's stepdaughter, Maxine Shean, and Jane Handler, long after her former neighbor had moved to the beach. At first Jane found the new mother overly timid, for she became alarmed at every little sneeze or cough. But Galina's caution paid off when mellow little Fedya grew into a healthy, precocious toddler. The Malas' lives, which revolved around him, were so full and happy it amazed them.

Actually, it was a good time for the world in general, for the awful war had ended. Although the economy slowed, the Depression era was well behind them. Movies remained big business at Twentieth Century Fox, where Darryl Zanuck had created a real galaxy of stars.[3] Among them on the

◀ **A SURPRISE.** After nine years of marriage, the birth of Theodore Mala in 1946 came as a delightful shock to Galina and Ray. "Little Fedya," as they called him in Russian, became the focus of their lives. Ray, who had helped bring up his younger sisters, was always eager to help the new mother who worried, needlessly it turned out, over her inexperience. *Mala Family Collection*

RAY TAKES ON A WOODEN INDIAN. When he couldn't find large parts, Ray was grateful for smaller ones like this assignment as a "bad" Indian in *Union Pacific*. The film was directed by Cecil B. DeMille, who would later invite the Eskimo to audition for bigger roles. *Photo courtesy of Ted Mala Jr.*

production side was Henry Koster, who, despite his narrow escape from Nazi Germany, had been considered an alien and had been confined to his house evenings during World War II. He had directed some excellent films in Berlin, however, and his early work in Hollywood was well received even before he fully mastered English. In 1947, he won an

Academy Award nomination for *The Bishop's Wife*, causing Fox to lure him away from RKO and give him some amusing scripts, for which he picked Joe LaShelle and Ray Mala to film. First up was *The Luck of the Irish*, involving a newspaperman and a grateful leprechaun with Anne Baxter and Tyrone Power. This he followed with *Come to the Stable,* a convent-based heart-warmer by Clare Boothe Luce, which starred Loretta Young, Celeste Holm, and Hugh Marlowe.

Henry Koster was very much in love with his second wife, the dynamic actress Peggy Moran, whom he had married in 1942. Family gatherings with their sons, Peter and Nicolas, and Robert from his earlier marriage to actress Kathe Kiraly, were important to them, and soon the Malas, an equally tight family, were included as friends.[4] In addition, there were excursions to visit Galina's uncle, Eugeny, and his new wife Marianna, who were now running a dairy farm up in Fallon, Marin County, near Petaluma and San Francisco, and the Malas also trekked north to visit grandparents, where all the news was not good.

Mary Liss was still doing well at her job in the garment district, in addition to assembling wonderful wardrobes for little Teddy in ever-growing sizes, but Bill Wise had become increasingly distant. During the war, Wise had lost considerable money to a crooked major with whom he was running the exchange at Steadman Air Force Base. He was hit hard again in 1945 when his mother, fearing burglars, accidently locked herself in her basement with daughter Nettie and failed to survive the frightening experience.[5] In 1947, Wise recovered his old bravado to team with Richard J. Dolwig, later a California state senator, to purchase the 1,640-acre estate of Alma De Bretteville Speckels in the Valley of the Moon. According to their press release, the property would be subdivided into homesites of 100 acres or more.[6] A month after the announcement, Wise issued a brief denial that they were selling the land to "nasty old John L. Lewis," then the American leader of organized labor, but nothing more came of the ambitious venture.[7] When May left Wise in 1948, he moved to the San Francisco Union Club, acting like all was fine, but that Christmas, Ray dropped by with Ted, thinking his father might need cheering up. At first Wise seemed pleased, but suddenly grew nasty, insisting that Ray pay for everything. Puzzled and hurt, Ray took his son to a nearby Catholic church, where they tried to enjoy the holiday service.[8]

It was also difficult for Mala to stay in touch with Johnny Weissmuller, whose divorce from Beryl had effectively cut off the swimming champ from their three children. Miserable, he'd taken to the golf courses again, where he met Allene Gates, a sixteen-year-old blonde he married four years later.[9] His *Tarzan* contract, which had passed from MGM to RKO in 1942, was canceled, but in 1948, on return from a lavish London honeymoon he could not afford, Weissmuller was hired by Columbia to play *Jungle Jim*. Finally winning a part where he could wear real clothes, he became preoccupied with shedding thirty-six pounds.[10]

Things went well with most of the Malas' other friends, including beleaguered Stan Laurel. Free at last from Virginia Ruth Rogers, he immediately wed Ida Kitaeva in Yuma, Arizona. The comic had already staged four weddings there, but this one would be different. Ida's previous husband, Gregory "Raphael" Matusewitch, had been a world-famous concertina virtuoso. His formal American debut in 1922 at Town Hall in New York City won great reviews, and even when he was later reduced to eking out a living on the vaudeville circuit during the Depression, she remained at his side.[11] A good-looking blonde, she had not considered remarriage after Raphael's unexpected death in 1939, until she fell in love with Laurel despite his stormy marital record.

LOVING PATIENCE

The Great Depression, followed by some disastrous investments of time and money, all but destroyed Bill Wise, although the former millionaire was apparently loath to admit he was struggling to make ends meet. May's divorce suit, ending what appeared to be a genuine love match, seemed to embitter him, and he became increasingly difficult to deal with, even on an occasional basis.

Yet Ray kept trying, sometimes going to see him with his little son, Ted, in tow because he knew the boy was Bill's pride and joy. Often burned and too well aware of his father's shortcomings, Ray also remembered how lonesome it was to face a hostile world without family, and he never gave up on trying to make the old man happy.

There would be no more divorces, Ida announced firmly to reporters after they tied the knot, and she kept her word.[12]

Also, enjoying a change of luck was Ewing Scott, who had managed to raise $165,000 to produce *Untamed Fury*, a drama about two lifelong friends and the disparate paths of their lives, set in great Okefenokee Swamp. The *New York Times* gave the film a back-handed review, claiming that it proceeded at a "slow crawl" with the usual shots of "coiled snakes, skulking alligators and sucking quicksand," but

A FAMILY EFFORT. Ray joined the close-knit Tuttle movie family, which worked hard to avoid work of any kind. Here they grapple with boat lines under the direction of Charles Laughton. *Mala Family Collection*

offered nothing of novelty.[13] However, *Fury* did well enough at the box office so that Scott soon undertook *Harpoon*, an Alaska-based epic.

His sponsors, brothers Abe, Ralph, and George Danches from Cleveland, had made so much money in the wholesale produce business—mainly selling eggs—that there were allegations of war profiteering. They loved the idea of investing in the film industry and purchased a $250,000 army patrol boat on Scott's behalf at the bargain surplus price of $40,000. Scott painted one side of the 104-foot craft white and the other black so that it could be filmed as two different vessels. Then he sailed it north from San Diego to Wales, Alaska, with seventeen actors, twenty-six technicians, and high hopes of making a great arctic adventure.[14]

Mala, who had too many family responsibilities to gamble on another acting job with no studio backing, declined to join in the venture with mixed feelings. He was enjoying his work as a cameraman at Fox, but his Alaska heritage was never far from his mind. Working on a film titled *Everybody Does It*, he'd come to know Linda Darnell, who was part Cherokee. "We Indians should stick together," she was always saying, which caused him to do some serious thinking. That actually seemed to be happening in Alaska, he knew. The territory had officially ended racial segregation in schools in 1938, and recently a brave half-Eskimo girl named Alberta Schenk had been jailed overnight because she refused to sit in the Native section of Nome's old Dream Theatre. Stubbornly, Alberta appealed to the territorial governor Ernest Gruening, who contacted the mayor of Nome. The incident would not be repeated, they were assured, and shortly thereafter, Schenk was elected queen for the local pageant.[15]

Yet the school system, integrated or not, remained substandard. Mala had discovered that Alaska Natives had the highest rate of tuberculosis in the world, after his sister Harriet learned that she was infected. There were still signs in many Alaskan bars and restaurants that read NO DOGS, NO COAST GUARD, NO NATIVES!

Yet Mala remained hungry for news of the Far North, anxious to hear from old friends there. One of his closest friends was Jimmie Ahkla who, having given up his stage career and switched from reindeer herding in Nome to fishing in Bristol Bay, was well pleased with life. He and his wife, Trixie, had changed their last name to Brandon after that of his birth father, when proprietors of the Bristol Bay

school system could not pronounce his children's Eskimo name. They raised six sons and a daughter, all of whom had done well.

Miles Brandon, the one that Ray had first welcomed into the world, was a gifted singer, back from army duty in the South Pacific, and in 1950, Ray invited him to visit Hollywood to try his luck. Miles was working at Boeing in Seattle at the time. When the company went on strike and he found himself with no income, Ray got him a job with a Hollywood furrier, and hosted the tall, good-looking vocalist for four months.

The Malas lived modestly, Miles recalled. Galina, with whom he felt immediately comfortable, favored blouses, well-tailored slacks, and sweaters. Both she and Ray loved to have parties and cooked out in the evening. Ray, working for Otto Preminger at the time, knew everyone. Through him, Brandon met Betty Grable and Gene Tierney, auditioned for a music director at Columbia, and found work on the *Eddie Cantor Show*. There were also some bit parts in *Wild Bill Hickok* serials, with Ray grandly chauffeuring Brandon in the studio Packard. But it was the closeness of the little Mala clan that impressed the visitor most. Galina came to look on him as a brother and really worried about him, afraid he might be taken advantage of by some gay "swish." "Ray always took the family if he was going to a party, and he took me," Brandon recalled. "For Russian Easter, we went to the Russian Orthodox Church and Little Ted was just fascinated. Ted and his dad were fantastic. It was beautiful. Then, there was the music at Columbia, a beautiful Russian soprano."

But there were problems, too. Galina had recently had pneumonia, which had taken a lot out of her. Ray showed Miles before and after photos and, while she was still beautiful, she had lost an unusual amount of weight. "Plus,

INTRODUCING FEDYA TO HOLLYWOOD MAGIC. Proud of his precocious young son, Ray spelled his wife on babysitting duties. Here they attend the Twentieth Century Fox Christmas party at Grauman's Chinese Theater. Galina's mother, who had become a professional seamstress, tailored the child's suit and coat. *Mala Family Collection*

Ray had a heart condition and knew it," Miles said. "Earlier in the year his doctor had given him medication and closed some lesion. He tried to hide it from Galina."

Still, nothing slowed them down. Galina was a wonderful housekeeper and hostess. Ray's job was a demanding one, which often required packing heavy camera gear over long distances for long hours. Yet he loved the work, and he loved what his life had become. One of

Brandon's best memories of his father's old friend was Mala toting his camera off duty, headed for a studio party for children at Grauman's Chinese Theater with little Fedya at his side. Although still in short pants, the excited boy wore a suit and topcoat tailored by his grandmother to look quite grown-up. Around his neck hung a light meter which he guarded protectively, ready to help his daddy get a picture of the magic fairy lady who had come to greet them.[16]

In 1951, Ray Mala was offered a part in Russian producer Boris Petroff's film *Red Snow*, with billing second only to superstar Guy Madison. It was a Cold War spy thriller that did double duty as an amazingly solid documentary of traditional Eskimo life. The assignment was too good to pass up. Joe LaShelle gave him leave and, after a ten-year hiatus as an actor, Mala found himself working once again with Ewing Scott in the Far North.

Scott's 1948 arctic film for the Danches brothers, *Harpoon*, had garnered bad reviews after months of accident-riddled production snafus. Ewing had crushed his foot when he was trying to hold two heavy boats apart, and he'd been hospitalized in Dutch Harbor, Alaska, for three expensive weeks. Then, Ernest Michens, the movie's villain, fell through a rotten stair and was so badly injured he had to be replaced. And film was scratched in shipping, which took an extra thirteen days and $30,000 to reshoot. The total bill came to more than $400,000, much of which the Danches (playfully referred to by the *New York Times* as the "Three Stooges") did not recover.[17] One reporter called the plot "hopelessly naive . . . directed and acted in such a painfully amateurish way that the best thing a generous reviewer can do is look the other way."[18]

But even sour reviews credited Scott with great outdoor and hunting scenes, so in 1949, Universal International backed him to produce *Arctic Manhunt,* the story of a desperate convict hiding out in an Eskimo village as a priest. To produce it, Scott reworked the northern footage he'd shot on his last trip to mix with studio shots with a new cast. Critics gave Carol Thurston credit for doing a fair job as the Eskimo heroine and made much of Quianna, a part-Eskimo girl named Wilma Bernhardt from Teller, who was that year's Miss Alaska. Good box office receipts proved there was renewed public interest in Alaska and Siberia, because of Iron Curtain tensions, so using the same formula, Scott followed up with *Arctic Flight,* about a bush pilot and a suspected international spy and white Eskimo Carol Thurston.[19]

Following Scott's lead, Boris Petroff, also an independent producer, invested $10,000 in new studio shots to recraft a plot-challenged 1935 arctic expedition film called *Tundra.* Adding a noble doctor who saves a plague-devastated Eskimo village, Petroff renamed the vehicle *Arctic Fury* to win fair reviews and an even better box office.[20] Then, finding himself with leftover footage, he hired Ewing Scott to shoot more and came up with the Cold War plot for *Red Snow,* which would feature Mala. Amazingly, the Eskimo had aged so little during the twenty plus years since Scott had filmed *Igloo,* some of his earlier scenes were incorporated with the *Red Snow* footage, which was also shot in the Arctic near Nome.

Dedicated to "loyal American Eskimos," *Red Snow* revolves around an air force investigation of strange lights and sounds in the Siberian Arctic. Inupiats are dispatched to find the bad guys, with Mala as Sergeant Koovuk at their head. En route, he manages to save residents of Little Diomede from starvation, stops the Soviet invasion of Alaska, and wins the hand of frisky little Gloria Saunders, a white actress gussied up as an Eskimo. Although the modern-day Russian spy epic included most of the old

IGLOO REVISITED. Although *Red Snow* is a Russian spy story set in Alaska off the Siberian coast following World War II, much of the footage was shot by Mala's old friend Ewing Scott for use in their film *Igloo* two decades earlier. Amazingly, Ray had aged so little that shots of him from the original were included in *Red Snow,* with the audience none the wiser. *Mala Family Collection*

Eskimo stereotypes, including the rubbing of noses to indicate romance, Petroff peddled the film to Columbia Pictures, which provided Mala with major studio backing and the start of a second acting career.[21]

Suddenly his own studio was negotiating with him for a part in *The Ten Commandments,* an all-star biblical epic with Cecil B. DeMille producing and directing. Television producers also beckoned. Mala had already gotten one role as a private detective, and he knew other offers were bound to follow in the fast-growing medium.[22]

"It looks like I can make a comeback," he wrote Maxine Shean happily. But he had been in the business too long to give up his day job, even when better offers started coming in.[23] Following the premiere of *Red Snow*, Mala finished shooting *Les Misérables* for Lewis Milestone, and headed with Joe LaShelle to make a new film in Mexico. The weather was steamy. It was tough, mountainous country deep in the interior. LaShelle wanted a long shot of the country from an unusually high vista. Ray was unloading cameras from their jeep as usual, when he got wobbly and collapsed. Their Mexican doctor pronounced him "very sick" and insisted he go home.

"I won't go home," LaShelle recalled the cameraman saying. "This is my job. I'm with you."

Getting back to civilization at that point would be a challenge at best, Mala argued reasonably. Since the Mexican government had required that LaShelle hire a full crew of local men, Joe made Ray promise to leave the heavy lifting to them. They shot for another three weeks. Ray limited his work to his unique focusing skills and seemed to have made a good recovery. On return to Hollywood, he saw his doctor and assured his boss all was well. But when LaShelle returned from a brief vacation, he was surprised to learn Mala was in Cedars of Lebanon Hospital and had been for a week or so. Ray had written his sister, Lorena, that he felt like a pincushion, but his illness didn't seem that serious.[24] In fact, he entertained a steady stream of visitors, including Anna and John Jobson, with whom he discussed ideas for a new story and his long overdue biography.

On the night of September 22, 1952, Joe LaShelle dropped by to find Ray sitting up in bed watching TV. They chatted casually for a bit, but Mala looked so well, his boss just couldn't resist talking shop.

"How soon will you get out of here?" LaShelle had asked. "We need you." Then, less than three hours later, Ray's doctor phoned to inform LaShelle that his cameraman was dead.[25] Ray Wise Mala was only forty-five.

The bond between Galina Liss Mala and her husband was so strong that she could not long survive him. Weakened by her earlier bout with pneumonia, and shielded by Ray from knowing how sick he was, she died earlier on July 3, 1953, leaving their six-year old son with no resources over which he had any control. Theodore's grandmother, Mary Liss, quickly cut him off from other relatives, including his father's father, who were anxious to rescue him. Theodore's bewilderment was heightened by the fact that he had so recently been the adored center of a close-knit, loving, highly social family. What saved him was his parents' early encouragement to make friends on his own and the fact that he quickly learned to keep his own council among warring factions.[26] ∎

▶ **FINAL PHOTO.** Three months before his death, Ray was interviewed by Henry Provisor of *8mm/16mm Home Movies Magazine*, discussing his pioneering work as a cinematographer. The article featured this photo plus one taken during his recent appearance in *Red Snow. Photo courtesy of Ted Mala Jr.*

BOATING EXPERIENCE COMES IN HANDY. Ray's early training as a sailor came in handy during the filming of *The Tuttles of Tahiti*.

Mala Family Collection

EPILOGUE

Theodore Mala has a habit of telling people who attempt to invade his privacy that he was "raised in the woods by wolves." In truth, he pretty much raised himself, and did a fair job of it. The Hollywood crowd, taken with the plight of the six-year-old in 1952, contributed generously to Ted's support, and a surprising number of family members and friends tried to adopt him. What happened to the contributions remains in question. His grief-stricken grandmother, Mary Liss, nimbly stonewalled all comers.

Ray's father, Bill Wise, became so desperate to see his grandson that, at age 69, he climbed in Ted's bedroom window under cover of darkness carrying presents, much to young Ted's delight.[1] Wise was also on hand to buy the boy his first suit with long pants but saw little of him beyond that.[2]

Believing Mary Liss's finances were tight, Wise's stepdaughter and her husband, Maxine and Bob Shean, inquired about adopting Ted, pointing out that Bob was a banker, but Liss refused to allow them even to see the child. "A rich home is not necessarily a loving home," she said.

Then she boggled their minds by shuttling Ted off to a series of military and religious boarding schools, where her permission was required to visit the boy.[3]

The Handlers had decided to dedicate their wealth and their lives to fighting poverty, collecting clothing, day-old bread, and canned goods to distribute in Mexico and contributing cash where needed. Occasionally, when they could spring Ted from school, they took him with them, strengthening his determination to do something useful for mankind.

Shortly after losing his grandfather in May and his grandmother in October 1968, Ted graduated from DePaul, a Catholic university in Chicago,[4] to major in medicine at Autonomous University, Guadalajara, Mexico, and he later earned his Master of Public Health degree from Harvard. When he finally worked his way to Alaska, he did so as its first male Inupiat doctor and was later appointed commissioner of the Alaska Department of Health and Social Services by Governor Walter Hickel.

Following that appointment, he worked in Oregon as a tribal CEO until he was brought home by Kevin Gottlieb, his adopted brother, and his wife Katherine, to work at Southcentral Foundation, an Alaska Native health corporation that co-manages the successful Alaska Native Medical Center in Anchorage. At this writing, Dr. Ted Mala serves as the Director for Tribal Relations and the Traditional Healing Clinic there, with a focus on traditional healing and mentoring future health professionals. In 2008, he was named Physician of the Year by the Association of American Indian Physicians.[5] His daughter, Galina Mala Liss is a business owner and also an actress/producer who has worked on several productions both in front and behind the camera like her grandfather. His son, Ted Junior, who has also appeared before the camera, works for NANA, his Native regional coporation in Alaska.

Most of the people who were important in Ray's life have long since passed. His stepfather, Johnny Herbert, sold his holdings at Candle in 1940 to join his wife, Hilda, who had earlier moved to the Seattle area. Despite a rough start, even Ray eventually gave Hilda credit for doing a good job of raising Johnny's two daughters by their Eskimo mother, and Hilda, in turn, was heard to claim that she had encouraged the Eskimo in his acting career. After Hilda died of heart problems in 1946, Herbert spent much of his time combing Washington State beaches for driftwood until his death in 1960, leaving a basement full of it to bewildered heirs, who could not fully understand what the trove would have been worth in the treeless land of Herbert's youth.[6]

Mala's sister, Harriet, later known as "Margaret," married a government telegraph operator named Don Chapman and had two children, Wayne and Marlene, before tuberculosis took her life. Lorena, the sister to whom Ray was the closest, married twice and survived him by more than three decades, leaving three children, Doris, whom she named after her stepsister, Lori, and Levi.[7] Their stepbrother, Uno, eventually took over Johnny Herbert's Candle business

and then retired in Seattle. Well before his death in May 2001, the little settlement became a ghost town.

Harriet and Lorena's two stepsisters, Doris Herbert Wright, eighty-four, and Mildred Herbert Richey, ninety-one, are still living in the Seattle area at this writing with good memories and driver's licenses to boot. Mildred remembers Ray from a brief meeting in the 1930s as a "nice man with an unusually soft voice."[8]

Jimmie Ahkla Brandon, whose family Ray called his own when he had none, moved to Anchorage at the insistence of his adventuresome wife, Trixie, who fell in love with Alaska's biggest town in the 1950s while on a dental visit. Well pleased with relocation, Jimmie remained there until his death from a heart attack in 1957. Trixie was still in residence in Anchorage, when she followed him thirty years later.

Most of the Ahkla-Brandons' surviving children were adults at the time of the Anchorage move and stayed in Bristol Bay, where they have done well as fishermen. The exception, Miles Brandon, decided against a career as a vocalist in Hollywood—perhaps after meeting too many of the "swishes" that Galina had warned him about. Although he never gave up singing for pleasure, he eventually became the first Eskimo police officer in Washington, D.C. Stationed at the White House while Eisenhower was in office, he was delighted to report that the president liked the smoked salmon that he often provided and that they had long conversations about Alaska statehood, which Ike finally backed after his initial rejection. Brandon later returned to Alaska to work in administrative positions for numerous government and Native agencies before his death of cancer in 2007.[9]

Frank Kleinschmidt, Mala's first mentor, died in Hollywood in 1949, long after the film industry passed him by. When he could no longer garner the funding to travel to Alaska, Kleinschmidt reedited his old movie footage to sell, but he gave his occupation to the 1930 census taker as a "salesman of magazine features." In a 1933 review of a movie Kleinschmidt variously titled *Eskimo Perils*, *Frozen Hell*, and *Blind Adventure*, Mordaunt Hall credited the filmmaker for "interesting glimpses of life in the Frozen North," and noted tersely, "Mrs. Kleinschmidt appears in the film, which was made in the frozen wilds." But Hall also observed the picture was accompanied by a running microphone comment. Obviously, Frank hadn't learned to deal with a sound track, something Ewing Scott and Ray Wise Mala had accomplished two years earlier with *Igloo*. Not surprisingly this was Kleinschmidt's last review of many in the *New York Times*.[10] Nor was there any more communication with Ray, who never recovered his disappointment that Frank and his wife, Essie, had sided with Gertrude Becker during his divorce. Twenty years later he mentioned his bitterness to Miles Brandon, who inquired about the once high-profile filmmaker whom he knew lived close by. "They told Gertrude to take me for everything I had," Mala remembered. "They never considered there might be two sides to the story."

Also alienated was Frank's first family. Immediately following his divorce from Margaret "Alaska" Young in 1917, Kleinschmidt had been attentive. "The twins will be 13 in June and Helen 8 in November," he wrote a niece who was planning to move in 1920. "If it hadn't been for the children I would have moved, too, long ago."[11] But California based and stressed for funding five years later, he apparently began to distance himself. In 1939, he wrote his family that both he and Essie had been down with pneumonia so he could not work, then noted casually that he had become a

grandfather since Grace, one of his twins, had just given birth to a son.[12] However, that grandson, Olney Webb, recalls his only contact with Kleinschmidt was a visit to California he made with his mother and little sister, Anne, in the late '40s just before the old man died. No one in the candid portrait taken on that event looks happy. Grace later sued the estate for lost child support and won, but Olney, about ten at the time, recalls that the lawyers got all the money.[13]

Explorer Knud Rasmussen, for whom Mala served as photographer at the end of the Dane's trek across the American Arctic in 1927, was planning his seventh Thule expedition six years later when he caught pneumonia after a bout with food poisoning and died at the age of fifty-four in Copenhagen. Rasmussen had been knighted by the King of Denmark and has gone down in history as "the father of Eskimology."[14]

John Hegness, champion dog racer and former mail boat captain, under whom Ray sailed for a season or two, spoke scores of different Eskimo dialects and was known throughout the Arctic as "besuktuak," meaning "great traveler." He had been a fixture there since he emigrated from Norway before the turn of the twentieth century, and most expected him to stay. It was Hegness who had mushed across the entire territory in the dead of winter to deliver Ray Mala's film of the 1925 Nome diphtheria epidemic to Pathé News. And it was Hegness, later based at a coastal trading post near Barrow, who had rescued pilot Russ Merrill during Mala's ill-fated Fox Studio expedition to film *Frozen Justice*.

But Hegness was also drawn to the southland. He moved there temporarily in 1930 with his wife and sixteen-year-old blonde, blue-eyed daughter, Brenda, as an advisor to Paramount Studios, which was filming *The Spoilers* by Rex Beach.[15] Although he continued to winter in the Arctic to trap and trade, he also enjoyed a career as a movie advisor, capping it with a year's employment as guide, hunter, and technician with MGM on the set of *Eskimo* and for later filming back on the studio lot. Although their paths seldom, if ever, crossed in later years, the captain lived not far from the Malas until he moved to Everett, Washington, where he died in 1960 at age eighty-three. [16]

Nor did Mala stay in touch with Merl LaVoy, the Pathé newsman he credited for his start in Hollywood. As Mala had predicted, LaVoy succeeded in his much-publicized Mount McKinley climb of 1932, bringing home to a grieving family the body of fallen mountaineer Theodore Koven. Then, turning his back on Alaska, with which he had so long been fascinated, LaVoy made a name for himself documenting the South Seas. By the time of his death at sixty-seven in Johannesburg, South Africa, he had produced notable films on all six continents. The *New York Times* referred to him as "an explorer-camera man," and a "modern Marco Polo," while spelling his name incorrectly in its 1953 obituary.[17]

Ewing Scott, who never could voluntarily turn his back on Alaska, shot his last footage there in 1951 for *Red Snow*. That would also be his final movie credit, as it was for his Eskimo colleague, although it was the fickleness of the film industry that ended the gambling producer's career. While Scott's arctic series had captured public fancy in the late 1940s, interest in the Far North quickly faded. Scott died estranged from the movie industry in San Diego just short of his seventy-fourth birthday in 1971.[18]

Edward Small, the publicity-shy producer who bailed out Scott and Mala by backing their production of *Igloo* when all else failed, had a better run. Moving from New York to Hollywood just before he picked up Scott's movie, Small went on to produce moneymakers like *Palooka*, *The Count of Monte Cristo*, and James Whale's *The Man with the Iron Mask*. Later

EARNING THAT STAR

Ray Mala qualifies for film star status, not only because he was a Hollywood pioneer in two fields, but because he remains the first and only traditionally raised Native American to reach international fame.

Linda Darnell was part Cherokee, but although the beautiful star readily acknowledged her roots, she was never exposed to an Indian lifestyle. Will Rogers, born into a prominent family of the Cherokee Nation in Oklahoma and raised there on a ranch, had far more white blood than Indian, and few fans in his lifetime were aware of his Native American ties.

In contrast, Mala, whose Jewish father claimed Siberian Eskimo blood and whose mother had nothing but, was so indoctrinated in his traditional upbringing that he thought of himself as Inupiat. In fact, never would he fail to introduce himself as Eskimo, even when the label was unpopular, for he was as proud of his roots as he was his Hollywood successes.

he served as chairman of the TV distribution company, Television Programs of America, but still continued to make movies. His last, *The Christine Jorgensen Story*, involving the world's most famous sex change operation, was released in 1970, seven years before his death at eighty-six.[19]

Despite his long career in films, Ray Wise Mala's greatest critical acclaim was for his role as Mala in *Eskimo*, for never again would he have the coaching of a director as attuned to his talents as Woody Van Dyke. Ultimately Van Dyke would direct four others—William Powell, Spencer Tracy, Robert Morley, and Norma Shearer—in Oscar-nominated performances. A Christian Scientist, he committed suicide in 1942 to escape a slow death by cancer.[20]

Van Dyke's inspiration also proved a high point for the rest of *Eskimo*'s credited minority cast who, like Mala, would find their careers blighted by racial stereotyping. LuLu Wong, who had watched her famous sister, Anna May Wong, quite literally driven to drink by the movie industry, dropped out early to marry well, become a traditional Chinese matron, and take firm charge of her large and varied family.[21]

Iris Yamaoka, who spoke fluent English as well as Japanese and showed considerable talent as a comedienne, picked up half a dozen minor parts, most of them uncredited, before being interned in the Heart Mountain Relocation Camp for Japanese in Cody, Wyoming, during World War II.[22] Thereafter, she, too, disappeared from the screen.

Most successful was Lotus Long who, despite her Japanese father, listed herself as white along with her Canadian filmmaking husband in the 1930 Los Angeles census[23] and then passed as part Chinese to escape internment during World War II. Yet Long stepped forward

happily in 1946 to star as *Tokyo Rose,* the Japanese radio announcer who did her best to discourage American soldiers during the conflict. She ended her career once again playing an Eskimo girl in *Rose of the Yukon* in 1949.[24]

Peter Freuchen had been promised a grand American movie career by MGM. Astonished that he was offered no real opportunity to continue after his work on *Eskimo*, he returned to his native Denmark, where he fought with the resistance during World War II and was eventually imprisoned by the Germans. Sentenced to death, he managed to escape to Sweden, and from there to the United States, where he married a fashion illustrator. In 1956, he won $64,000 on a quiz show. He died on a return trip to Alaska in 1957.[25]

Gertrude Becker, who left Mala during his *Eskimo* fame, and Hollywood shortly thereafter, did not return to Alaska as expected, for she had become a sophisticated young woman and was eager to see more of the world. In 1940, she fell in love with Jack Lundstam, a trombone player who was a member of the U.S. Navy Band. Marrying him, she enjoyed a migratory career as a military wife and stayed with him when he became a civilian musician.[26]

Mamo Clark, the Hawaiian beauty whose movie career in many ways paralleled Mala's, never got a real break after her lead in *Robinson Crusoe of Clipper Island*, and quit acting in 1940. Earlier an actor named James Rawley had seen her in *Mutiny on the Bounty,* and decided to marry her even though they'd never met. Following through, he won her heart. Their marriage was a happy one despite the fact that he was away much of the time serving in the U.S. Air Force during World War II and the Korean War. On discharge, Rawley resumed his career in television, worked as a record company executive, and later got his master's in theater arts at UCLA to become a high school drama teacher. After raising their son, James Jr., Mamo earned a degree in cinematography from the same school and later wrote a book, *Not Their Sun*, on the lives of her parents and their early days in Hawaii.

Mamo Clark had been adopted. Her natural mother is thought to have been Princess Evalina of the Hawaiian royal family, and in later years Mamo won a precedent-setting lawsuit that validated her traditional adoption, much to the relief of fellow Hawaiian Natives who had similar problems. Until her death of cancer in 1972, she remained in touch with a few close friends from her movie days and also with her homeland, but content with the life she later made for herself in California, she never spoke of missing either. Her ashes were scattered off the island of Oahu in an elaborate service that involved traditional outrigger canoes and teams of rowers led by Princess Abigail Kinoiki Kekaulike Kawananakoa.[27]

Lupe Vélez, the second wife of Johnny Weissmuller, committed suicide in 1944 after discovering she was pregnant by a young and handsome actor who refused to marry her. Johnny, who still loved her, was the first person Lupe's housekeeper called for help. Later he arranged for a memorial in her honor in her hometown of San Luis Potosi, Mexico.[28]

In the mid-1950s, Weissmuller discovered he was broke. The shock coincided with the end of his *Jungle Jim* television series and his film career.[29] From that point, the champion swimmer depended on his considerable celebrity status to eke out a living with guest appearances, bit parts, and anything else that came his way. Allene Gates divorced him after he sold their membership in the prestigious Lakeside Golf Club without telling her, but another member, Maria Theresia Brock Mandell, born Bauman, who claimed royal blood, moved in to become wife number five. Weissmuller was living with her in Mexico when he died of heart failure in 1984.[30]

FORTY YEARS AFTER HIS DEATH. This photo of Mala taken in 1929 appeared in the Eightieth Anniversary edition of the American Cinematographers annual publication sponsored by Lenhoff & Lenhoff, a long-established Hollywood talent agency. Ironically, it captures the young Inupiat in his two favorite but conflicting roles: as a traditional Eskimo and as a highly skilled cameraman. *Courtesy of Lenhoff & Lenfoff and Robert Koster.*

After four divorces, comic Stan Laurel finally found peace with Russian opera singer Ida Kitaeva, with whom he enjoyed nearly two decades of marriage before his death following a heart attack in 1965.

John Jobson, perhaps Mala's closest friend, settled for just one wife, Anna, but eventually traded his assignment as a Hollywood publicist for a simpler life in the out of doors. In 1962, he became an editor for *Sports Afield*, a job that often took him back to Alaska and one he thoroughly enjoyed until his death in 1979.[31]

In contrast, Joseph LaShelle and Henry Koster stuck it out in Tinseltown. When the cinematographer finally retired in 1969, he was credited with shooting nearly 100 films and had garnered eight more Oscar nominations. Koster, who retired three years earlier with writing and producing credits on more than 100 films, had no Oscars to show for his work but he did have the honor of directing seven stars who were nominated for them. In addition, his name lives on in the industry through son Nicolas who became a child star; son Robert, a director and production manager who retired to teach at UCLA Extension and wrote a textbook on the subject; and Robert's son Kevin who continues to rack up directing and producing credits today.[32]

Hollywood, California, remains the dream capital of America, just as it was when Mala discovered it, although its star system is a bit faded and major studios no longer have complete control over destinies of those they contract. As Mala foresaw, television provided welcome new options for both young actors and fading stars, as would an increasing number of independent productions like he pioneered with Ewing Scott and Boris Petroff.

The biggest changes since Mala's death, however, have happened in his beloved Far North. Following statehood in 1959, Alaska's indigenous people—Eskimos, Indians, and Aleuts—finally joined forces, just as part-Cherokee actress Linda Darnell had suggested so often to Ray. In 1971, never having signed any treaties or lost any major wars, they won from Congress the largest claims settlement in the history of America—one billion dollars and forty-four million acres.[33] Today Alaska's Natives are the state's biggest land owners, and many wield enormous power through large corporations they established to manage their wealth.

The slur "half-breed" is no longer politically acceptable. Although those of mixed race are probably in the majority, Alaska's indigenous people are best referred to as "Native"

with a capital "N." When lowercased, it refers to a person born in the state, who may or may not be an Alaska Native.[34]

As for the state's education system, it is a mixed bag. Some school districts are ahead of their stateside counterparts while others still lag. But all are controlled by local school boards, and Alaska Natives play a major role in most. None are now under the dictatorship of missionaries or the federal government.

Ray Wise Mala never got home to see these changes. He is buried in California, not far from Hollywood Boulevard, where his family and friends are hoping a star will one day be placed in his honor as the first Native American to crack the system. He was not, in the usual sense, a social activist. He seldom spoke out unless he was asked. Many of the parts he played reinforced racial stereotypes that he hated, and he played them without protest. Yet Mala tried in his quiet way to educate the public by setting a good example and being gracious in his dealings with the press. Shortly after *Eskimo* became a hit, Mala gave a lengthy interview to Barrett Keisling of the *Los Angeles Times* that is typical of his approach.

"People down here ask me all sorts of questions about my life as an Eskimo," he began. "They think it is very funny. When I give them my answers to anything they say: 'What a terrible way to live. What strange people!' It never occurs to them that I, in turn, think their existence equally incredible."

While conceding that life in the Arctic could be tough, he tried to explain the simple joy a successful hunt and a full stomach could bring. He also had a few harsh but carefully chosen words on the unhappiness he found in a more complicated world laid low by the Depression.

"To an Eskimo, all this fuss you people in the United States have been making about money is silly," he insisted.

SAVING A DAMSEL IN DISTRESS. Ray cheerfully proved he could play villainous parts, but truly was at his best as the good guy, as in the role of Air Force Sergeant Koovuk rescuing Gloria Saunders in *Red Snow*. The "Eskimo" leading lady, with whom the script required him to rub noses, was not a Native. *Mala Family Collection*

"When I return to the North, I won't even try to explain about why the United States of America went off the gold standard. I won't relate any stories about this country, where big strong men starve because there is no work to bring them little pieces of gold and silver. To an Eskimo, the misery of crowded civilization is incomprehensible."[35]

What made Ray Wise Mala a hero in his own time among his Native people, however, was not that he championed their values, but that he had the courage to dream an audacious dream and he had faith enough in himself to pursue it. And, while it may be difficult today to realize how hard the going must have been for him or the full extent of the prejudices Mala faced, we can still appreciate the dream and the amazing way he fulfilled it. ∎

FILMOGRAPHY

RAY WISE MALA'S MOVIE CREDITS

Note to the reader: I used the Internet Movie Database to research information on these films. Movies in which Ray Mala had an acting part are underlined. He worked on the other listed movies as a cameraman. The films are arranged by release date, with the most recent first.

1966, *Lost Island of Kioga*. Reedit of *Hawk of the Wilderness* (1936) for television. Republic Pictures.[1]

1952, August 30, *Something for the Birds*. Robert Wise, director. Starring Victor Mature and Patricia Neal. Cinematography by Joseph LaShelle. Twentieth Century Fox.[2]

1952, August 14, released in New York, *Les Misérables*. Lewis Milestone, director. Starring Debra Paget and Michael Rennie. Cinematography by Joseph LaShelle. Twentieth Century Fox.[3]

1952, July 7, *Red Snow*. Ray Mala cast as Sergeant Koovuk. Director, Boris Petroff. Also starring Guy Madison and Carole Mathews. Cinematography by Paul Ivano; Ewing Scott, Second Camera Unit Alaska. An All American Film released by Columbia.[4]

1952, June, *Run for the Sun*. Roy Boulting, director. Starring Richard Widmark, Trevor Howard, and Jane Greer. Cinematography by Joseph LaShelle. Not released by United Artists until 1956, well after the death of Ray Wise.[5]

1952, May 16, *The Outcasts of Poker Flat*. Joseph M. Newman, director. Starring Anne Baxter and Dale Robertson. Cinematography by Joseph LaShelle. Twentieth Century Fox.[6]

1951, October, *Meet Me After the Show*. Richard Sale, director. Starring Betty Grable, Macdonald Carey, with Gwen Verdon, Eddie Albert, and Rory Calhoun. Cinematographer, Arthur Arling, Twentieth Century Fox.[7]

1949, November 10, *Happy Land*. Irving Pichel, director. Starring Frances Dee and Don Ameche, with Natalie Wood in a bit part that was her first movie role. Cinematography by Joseph LaShelle. Twentieth Century Fox.[8]

1949, October 25, *Everybody Does It*. James Cain and Nunnally Johnson, directors. Starring Linda Darnell, Paul Douglas, Celeste Holm, and Charles Coburn. Mala's neighbor Jane Handler also had a small role. Cinematography by Joseph LaShelle. Twentieth Century Fox.[9]

1949, September 1, *Come to the Stable*. Henry Koster, director. Starring Loretta Young, Celeste Holm, and Hugh Marlowe. Cinematography by Joe LaShelle. Twentieth Century Fox.[10]

1949, April 1, *The Fan*. Otto Preminger, director. Starring Jeanne Crain and George Sanders. Cinematography by Joseph LaShelle. Twentieth Century Fox.[11]

1948, September 15, *The Luck of the Irish*. Henry Koster, directing. Starring Tyrone Power, Anne Baxter, and Lee J. Cobb. Cinematography by Joe LaShelle. Twentieth Century Fox.[12]

1945–1948. During this period, LaShelle filmed *Claudia and David*, *Cluny Brown*, *The Late George Apley*, *The Foxes of Harrow*, and *Deep Waters*. It seems likely that Mala worked with him on most of these films, but since there are no credits or mention of them in the family scrapbooks, they are not on this list as part of his work. Also missing for the same reasons are nine films LaShelle made between 1950 and 1951, although it is reasonable to assume they also should be included.[13]

1945, August 24, *Thunderhead, Son of Flicka*. Louis King, director. Starring Roddy McDowell, Preston Foster, and Rita Johnson. Cinematography by Charles G. Clarke. Twentieth Century Fox. The movie was later known simply as Son of Flicka.[14]

1945, January, *Doll Face*. Lewis Seiler, director. Starring Vivian Blaine, Dennis O'Keefe, and Carmen Miranda. The show was from the work of Gypsy Rose Lee, who was the mistress of Otto Preminger at the time. Cinematography by Joseph LaShelle. Twentieth Century Fox.[15]

1944, October 11, *Laura*. Otto Preminger, director. Starring Gene Tierney, Dana Andrews, Clifton Webb, and Vincent Price. Cinematography by Joseph LaShelle, Twentieth Century Fox. This movie was originally planned as a Class B picture. Joseph LaShelle had been a chief cinematographer for less than a year, but won an Oscar for his work on this film. Preminger was also nominated for his direction, Webb for his work as a supporting actor, and the writers, and interior decorators for the film. Only LaShelle won.[16]

1944, January 19, *The Lodger*. John Brahm, director. Starring Merle Oberon, George Sanders, and Sir Cedric Hardwicke. Cinematography by Lucian Ballard. Twentieth Century Fox.[17]

1943, August 16, *Shadow of a Doubt*. Alfred Hitchcock, director. Starring Joseph Cotton, Teresa Wright, and Macdonald Carey. Cinematography by Joseph Valentine. Skirball Productions for Universal Studios. The film was nominated for an Academy Award for writing and direction, but failed to win.[18]

1943. Mala and Ray Cannon held a press conference in San Francisco to announce Ray would star in their film titled *The Mongolian Empire*. Although they apparently spent considerable time researching it, the movie never materialized.[19]

1942, November 13, *Nightmare*. Tim Whelan, director. Starring Diana Barrymore and Brian Donlevy. Cinematography by George Barnes. Universal Pictures.[20]

1942, April 29, *The Tuttles of Tahiti*. Mala cast as Native islander. James Vidor, director. Starring Charles Laughton, Jon Hall, and Peggy Drake. Cinematography by Nicholas Musuraca. RKO Studios lost money.[21]

1942, April 16, *The Girl from Alaska*. Mala cast as an Eskimo named Charley. Nick Grinde and William Witney, directors. Starring Jean Parker, Ray Middleton, Ace the Wonder Dog, and Iron Eyes Cody. Cinematography by Jack A. Marta and Bud Thackery. Republic Pictures.[22]

1942, February 27, *The Mad Doctor of Market Street*. Mala cast as Bareb, a South Seas islander. Joseph Lewis, director. Starring Lionel Atwell and Una Merkel. Cinematography by Jerome Ash. Universal Studios.[23]

1942, January 29, *Son of Fury: The Story of Benjamin Blake*. Ray Mala cast as a Marnoa, a Native islander. John Cromwell, director. Starring Gene Tierney, John Carradine, Tyrone Power, George Sanders, Roddy McDowall, and Elsa Lanchester. This would be Frances Farmer's last film. Cinematography by Arthur C. Miller. Twentieth Century Fox.[24]

1941, February 26. Ray Wise Mala and Ewing Scott hold a press conference in Seattle to announce Mala would star in *Son of Nanook* under Ewing's direction. Although they apparently scouted the movie in Alaska, it was never filmed.[25]

1941, December 11, *Honolulu Lu*. Mala cast in uncredited part of a Native policeman. Charles Barton, director. Starring Lupe Vélez and Bruce

Bennett. Cinematography by Franz Planer. Columbia Pictures.[26]

1941, September 26, *Hold Back the Dawn*. Mala cast in uncredited part of young Mexican bridegroom. Mitchell Leisen, director. Starring Charles Boyer, Olivia de Havilland, and Paulette Goddard. Cinematography by Leo Tover. Paramount Pictures.[27]

1940, November 1, *The Devil's Pipeline: Isle of Missing Men*. Mala cast as Talamu, a local Native. Christy Cabanne, director. Starring Richard Arlen, Francis McDonald, and Andy Devine. Cinematography by John W. Boyle. Universal Pictures.[28]

1940 , October 22, *North West Mounted Police*. Mala cast in uncredited part as a Native policeman. Cecil B. DeMille, director. Starring Gary Cooper, Lon Chaney, and Paulette Goddard. Cinematography by Victor Milner and W. Howard Green. Paramount Pictures.[29]

1940, July 30, *Girl from God's Country*. Mala cast as Joe, a local Native. Sidney Salkow, director. Starring Chester Morris and Jane Wyatt. Mamo Clark also played an uncredited role. Cinematography by Jack Marta. Republic Pictures.[30]

1940, July 19, *South of Pago Pago*. Mala, cast as a Native diver, uncredited. Alfred E. Green director. Starring Victor McLaglen, Jon Hall, and Frances Farmer. Cinematography by John Mescall. Edward Small Productions for United Artists.[31]

1940, July 11, according to the *Los Angeles Times*, Mala tested at Warner Brothers for the part of a Mayan in *The Letter* with Bette Davis. It does not appear that he won the part.[32]

1940 March 8, *Zanzibar*. Mala cast as a Malaysian in this jungle epic. Harold Schusler, director. Starring Lola Lane and James Craig. Cinematography by Milton Krasner. Universal.[33]

1940, March 3, *Flash Gordon Conquers the Universe*. Mala, uncredited, cast as Prince of the Rock People. Ford Beebe and Ray Taylor, directed this sci-fi classic. Starring Buster Crabbe as Flash Gordon and Carol Hughes. Cinematography by Jerome Ash and William Sickner. Universal.[34]

1940, January 26, *Green Hell*. Mala cast as jungle Native as is Iron Eyes Cody. James Whale directed the all-star cast in this film disaster. Starring Douglas Fairbanks Jr., Joan Bennett, George Sanders, and Vincent Price. Cinematography by Karl Freund. Universal.[35]

1939, September 1, *Desperate Trails*. This film may have been one where Mala worked as an extra, but his name is not shown in the lengthy listing. Albert Ray, director. Starring Johnny Mack Brown, Bob Baker, Fuzzy Knight, and Frances Robinson. Cinematography by Jerome Ash. Universal.[36]

1939, September 1, *Mutiny on the Blackhawk*. Mala cast as Wani, Native slave leader. Christy Cabanne, director. Starring Richard Arlen, Andy Devine, and Constance Moore, with Mamo Clark in a walk-on. Cinematography by John W. Boyle. Universal.[37]

1939, August 4, *Coast Guard*. Mala cast in uncredited part as the Eskimo driver. Edward Ludwig, director. Starring Frances Dee, Randolph Scott, and Ralph Bellamy. Cinematography by Lucian Ballard. Columbia Pictures.[38]

1939, May 5, *Union Pacific*. Mala cast in uncredited part as a marauding Indian. Cecil B. DeMille, director. Starring Joel McCrea and Barbara Stanwyck, with Anthony Quinn as a thug. Cinematography by Victor Milner. Paramount.[39]

1938, December 3, *Hawk of the Wilderness*. Mala cast as Kias, the good Native. John English and William Witney, directors. Starring Herman Brix, with Monte Blue as the bad Indian, Yellow Weasel. Then there is Tuffie the Dog, who also got billing. Cinematography by William Nobles and Edgar Lyons. Republic.[40]

1938, June 30, *The Great Adventures of Wild Bill Hickok*. Mala cast as Indian Little Elk. Sam Nelson and Mack V. Wright, directors. Starring Bill Elliott with Monte Blue and Carol Wayne. Cinematography by Benjamin Kline and George Meeham. Columbia.[41]

1938, April l8, *Call of the Yukon*. Mala cast as Eskimo Olee John. B. Reeves Eason, director. Starring Richard Arlen, Beverly Roberts, and Buck the Saint Bernard. Cinematography by Ernest Miller. Republic.[42]

1937, November 2, *The Barrier*. Mala mentioned going to Washington to do this but his name cannot be found in the credits and Sally Marks Martin, who played the role of a child, cannot remember him, although she had also been cast with him earlier as the younger version of Dorothy Lamour in *Jungle Princess*. Lesley Selander, director. Starring Leo Carrillo and Jean Parker. Cinematography by George Barnes. Paramount.[43]

1936, December 24, *The Jungle Princess*. Mala cast as Melan, a Malaysian Native. Wilhelm Thiele, director. Starring Dorothy Lamour and Ray Milland. Cinematography by Harry Fischbeck. Paramount.[44]

1936, November 14, *Robinson Crusoe of Clipper Island*. Mala starred as government agent in this fourteen-part serial. Ray Taylor and Mack V. Wright, directors. Also starring Mamo Clark, Rex the Wonder Horse, and Buck the Saint Bernard. Cinematography by William Nobles and Edgar Lyons. Republic Pictures.[45]

1935, December 20, *Last of the Pagans*. Mala cast in lead as warrior. Richard Thorpe, director. Also starring Lotus Long. Cinematography by Clyde De Vinna. Metro-Goldwyn-Mayer.[46]

1934, January 10, *Eskimo*. Mala cast without credit as Mala, the Eskimo hero. W. S. Van Dyke, director. Also starring Edgar Dearing, Edward Hearn, Peter Freuchen, Lotus Long, Lulu Wong, and Iris Yamaoka. Cinematography by Clyde De Vinna, George Nogle, Josiah Roberts, and Leonard Smith. This was the first film ever to win an Academy Award for editing. The honor went to Conrad Nervig. Metro-Goldwyn-Mayer.[47]

1932, July 1, *Igloo*. Mala cast in starring role as Chee-Ak, the tribal leader. Ewing Scott, director. A Barrow girl, billed only as "Dortuk, the Garbo of the North," played the female lead. Cinematography by Roy H. Klaffki. Produced by Scott Arctic Productions, which sold the film to Edward Small Company, which got Universal to release the film.[48]

1930, November 1, *The Big Trail*. Raoul Walsh, director, with Ewing Scott as one of six assistant directors. Starring John Wayne in his first major role with Ruth Cameron, and Tyrone Power Sr. Cinematography by Lucien Andriot and Arthur Edeson.[49] While sweating out this film in the California desert, Mala and Scott decided to do an independent production in Alaska.

1929, March 24, *Girls Gone Wild*. Lewis Seiler, director. Starring Sue Carol and Nick Stuart, with Hedda Hopper in a bit part. Cinematography by Arthur Edeson and Irving Rosenberg. William Fox, presenter.[50]

1928, September 30, *Air Circus*. Howard Hawks and Lewis Seiler, directors. Starring Arthur Lake and Sue Carol, with Marie Dresser as a supporting actress. This was the first feature film that used sound, although there was only fifteen minutes of dialogue. The flying sequences, with Daniel B. Clark as chief cameraman, was considered a real breakthrough in cinematography. William Fox, presenter.[51]

1927, September, *Two Girls Wanted*. Alfred E. Green, director. Starring Janet Gaynor and Glenn Tryon. Cinematography by Irving Rosenberg. William Fox, presenter.[52]

1927, May. Ray Wise headed for Alaska with cinematographer Charles G. Clarke, documentary cameraman Capt. Jack Robertson, and producers Virgil Hart and Ewing Scott, to shoot preliminary footage for *Frozen Justice*, a best seller for which William Fox had just purchased movie rights. Two planes hired to ferry the crew and gear out of Fairbanks crashed en route to Barrow with Clark, Hart, and Robertson aboard. Ewing and Wise, who were waiting for a second run, were unable to locate them for almost a month. Although everyone survived, they were in bad shape, and Fox decided against making the movie in Alaska.[53] In 1928, Mala tested for a role in the film but was rejected because the studio decided to use an all-white cast.[54]

1927, May 8, *Heart of Salome*. Victor Schertzinger, director. Starring Walter Pidgeon and Alma Rubens. Cinematography by Glen MacWilliams. William Fox, presenter.[55]

1927, May, *Primitive Love*. Frank Kleinschmidt, director and producer. Starring Mala as the brave young hunter, with Eskimos from Nome in cast uncredited. Mala also took the part of a woman, and served as cameraman when he was not before the camera.[56]

1926, early. Ray Wise went to work for William Fox Studios, first as a laborer, but within a couple of months became an assistant cameraman.[57] Since assistant cameramen were seldom, if ever, credited, it is difficult to guess which films he worked on, but Fox was one of the busiest studios in town and up to its ears in productions. The specific films we have documented here are those on which Ray sent production stills to his sister, but since he worked full time for the studio, he no doubt shot many more. One of the most interesting stills he sent home was that of himself with Ben Johnson, who was head of Fox Studio. The fact that Johnson posed with Ray (at least twice), indicated he was a valued member of the crew.

1925, March, *How Death Was Cheated in the Great Race to Nome*. Cinematographer, Ray Wise. Pothé News.

BIBLIOGRAPHY
BOOKS AND ARTICLES

Andrews, Clarence Leroy. *The Eskimo and his Reindeer in Alaska*. Caldwell, Idaho: The Caxton Printers Ltd., 1939.

Barbas, Samantha. *The First Lady of Hollywood: A Biography of Louella Parsons*. Berkeley: University of California Press, 2005.

Cahan, Abraham. *The Rise of David Levinsky*. New York: Penguin Books, 1993.

Cannom, Robert. *Van Dyke and the Mythical City, Hollywood*. Culver City, California: Murray & Gee, 1948.

Cannon, Raymond. *The Sea of Cortez*. Menlo Park, California: Lane Magazine and Book Co., 1966.

Clarke, Charles G. *Highlights and Shadows: The Memoirs of a Hollywood Cameraman*. Metuchen, New Jersey: The Scarecrow Press, 1989.

Cole, Terrence. *Nome: City of the Golden Beaches*. Vol. 11, No. 1. Anchorage: Alaska Geographic, 1984.

Davis, Mary Lee. *Uncle Sam's Attic*. Boston: W. A. Wilde Co., 1930.

Davis, Ronald L. *Hollywood Beauty: Linda Darnell and the American Dream*. Norman: University of Oklahoma Press, 1991.

Fienup-Riordan, Ann. *Freeze Frame: Alaska Eskimos in Movies*. Seattle: University of Washington Press, 1995.

Freuchen, Peter. *Eskimo*. New York: Grosset and Dunlap, 1931.

Freuchen, Peter. *Vagrant Viking: My Life and Adventures*. New York: Julian Messner, 1953.

Gehring, Wes D. *Laurel and Hardy: A Bio-Bibliography*. New York: Greenwood Press, 1990.

Graf, Linda. *Rex, King of the Wild Horses*. Jefferson, North Carolina: McFarland, 2011.

Harmetz, Aljean. *The Making of the Wizard of Oz*. New York: Dell Publishing, 1989.

Harkey, Ira. *Pioneer Bush Pilot: The Story of Noel Wien*. Seattle: University of Washington Press, 1963.

Harrison, E. S. *Nome and Seward Peninsula; History, Description, Biographies, and Stories*. Seattle: E. S. Harrison, 1905.

Hensley, William L. *Fifty Miles from Tomorrow: A Memoir of Alaska and the Real People*. New York: Sarah Crichton Books, Farrar, Straus and Giroux, 2009.

Hodges, Graham Russell Gao. *Anna May Wong: From Laundryman's Daughter to Hollywood Legend*. New York: Palgrave MacMillan, 2005.

Jackson, Sheldon. *Report on the Introduction of Domestic Reindeer into Alaska*. 55th Congress Senate Document #34. Washington, D.C.: U.S. Government Printing Office, 1898.

Johnson, Susan Hackley, "When Movie Makers Look North." *Alaska Journal*, Winter 1979: 12–33.

Kawin, Bruce. *How Movies Work*. Berkeley: University of California Press, 1992. (First edition, 1978).

Kira, Gene. *The Unforgettable Sea of Cortes*. Torrance, California: Cortez Publications, 1999.

Lamour, Dorothy, with Dick McInnes. *Dorothy Lamour: My Side of the Road*. New Jersey: Prentice-Hall, 1980.

Lontz, Vernon. *Arctic Interlude: True Stories of Alaska*. New York: Vantage Press, 1990.

Louvish, Simon. *Stan and Olie, The Roots of Comedy: The Double Life of Laurel and Hardy*. New York, St. Martin's Press, 2002.

McCurdy, H. W. "Maritime Events of 1924," *Marine History of the Pacific Northwest*. Seattle: Superior Publishing Company, 1966.

Mikkelsen, Ejnar. *Frozen Justice*, translated from Danish by A. G. Jayne. New York: Alfred A. Knopf, A. L. Burt Company, 1922.

Morgan, Lael. *The Kotzebue Basin.* Vol. 8, No. 3. Seattle: Alaska Geographic, 1981.

Pinson, Elizabeth Bernhardt. *Alaska's Daughter: An Eskimo Memoir of the Early Twentieth Century.* Logan: Utah State University Press, 2005.

Potter, Jean. *The Flying North.* New York: Bantam, 1984 (originally published in 1947).

Provisor, Henry. "Ray Mala Was an Amateur Once." *Home Movies,* July 1952.

Rasmussen, Knud. *Across Arctic America: Narrative of the Fifth Thule Expedition.* New York: G. P. Putnam's Sons, 1927.

Rawley, Mamo Clark. *Except Their Sun.* Honolulu: Abigail Kekaulike Kawananakoa Foundation, 1994.

Roberts, Arthur O. *Tomorrow is Growing Old: Stories of the Quakers in Alaska.* Newberg, Oregon: Barclay Press, 1978.

Rossman, Earl. *Black Sunlight: A Log of the Arctic.* New York: Oxford University Press, 1926.

Ruskin, Evey. "Memories of a Movie Star: Ray Mala's Life in Pictures," *Alaska Journal,* Spring 1984: 33.

Salisbury, Gay, and Laney Salisbury. *The Cruelest Miles: The Heroic Story of Dogs and Men in a Race Against an Epidemic.* New York: W. W. Norton, 2003.

Weissmuller, Johnny Jr., with William Reed and W. Craig Reed. *Tarzan: My Father.* Toronto, Canada: ECW Press, 2002.

Whitney, William. *In a Door, Into a Fight, Out a Door, Into a Chase: Moviemaking Remembered by the Guy at the Door.* Jefferson, North Carolina: McFarland & Company, 1996.

Ungermann, Kenneth A. *The Race to Nome.* New York: Harper and Row, 1963.

Young, S. Hall. *Hall Young of Alaska.* New York: Flemming H. Revell Co., 1927.

INTERVIEWS & CORRESPONDENCE

Ayotte, Paul, great-grandson of Jimmie Ahkla, Anchorage, Alaska. June 20, 2009. Phone interview by author.

Brandon, Art, son of Jimmie Ahkla, in Anchorage, June 23, 2009. Phone interview by author.

Brandon, James, son of Jimmie Ahkla, Ekwok, Alaska, June 25, 2009. Phone interview by author.

Brandon, Mable, daughter-in-law of Jimmie Ahkla and wife of Ed Brandon, Dillingham, Alaska, June 23, 2009. Phone interview by author.

Brandon, Miles, son of Jimmie Ahkla, Anchorage, Alaska, 1981. Interview by author.

Coats, Lorena, half-sister of Ray Wise Mala, and Emma Black, about 1983 in Fairbanks. Interview by author.

Handler, Jane, and Allen Handler, October 1981, in Malibu, California. Interview by author.

Jobson, Anna M., widow of John Jobson, Layton, Utah, March 26, 1984. Phone interview by author.

LaShelle, Joseph. Interview by author in Hollywood, California, 1982.

Lundstam, Gertrude Becker, Snohomish, Washington, March 1985. Interview by author.

Mala, Dr. Ted, of Anchorage, Alaska, son of Galina and Ray Wise Mala. Interviewed many times since the early 1980s by author.

Marks, Sally Martin, who appeared as a young girl in *The Barrier,* e-mail to the author July 15, 2009, and later follow-ups.

Rawley, James McKee, son of Mamo Clark Rawley, e-mail interview by author, February 28, 2009.

Richey, Mildred E. Herbert, daughter of Johnny and Hilda Herbert of Candle, now of Ferndale, Washington. Interviewed by author, May 10, 2009.

Sarrett, Ruth, of Brick, New Jersey. A descendant of Frank Kleinschmidt, she has worked with the author via phone and mail since 2006 to piece together a history of the pioneering filmmaker.

Shean, Maxine, stepdaughter of Bill Wise. Interviewed by author in Larkspur, California, 1983.

Teters, Mary, a neighbor of the Herbert family in Candle, now of Wilsonville, Oregon. Interviewed by phone by author, June 22, 2010.

Wright, Doris, daughter of Hilda and John Herbert of Candle, Alaska, now of Seattle. Interviewed by phone by author, April 24, 2009.

ENDNOTES

CHAPTER 1

1 Erskine Johnson, "Eskimo Vivid Story of Primitive Passions," *Los Angeles Times*, November 25, 1933.

2 Peter Freuchen, Vagrant Viking: My Life and Adventures (New York: Julian Messner, 1953), 246.

3 Robert Cannom, Van Dyke and the Mythical City of Hollywood (Culver City: Murray & Gee, 1948), 248.

4 "When Man Meets Wolf," *New York Times,* July 16, 1933.

5 Freuchen, 263.

6 Susan Hackley Johnson, "When Movie Makers Look North," *Alaska Journal* (Winter 1979), 18.

CHAPTER 2

1 *William L. Hensley, Fifty Miles from Tomorrow: A Memoir of Alaska and the Real People* (New York: Sarah Crichton Books, Farrar, Straus and Giroux, 2009), 12.

2 Abraham Cahan, *The Rise of David Levinsky,* first published in 1917 by Harper & Brothers, focuses briefly on this murder which touched off a major migration of Jews from Russia, and ultimately the Russian Revolution. See a later edition (New York: Penguin Books, 1993) for an introducton by Jules Chametzky, xii–xiii, and Cahan, 60 and 382.

3 Interviews with Dr. Ted Mala, grandson of Bill Wise (1980). Also see passenger list of the Virginia, March 31, 1937, Ancestry.com New York passenger Lists, Microfilm serial: T715; Microfilm roll: T715 5956; Line 29, notes that passenger William Wise acquired his U.S. citizenship through his father. Census listings for San Francisco in 1900 (Roll 623_100 Page: 2B; Enumeration District: 22, show Bill, his mother, and sister Theresa were naturalized in 1890.)

4 Interview with Maxine Shean, stepdaughter of Bill Wise, Larkspur, California, 1983. Maxine did not know the name of the older son but it was probably Abraham Wise, listed as a musician employed at a San Francisco restaurant in the 1910 census. Roll T626-99; Page 3A, Enumeration District 192; Image 697.

5 Interviews with Mala (1980) and Shean (1983).

6 Interview with Shean (1983).

7 Geological Survey, Professional Paper 567, *Dictionary of Alaska Place Names* (Washington: United States Government Printing Office, 1967) 542. More recent Eskimo translators report the name as Qikiqtagruk. However the settlement was recorded as Kikikhtagyut in the l880 U.S. Census with a population of 200, very much the same as it was when Wise landed. Lieutenant Zagoskin, the first explorer on the scene (in 1847) reported it as Kikikhtagyut.

8 Lael Morgan, The Kotzebue Basin (Seattle: *Alaska Geographic*, 1981), Vol. 8, No. 3. 71. Singer Margaret "Gretchen" Echardt was one of very few white women in the town, but a good example of how unusual the newcomers were. Many of the European men were fleeing military conscription. Also see Earl Rossman, Black Sunlight (New York: Oxford University Press, 1926), 38–39.

9 Geological Survey, 179.

10 Vernon Lontz, *Arctic Interlude: True Stories of Alaska* (New York, Los Angeles: Vantage Press, 1990), 90.

11 He is listed as age fifty, with a wife named Charlotte, forty-five, with both unable to read or write in the 1930 census, Noatak Kobuk, Second Judicial District, Roll: T625_2031; Page: 3B, Enumeration District: 6; Image 1511.

12 Mala as told to Barrett C. Keisling, "Look Homeward Simple Eskimo," *Los Angeles Times*, January 28, 1934, H3.

13 Ray Wise death certificate, State of California 52-076930, September 23, 1952, lists her as "Constance Unknown." Her oldest daughter, Lorena Coats, interviewed about 1983 in Fairbanks, maintained her name was Ellen but that she was always known as Casina. When Ray let the *Los Angeles Times* publish her photo in an article titled "Look Homeward Simple Eskimo," on January 28, 1934, he gave her name as Karenak.

14 Phone interview with Mary Teeters, Wilsonville, Oregon, June 22, 2010. A neighbor of Herbert's in Candle, Teeters recalls the grave of his first wife stood out in the Candle cemetery.

15 Interview with Lorena Coats (about 1983).

16 Henry Provisor, "Ray Mala was an Amateur Once," *Home Movies*, July 1952, and Coats.

17 Interview with Lorena Coats (about 1983). In the family scrapbook, there is a photo of a sod house fronted by vertical logs with an unnamed older Eskimo who is probably Nancy Armstrong posing outside, which might be the family's winter home.

18 Eskimo babies traditionally shared their mother's parkas following birth, but a picture of Ray as a newborn, treasured by his sister Lorena, shows him in an elaborate dress and lacy cap.

19 Eleanor Barnes, "Living Is Cheap in Arctic. Housekeeping Is Simple." Clipping in family scrapbook does not name publication but the interview with Ray is dated February 16, 1932. During the interview, Wise refers to the woman who died as his "grandmother." According to Ray Wise's son, Dr. Ted Mala, Ray's mother's mother lived to a ripe old age, so it might have been a great-grandmother or simply a neighbor the boy regarded in the same way.

20 Phone interview with Herbert's youngest daughter, Doris Herbert Wright, Seattle, Washington, April 24, 2009.

21 1910 Census, Fairhaven Division 4, Alaska Roll T624, Page 22A, Enumeration District: 6: Image 122, lists Anna Herbert at John Herbert's residence as a "partner."

22 Anna Herbert is listed as a married inmate of Morningside Hospital in the 1920 census, Russellville, Multnomah, Oregon; Roll: T625_1503; Page: 16B; Enumeration District 194: Image 795.

23 Phone interview with Herbert's daughter, Mildred Herbert Richey, Ferndale, Washington, May 3, 2009.

24 Interview with Lorena Coats and Emma Black in Fairbanks (1983).

25 Arthur O. Roberts, Tomorrow is Growing Old: Stories of the Quaker in Alaska (Newberg, Oregon: Barclay Press, 1978), 250. This missionary history names John 'Punnak' Armstrong as engaged in evangelistic missionary work in the Candle mining district with a church "of short duration" at Kiwalik." "He was another valiant 'Jesus man,' " according to that account.

26 Maxwell Styles, "Deer Races, Finger Pulling, Eating, Favored Eskimo Sports" in an undated newspaper interview with Wise in family scrapbook, probably published about 1932.

27 Interview with Lorena Coats and Emma Black (1983).

28 While there is no record that Wise was enrolled, most of his memories of missionary teachers center on Charles Replogle, who based in Noorvik and made only occasional appearances at the Kotzebue school. The description of the village comes from Knud Rasmussen, *Across Arctic America* (New York: G. P. Putnam's Sons, 1927), 337–8, who visited just after Wise would have been there.

29 Interview with Black and Coats (1983).

30 Mike Leavitt, Secretary of Health and Human Services, Opening Remarks at the Pandemic Planning Summits held in Alaska April 13, 2006. Online at http://www.pandemicflu.gov/general/grandpandemic.html

31 Roberts, 271.

32 Ray recounted his lumber camp experience to Hollywood columnist Maxwell Styles. We're not sure how he got south or exactly where he landed in the Pacific Northwest. "Portrait of an Actor," *New York Times*, July 24, 1932, X3. The author reported that after Wise ran away, he tried his luck "as dishwasher in a restaurant, as assistant cook on a small schooner and later as first engineer when the first engineer quit." An undocumented clipping authored by Lloyd Pantages in the same collection says Ray was chief engineer of an Alaska schooner at age eleven and held down his post for nearly a year.

33 Interview with Richey, and 1930 census on the Herberts, Fairhaven, Second Judicial District, Alaska Territory; Roll: 2627; Page: 5A; Enumeration District 7; Image 162.0.

34 Annual Report-B to the Commissioner of Education of the Candle Public School, Territory of Alaska for the year ending June 4, 1920, in the family collection shows fifteen students enrolled with nine withdrawing during the year. Ray is listed as being promoted to the sixth grade.

35 "Portrait of an Actor"; and Black (1983), who recalled his trip to Nome with a shudder.

CHAPTER 3

1 Terrence Cole, chief editor, *Nome: City of the Golden Beaches* (Anchorage: Alaska Geographic, Vol. Number 1/ 1984), 106.

2 Elizabeth Bernhardt Pinson, *Alaska's Daughter: An Eskimo Memoir of the Early Twentieth Century* (Logan: Utah State University Press, 2005), 43.

3 Cole, 111.

4 Interview with Miles Brandon, Anchorage, Alaska, 1981. Jimmie Ahkla, 1920 Census, Second Judicial District, Alaska Territory; Roll T625_2031; Page 1A; Enumeration District: 4; Image 989. Akhla is listed as 24 years old but family members say he was born in 1898 which would make him 22.

5 Pinson, 83–4.

6 Sheldon Jackson, "Report on the Introduction of Domestic Reindeer into Alaska," 55th Congress Senate Document #34 (Washington, D.C.: U.S. Government Printing Office, 1898), 129.

7 E. S. Harrison, Nome and Seward Peninsula; History, Description, Biographies and Stories (Seattle: E. S. Harrison, 1905), 51.

8 Phone interviews with Paul Ayotte, great grandson of Jimmie Ahkla, and Art Brandon, Paul's grandfather, in Anchorage, and with Mrs. Ed (Mable) Brandon, one of Ahkla's daughters-in-law, Dillingham, June 23, 2009. Also see C. H. Brandon, 1900 Census: Nome, Northern Supervisors District, Alaska; Roll T623_1828 Page: 26B; Enumeration District: 3. Brandon is listed as single, a transient miner and a pharmacist from Elmira, Illinois. His birthdate is given as 1862. There is a Cole W. or H. Brandon listed in the 1930 Census with a birthdate of about 1864; Bellingham, Whatcom, Washington; Roll 2521; Page: 5A; Enumeration District: 18; Image: 1067.0. He lists his occupation as pharmacist and owns his own pharmacy and store. His wife, Fredia Lean, 46, was born in Illinois and they have a son named Richard, age 26, who is a radio announcer.

9 Clarence Leroy Andrews, *The Eskimo and his Reindeer in Alaska* (Caldwell, Idaho: The Caxton Printers Ltd., 1939). In Chapter 28, "The Seward Peninsula District," the author expresses disappointment in the Nome reindeer men who sometimes ignore their herds for years at a time.

10 Interview with Miles Brandon, and phone interview with James Brandon, one of Jimmie's sons, Ekwok, Alaska, June 25, 2009.

11 H. W. McCurdy, "Maritime Events of 1924," *Marine History of the Pacific Northwest* (Seattle: Superior Publishing Company, 1966), 35.

12 Cole, 57; Pinson, 15; and Gay and Laney Salisbury, *The Cruelest Miles: The Heroic Story of Dogs and Men in a Race Against an Epidemic* (New York: W. W. Norton, 2003), 5.

13 Interview with Gertrude Becker Lundstam, Snohomish, Washington, March 1985. John Becker, 57, is listed in Nome's 1920 census with wife Ella, 32; and children Charles K., 12; Edward, 10; Gertrude, 7; and Andrew, 2 months.

14 An umiak is a large Eskimo boat crafted of walrus skins stretched over a driftwood frame and sewed in place with sinew.

15 Knud Rasmussen, *Across Arctic America: Narrative of the Fifth Thule Expedition* (New York, London: G. P. Putnam's sons, 1927), 341–2.

16 Cole, 170 and 154.

17 Phone interview with Doris Wright, daughter of Hilda and John Herbert, Seattle, April 24, 2009.

18 Henry Provisor, *Home Movies*, July 1952, 238; and Salisbury, 6.

19 Earl Rossman, *Black Sunlight: A Log of the Arctic* (New York: Oxford University Press, 1926), 27.

20 Provisor. The Dream Theatre remained segregated until 1943. See Cole, 170.

21 Rasmussen, 358.

22 "Report Cruelty in Siberia," *New York Times*, July 30, 1923, 3.

23 Kleinschmidt is listed in the *Dawson Polk Directory* of 1901 as the owner of both the Diamond K and the Diamond L. By 1907, he is listed in the Polk Directory for Teller as the captain of both boats, in residence at Laurence Hotel. Presbyterian missionary S. Hall Young, who sailed with Kleinschmidt in 1914, speaks well of his son-in-law in his autobiography, *Hall Young of Alaska:"The Mushing Parson"* (New York: Fleming H. Revell Company, 1927), 407–8 and 423–5. Kleinschmidt married Young's daughter in 1904.

24 "Alaska-Siberia Motion Pictures," a poster and postcards promoting the show in possession of the author. *New York Times*,

March 2, 1912, 8; March 29, 1912, 13; May 17, 1912, 13. Kleinschmidt's passport application #42112 in 1914 shows he was 5 feet 7 inches.

25 *New York Times*, November 11, 1913, 6.

26 Ann Fienup-Riordan, *Freeze Frame: Alaska Eskimos in Movies* (Seattle, University of Washington Press, 1995), 42.

27 "The Will Hudson Collection," http://www.whatcommuseum.org/pages/archives/hudson.htm, accessed February 2, 2009, and Will E. Hudson, "Thinks Stefansson's Ship is Lost," *New York Times*, February 1, 1914, 10.

28 "Fred LeRoy Granville at http://www.imdb.com/title/tt0004528/ and "Fred LeRoy Granville" at http: //www.theasc.com/magazine/aug04/founding/page4.html, accessed February 2, 2009.

29 "Praises Germans' Military Methods," *New York Times*, February 27, 1916, 3.

30 "Carnegie Hall is About to be Sold, but Won't Close Yet," *New York Times*, January 30, 1925, 2.

31 "Austrian Arrested and Weapons Found," *New York Times*, November 25, 1917, 7.

32 Hal Erickson, "All Movie Guide," *New York Times* Movies, http://movies.nytimes.com/movie/236467/The-War-on-Three-Fronts/overview, and the Internet Movie Database, http://www.imdb.com/title/tt0009150/ accessed April 27, 2009.

33 "Adventures in Far North," *Variety*, Film Review, September 13, 1932, and "Portrait of an Actor" *The New York Times*, July 24, 1932, X3.

34 "Portrait of an Actor." *New York Times*, July 24, 1932. According to the interview, Kleinschmidt was en route to Seattle as passenger on the Silver Wave when he met Wise, who was hired as the cook.

35 Letter from Frank Kleinschmidt to Minnie Louise Bismarck (née Wagner-Kleinschmidt) provided by Mary Katherine Ellison (nee Otterbein-Bismarck), April 19, 1924, from a genealogy material provided by Mrs. Ruth L. Sarrett (née Otterbein-Bismarck) who is working on Kleinschmidt genealogy, Brick, New Jersey, September 2008.

36 Provisor, 226, 238

37 *Variety*, September 13, 1932.

38 Ann Fienup-Riordan does an excellent job of discussiing reactions to Flaherty's work. See *Freeze Frame*, 3, 47–53.

39 Rossman, 1.

40 Kleinschmidt, April 19, 1924.

41 Frank E. Kleinschmidt, "The White Tyrant of the North," *Los Angeles Times*, November 8, 1925, K11.

42 Frank, Kleinschmidt (no title), *New York Times*, October 26, 1924, RPB2.

43 Promotion handout for *Primitive Love*, courtesy of Ruth L. Sarrett.

44 In 1985, a group of Eskimos at the Nome Senior Center regaled this writer with accounts of Kleinschmidt and Wise's beachfront filming, which had most definitely amused them.

45 "Johan Hegness," typed manuscript labeled

"English Translation" but unsigned in the John Hegness File, Carrie M. McLain Memorial Museum, Nome.

46 Rasmussen, 339, and Joseph F. Bernard, Untitled log, Archives, University of Alaska, Joseph F. Bernard Collection, Folder 17, 2 and Joseph F. Bernard, "Captain Joseph Bernard and Rasmussen Trip to Siberia" Archives, University of Alaska, Joseph F. Bernard Collection, Folder 17, 2, 5–7.

47 Rossman, 162.

48 Bernard, "Captain Joseph Bernard and Rasmussen Trip to Siberia," 5.

49 Rossman does not mention Edna Claire Wallace in his book on Alaska, but Margaret B. Blackman in her biography of Sadie Brower Neakok, notes she lived in the home of Sadie's father, Charles Brower, who was Barrow's wealthiest trader, for a year or so and that Brower's wife and children disliked her intensely. Later, according to Sadie, Wallace moved in with Jim Allen, another well-heeled trader at Wainwright. See *Sadie Brower Neakok, an Inupiaq Woman* (Seattle, University of Washington Press, 1989), 47. Throughout her arctic stay, Wallace claimed to be writing a book. Her "Nineteen Degrees South of the North Pole: An Adventure in Bowhead Whaling, which Almost Had A Fatal End on Drifting Ice" was published in 1925 by *Asia Magazine*, 573–582. Later she wrote another piece for them titled "Little Female 'Nanook,' " "Current Magazines," *New York Times*, June 20, 1926, BR20.

50 Today known as Uelen.

51 Bernard, "Captain Joseph Bernard and Rasmussen Trip to Siberia," 11–13

52 Provisor, 238.

53 Rasmussen, 381, and Mary Lee Davis, *Uncle Sam's Attic* (Boston: W.A. Wilde Co., 1930), 149.

54 Rossman, 27–28.

55 James Brandon.

56 Cole, 141–2, and Salisbury, 9.

57 "Authorizes Flyer to Make Nome Dash," *New York Times,* January 31, 1935, 1.

58 "Dogs Rush Anti-Toxin for Nome Epidemic," *New York Times*, January 29, 1925, 4.

59 Salisbury, 56–79.

60 Salisbury, 225.

61 Cole, 142-3; "Blizzard Delays Nome Relief Dogs in the Final Dash," *New York Times*, February 2, 1925, 1; and Kenneth A. Ungermann, *The Race to Nome* (New York, Harper and Row, 1963).

62 Provisor, 238.

63 Salisbury, 245.

64 Provisor, 238.

CHAPTER 4

1 Mathew Strum, "Climbing into Catastrophe," Heartland, *Fairbanks News-Miner*, January 9, 2009, 1, and "History Timeline for Denali Park

and Preserve," http://www.nps.gov/dena/upload/Park%20History%20Timeline.pdf, accessed January 1, 2008.

2 Wise was an adolescent when he met Kleinschmidt, age 50, who always seems to have thought of him as a youngster. Knud Rasmussen was 45 and too distracted by his encounter with the Russians to give the lad much attention. Although LaVoy, 43, would spend most of his life traveling, he was more a professional cameraman, than an adventurer, and encouraged other talented shooters. LaVoy's first name is spelled both Mernl and Merle by the New York Times. Universities that feature collections of his work spell it Merl.

3 Henry Provisor, "Ray Mala Was an Amateur Once," Home Movies magazine, July 1952, 239.

4 "Balto," The Internet Movie Database, http://www.imdb.com/title/tt01124531/, accessed May 6, 2009. The dogs Gunnar had used for the serum run actually belonged to Leonhard Seppala, who eventually sold them to Hollywood producer Sol Lesser.

5 "Lance Jensen, Seppala Tour," http:www.workingdogweb.com/Balto-Togo-Goodby-Nome.htm, accessed May 6, 2009.

6 Phone interview with Paul Ayotte, grandson of Jimmie Ahkla, Anchorage, June 23, 2009.

7 Interview with Lorena Coats and her cousin, Emma Black, in Fairbanks, about 1983.

8 Jane Holtz Kay, Asphalt Nation: How the Automobile Took Over America and How We Can Take It Back (New York: Crown Publishers, 1997), 178.

9 "Ask American Profile." American Profile, November 7–13, 2010, 1.

10 "Portrait of an Actor," New York Times, July 24, 1932, X3.

11 Brett L. Abrams, "Latitude in Mass-Produced Culture's Capital: New Women and Other Players in Hollywood, 1920–1945." http://findarticles.com/p/articles/mi_qa3687/is_200401/ai_n9381281/, accessed July 3, 2008, 2.

12 Ronald L. Davis, Hollywood Beauty: Linda Darnell and the American Dream (Norman: University of Oklahoma Press, 1991) 33, and "Seeing Stars," http://www.seeing-stars.com/studios/foxstudios.shtml, accessed July 3, 2008.

13 Provisor, 226.

14 Bruce Kawin, How Movies Work (Berkeley: University of California Press, 1992, originally l978), 380. Charles Clarke, Highlights and Shadows: The Memoirs of a Hollywood Cameraman (Metuchen, New Jersey: The Scarecrow Press, 1989), 50.

15 William Whitney, In a Door, into a Fight, Out a Door, into a Chase: Moviemaking Remembered by the Guy at the Door (Jefferson, North Carolina: McFarland & Company, 1996), 24.

16 Provisor, 226.

17 Ray Wise is listed in 1930 census as a lodger with Elmer A. and Laura D. George at 4048 Edenhurst Street. Also interview with Gertrude Becker Lundstam, Snohomish, Washington, March 1985, who said Wise had lived there for years when she married him. About 1927, the Kleinschmidts moved from 220 West 42nd Street in New York City to 6019 Carlos Avenue, Hollywood, an address featured on Frank's motion picture fliers. It was less than four miles from the Georges.

18 Samantha Barbas, The First Lady of Hollywood: A Biography of Louella Parsons (Berkeley: University of California Press, 2005), 117.

19 Whitney, 24.

20 Mordaunt Hall, "The Screen," New York Times, June 29, 1925, 8, wrote that the show "melts into mediocrity when compared with Robert J. Flaherty's masterpiece, 'Nanook of the North.' "

21 Earl Rossman, Black Sunlight: A Log of the Arctic (New York: Oxford University Press, 1926), 144.

22 "At 85 She Loops the Loop," New York Times, August 26, 1922, and Ann Fienup-Riordan, Freeze Frame: Alaska Eskimos in Movies (Seattle, University of Washington Press, 1995), 42. Robinson and Young released two travelogues, The True North in 1925 and Alaskan Adventures in 1926.

23 Fienup-Riordan, 60.

24 Mordaunt Hall, "The Screen," New York Times, May 30, 1927.

25 June 1, 1927.

26 The treatment is preserved in family collection.

27 Ejnar Mikkelsen, Frozen Justice, translated from Danish by A. G. Jayne (New York; Alfred A. Knopf , A. L. Burt Company, 1922).

28 "F. W. Murnau Killed in Coast Auto Crash," New York Times, March 12, 1931.

29 Clarke, 76.

30 Alma Whitaker, "Movies in the North," Los Angeles Times Magazine, July 17, 1932.

31 Clarke, 88

32 Ira Harkey, Noel Wien: Alaska Pioneer Bush Pilot (Fairbanks: University of Alaska Press, 1974, originally printed by University of Washington Press, 1963), 210.

33 Harkey, 208–10.

34 Harkey, 213–14.

35 Clarke, 118.

36 Harkey, 218–19.

37 Ibid, 219.

38 "Nieminen Returning to Kotzebue Brings Report Frantic Search—Rescues," Fairbanks News-Miner, June 5, 1928.

39 Clarke, 114.

40 Clarke, 122–24, and Whitaker.

41 Clarke ,119, and interview with Wise's sister, Lorena Coats, in Fairbanks about 1983.

42 Hal Erickson, "All Movie," New York Times," no date given, http://movies.nytimes.com/movie/110269/The-Sin-Sister/overview accessed May 9, 2009. Clarke, 125.

43 "Virgil Hart" The Internet Movie Database, http://www.imdb.com/name/ nm0366576/, accessed May 9, 2009.

44 "The Woman from Hell," The Internet Movie Database, http://www.imdb.com/title/tt0020600/ accessed May 9, 2009.

45 "Moana," The Internet Movie Database, http://www.imdb.com/title/tt0017162/, accessed May 9, 2008.

46 " Frozen Justice," The Internet Movie Database, http:// www.imdb.com/title/tt0019907/, accessed May 9, 2008, and Fienup-Riordan, 66.

CHAPTER 5

1 Harrison Caroll, "Behind the Scenes," June 12, 1932, publication not named. A clipping in the family scrapbook.

2 Interview with Gertrude Becker Lundstam, Snohomish, Washington, March 1985.

3 Interview with Lorena Coats and her cousin, Emma Black, in Fairbanks about 1983.

4 "Credit Seventy-Five Years of History of the Atlanta Fox, The City of Atlanta, the Movie Industry, Gone with the Wind," author, who claims to have worked for Fox in the early days, gives only his e-mail address (ThunderChild@dobywood.com), http://whitenberg.de/FoxTheatreAtlanta/FoxHistory.html accessed May 9, 2009, and "Fox Up," Los Angeles Times, December 7, 1929, 1.

5 Mildred Adams, "The City of Angels Enters its Heaven," New York Times, August 3, 1930, 69.

6 Brett L. Abrams, "Latitude in Mass-Produced Culture's Capital: New Women and other Players in Hollywood, 1920–1941," Frontiers: A Journal of Women Studies, Volume 25, Number 2, 2004.at http:// http://findarticles.com/p/articles/mi_qa3687/is_200401/ai_n9381281/ accessed July 3, 2008.

7 Samantha Barbas, The First Lady of Hollywood: A Biography of Louella Parsons (Berkeley: University of California Press, 2005), 147.

8 The American, Waterbury, Connecticut, May 25, 1929, taken from family scrapbook with a similar piece by Coons from the St. Joseph Missouri New Press, M3, 1929.

9 Charles Clarke, Highlights and Shadows: The Memoirs of a Hollywood Cameraman (Metuchen, New Jersey: The Scarecrow Press, 1989), 128–31.

10 "Ewing Scott," The Internet Movie Database at http://www.imdb.com/name/nm0779131/, accessed June 17, 2008.

11 Peter Rivendell, "Friedrich Wilhelm Murneau," Gay for Today, http://gayfortoday.blogspot.com/2007/12/f-w-murnau.html, accessed May 11, 2009.

12 "The Big Trail," Wikipedia, http://en.wikipedia.org/wiki/The_Big_Trail, accessed May 11, 2009.

13 According to "Virgil Hart," The Internet Movie Database, http://www.imdb.com/name/nm0366576/, accessed July 4, 2008, Hart carried the title of assistant from the beginning of his career in 1926 to his final film in 1957, with the exception of a couple of gigs as production manager.

14 Alma Whitaker, "Movies in the North," *Los Angeles Times Magazine*, July 17, 1932, and "Portrait of an Actor," *New York Times*, July 24, 1932, X3.

15 Robert S. Birchard, "The Founding Fathers," American Cinematographer, 85th Anniversary Edition, August 2, 2004, at http://www.theasc.com/society/downloads/AC_85th_Anniversary_Excerpts.pdf, accessed May 12, 2009, and the 1030 U.S. Census, Roy H. Klaffki, Los Angeles Assembly District 63, Roll: T625_106, page 7B.

16 Kevin Brownlow and Patrick Stanbury, Le Giornate del Cinema Muto, http://www.cinetecadelfriuli.org/qcm/ed_precedenti/edizione1999/stro_wedd.html, accessed May 12, 2009.

17 "Hell's Angels," Internet Movie Database, http://www.imdb.com/title/tt0020960/, accessed May 12, 2009.

18 "Scott Party to Fly to Arctic," *Fairbanks News-Miner*, March 9, 1931.

19 Whitaker, 3; "Alaska Epidemic Grows," *New York Times*, April 5, 1931, 15; and *Time*, July 4, 1949 "Died. Joe Crosson, 45, veteran bush pilot" at http://www.time.com/time/magazine/article/0,9171,888589,00.html, accessed May 14, 2009.

20 In ensuing interviews, Ewing never named Klaffki as the miserable crew member, but the cinematographer was California born while Scott, who was raised in Nebraska, and Wise were both used to the cold. To Klaffki's credit, it should be noted that more than a decade later, Scott was able to sell the fine footage he shot under duress for *Red Snow*, distributed by Columbia Pictures.

21 Whitaker, 15, and 1930 U.S. Census, Noatak Kobuk, Second Judicial District, Alaska Territory' Roll: 2627, Page 4B. Phone interview with granddaughter Ann Whipple, Nome, Alaska, October 24, 2009.

22 McNeil Island Penitentiary Records of Prisoners Received, 1887–1951 (National Archives microfilm Publication M 1619, 4 rolls); records of the Bureau of Prisons, Record Group 129; National Archives, Washington, D. C. Accessed through http://Ancestry.com.

23 Interviews with Lorena Coats and Emma Black, about 1983.

24 Correspondence from Paul Ayotte, Anchorage, Alaska, June 29, 2009. Ayotte has some of the notes Jimmie made as an informant for Jacobs.

25 Phone interview with James Brandon, son of Jimmie Ahkla, from Ekwok June 25, 2009.

26 Interview with Lundstam.

27 "Lost Film Party Safe in North," *Los Angeles Times*, August 17, 1931.

28 Whitaker, 15, and "Biography for Edward Small," The Internet Movie Database, http://www.imdb.com/name/nm0806448/bio, accessed May 12, 2009.

29 Eleanor Barnes, "Cameraman to Exhibit His Eskimo Photos," no publication source given, October 2, 1931, Clipping in family scrapbook.

30 Harrison Carroll, "Universal Studio Buys 'Igloo' for Release," *Los Angles Evening Herald and Express*, June 1, 1932.

31 "The New Pictures," Time, August 1, 1932, and "Portrait of an Actor," *New York Times*, July 24, 1932.

32 W. E. Oliver, " 'Igloo' True, Powerful story of Eskimo Tribe," *Los Angeles Times*, June 1, 1932.

33 Robbin Coons, "Hot Weather Release Due for Igloo," undated and sourceless clipping in family scrapbook.

34 Eleanor Barnes, "Living is Cheap in Arctic," February 16, 1932, no publication mentioned in family scrapbook.

35 "An Eskimo Beholds Hollywood," May 1932, no publication data, in family scrapbook.

36 "Cinématters," *New Telegram*, September 5, 1932, from family scrapbook.

37 " 'Igloo' Brings Sensation of Arctic Drama to Films," *The Charleston Gazette*, June 19, 1932, and undated ad for *Igloo* in family scrapbook.

38 " 'Igloo' Director," undated clipping in family scrapbook, and "Universal Buys 'Igloo' for Release."

39 Undated, unreferenced clips in family scrapbook by Jerry Hoffman and W. E. Oliver.

40 Ann Fienup-Riordan, *Freeze Frame: Alaska Eskimos in the Movies* (Seattle: University of Washington Press, 1995), 70.

41 Peter Rivendell.

42 "Ewing Scott," The Internet Movie Database, http://www.imdb.com/name/nm0779131.

43 Suit against Ewing Scott by Ray Wise, July 1, 1933, Los Angeles Hall of Justice.

44 Robert S. Birchard, "The Founding Fathers," *American Cinematographer*, 85th Anniversary Edition, August 2, 2004; and "Roy H. Klaffki," The Internet Movie Database, http:// http://www.imdb.com/name/nm0458165/, accessed May 12, 2009.

45 Robert Cannom, *Van Dyke and the Mythical City*, Hollywood (Culver City: Murray & Gee, 1948) 160–164.

46 Cannom, 248.

CHAPTER 6

1 "Schooner Nanuk Going North to be Used in Film Drama," undated, or referenced clipping courtesy of the Carrie McLain Memorial Museum, Nome, Alaska, and Peter Freuchen, *Vagrant Viking* (New York: Julian Messner, 1953), 242–3.

2 Robert Cannom, *Van Dyke and the Mythical City*, Hollywood (Culver City: Murray and Gee, 1948), 255.

3 Peter Freuchen letter to Robert Grant, from Teller, Alaska, October 14, 1932, Boston Public Library.

4 Freuchen, *Vagrant Viking*, 252.

5 Cannom, 242–245.

6 Freuchen in letter to Rockwell Kent, July 14, 1932, Bering Sea, Boston Public Library.

7 Stanton Patty, "Filming Eskimo Saga Was More Adventuresome than the Script," *Seattle Times*, July 26, 1981, F14.

8 Cannom, 246–8.

9 Mala family papers.

10 "To Seek Koven's Body," *New York Times*, July 9, 1932, 28, and "Koven's Body Recovered," *New York Times*, August 23, 1932.

11 "Actors Get to Help Filming Arctic Movie," *Anchorage Daily Times*, July 29, 1932.

12 Cannom, 248.

13 Cannom, 181.

14 "W. S. Van Dyke," The Internet Movie Database, http://www.imdb.com/name/nm0886754/bio accessed July 4, 2008.

15 Cannom, 252–4.

16 Freuchen, *Vagrant Viking*, 235.

17 Freuchen, *Vagrant Viking*, 199–200.

18 Freuchen, letter to Kent Rockwell.

19 A photo of the two standing together is telling. "Pictorial California," no publication data, Mala family scrapbook.

20 "To Make Color Film in South Seas," *New York Times*, July 7, 1929, 95.

21 Most records claim Knott met Lotus on the Eskimo set; however an earlier census shows them already wed. Census of 1930, William James Knott, Los Angeles, Los Angeles, California; Roll: 133; Page 4B; Enumeration District: 45: image 741.0.

22 Census of 1930, Iris Yamaoka, Los Angeles, Los Angeles, California; Roll: 133; Page 4B; Enumeration District: 45: Image 738.0

23 Freuchen, *Vagrant Viking*, 249.

24 *MGM Eskimo News*, Volume 1, 1932, Teller, Alaska, in family collection.

25 Freuchen, letter to Rockwell Kent.

26 Freuchen, *Vagrant Viking*, 253.

27 Freuchen, *Vagrant Viking*, 244.

28 Graham Russell Gao Hodges, *Anna May Wong* (New York: Palgrave MacMillan, 2004), 181.

29 Wong never appeared in another Hollywood film. Instead, two years later she got a job in the Chinese Customs Office in Hong Kong. Graham Russell Gao Hodges, 155.

30 When Van Dyke took on the assignment directing Johnny Weissmuller in *Tarzan*, he told the studio not to bother with a screen test. "This is the guy I want for the Tarzan role," he said. "He looks the part, and he

doesn't really have to act much, anyway. All he has to do is take orders." Johnny Weissmuller Jr., *Tarzan My Father* (Toronto: ECW Press, 2002), 55.

31 Freuchen, *Vagrant Viking*, 254-5.

32 Freuchen, 249.

33 Booth, who was ill for six years and never worked again in films, eventually sued MGM for more than a million dollars and won an out-of-court settlement. "Edwina Booth," The Internet Media Database, http://www.imdb.com/name/nm0095693/bio, and "Trivia for Trader Horn," The Internet Movie Database, http://www.imdb.com/title/tt0022495/trivia, accessed May 23, 2009.

34 "Shooting of Water Scenes for Motion Pictures Offers Thrills," undated clip from Coos Bay Harbor with dateline Hollywood, August 18, the Michael Phillips Collection, University of Alaska Anchorage Archives and Manuscript Collection.

35 Cannom, 261–3.

36 George Tilden, "Into a White Hell for a Movie," undocumented, Mala collection.

37 Freuchen, *Vagrant Viking*, 251.

38 Peter Freuchen letter to Rockwell Kent, Teller, Alaska, September 1, 1932.

39 Mike Phillips sent an undated clipping of the lie to the Coos Bay Harbor newspaper that was running a series on his Eskimo tenure. His column was datelined Teller, August 24, 1932. Michael Phillips Collection, University of Alaska Anchorage Archives.

40 Pictorial, California caption, Mala family scrapbook.

41 Freuchen, *Valant Viking*, 255.

42 Col. W. S. Van Dyke, "Director of 'Eskimo' Writes of Horrors in Great, Icy Wasteland." Undated with no attribution, Mala Collection.

43 *MGM Eskimo News*.

44 Cannom, 262.

45 Freuchen, *Vagrant Viking*, 256.

46 "MGM vs. PAA," *Nome Nugget*, February 4, 1933, 1–2.

47 "Premier Performance of 'Follies Novelle' Last Saturday Big Success," *Nome Nugget*, February 18, 1933, 2.

48 "Surprise Wedding," *Nome Nugget*, February 18, 1933, 1, and interview with Gertrude Becker Lundstam, Snohomish, Washington, March 1985.

49 Freuchen, *Vagrant Viking*, 257–8.

50 Freuchen, 260.

51 Lundstam.

52 Grace Kingsley, "Hobnobing in Hollywood, *Seattle Times*, April 4, 1938, 9.

53 The 1930 census finds Kleinschmidt in residence with Essie at 391 Audubon Avenue in Manhattan, but from earlier family correspondence it is clear they called their California residence home. Correspondence with family genealogist Ruth Sarrett shows Kleinschmidt dispatched postcards to niece Minnie Louise Bismarck in 1928–29 from such far-flung

locations as Jacksonville, Florida, June 1928; Toronto, Canada, July 20, 1928; and Chinatown, San Francisco, July 20, 192?; while promoting his films. Two years later he garnered what appears to be his last *New York Times* movie review, for a film he called *Eskimo Perils* or *Frozen Hell*, Mordaunt Hall, October 31, 1933. Following this, there is no mention of him in the family papers until 1939, when a letter has been preserved saying both he and Essie have had pneumonia. Gertrude Becker Lundstam's description of the Kleinschmidts' California house is the same as the one described by Kleinschmidt's grandson, Olney Webb, Ketchikan, Alaska, e-mail to author May 11, 2009, who visited just before Kleinschmidt died March 25, 1949.

54 Mordaunt Hall, 'The Screen," January 12, 1934, 29. Kleinschmidt received credit as technical director, "Man of Two Worlds," The Internet Movie Database, http://www.imdb.com/title/tt0025457/ accessed May 24, 2009.

55 Lundstam and "Francis Lerderer Makes His American Film Debut as Fearless Eskimo Hunter, *New York Times*, January 12, 1934.

56 Grace Kingsley, "Hobnobbing in Hollywood," *Los Angeles Times*, September 29, 1933, 9.

57 Lundstam.

58 Phone interview with Anna M. Jobson, Layton, Utah, March 26, 1984.

59 Weissmuller Jr., 46.

60 Weissmuller Jr., 56–57.

61 Lundstam.

62 " 'Eskimo' Wins Preview Praise," newspaper name missing, November 11, 1933, from Mala family collection.

63 Cannom, 273.

64 "Want Ray Wise for 'Good Earth' Lead," undocumented clip in family collection, October 17, 1933.

65 "Good Earth," The Internet Movie Database, http://www.imdb.com/title/tt0028944/ accessed May 26, 2009.

CHAPTER 7

1 "Looking for Mabel Norman, Madcap Mabel Normand," at http://www.freewebs.com/looking-for-mabel/spurr.htm, accessed June 27, 2009.

2 Samantha Barbas, *The First Lady of Hollywood: A Biography of Louella Parsons* (Berkeley: University of California Press, 2005), 148.

3 Ronald L. Davis, *Hollywood Beauty: Linda Darnell and the American Dream* (Norman: University of Oklahoma Press, 1991), 40.

4 Barbas, 30.

5 Feg Murray, "Seeing Stars," undocumented clipping in family collection; "Florine McKinney," The Internet Movie Database, http://www.imdb.com/name/nm0571868/, accessed June 28, 2009; and "Edgar Allan Woolf," Answers.com, http://www.answers.com/topic/edgar-allan-woolf, accessed June 28, 2009.

6 Interview with Maxine Shean, stepdaughter of

William Wise, Larkspur, California, 1983.

7 January 28, 1934, H3.

8 Mala family collection of clippings include many bylined columns by Stiles and Kingsley, almost all undated.

9 Johnny Weissmuller Jr., *Tarzan: My Father* (Ontario, Canada: ECW Press, 2002), 90.

10 James E. Mitchell, "Close Ups," undocumented clip in family collection.

11 Mordaunt Hall, "Man of Two Worlds," *New York Times*, January 12, 1934, and *New York Times* Movies, http: http://movies.nytimes.com/movie/101315/Man-of-Two-Worlds/overview, accessed June 28, 2009.

12 Interview with Gertrude Becker Lundstam, Snohomish, Washington, March 1985.

13 Family members suspect Wise Senior had earlier become aware of Ray's stardom, but Maxine Shean, his stepdaughter, was certain that Ray's initial visit was a complete surprise.

14 Interview with Maxine Shean, 1983.

15 "Mother Found by Rich Miner," *San Francisco Examiner*, December 14, 1933, from a file on William Wise in the San Francisco Public Library to which this author is indebted.

16 "Couple Are Wedded at Hotel, Three Hundred See Ceremony," *San Francisco Chronicle*, December 12, 1915.

17 May 7, 1916, clipping with documentation missing from file of William Wise, San Francisco Public Library.

18 "Mrs. Wise Divorced from Hotel Manager," May 19, 1916. Name of publication illegible.

19 "Mrs. E.S.C. Wise Will Seek Divorce," *San Francisco Examiner*, no date, William Wise file, San Francisco Public Library.

20 Interview with Maxine Shean.

21 "Hotel Man Sued for Girl's Coat Payments," March 19, 1920, no attribution, San Francisco Public Library file on William Wise.

22 Interview with Maxine Shean.

23 "Pismo Beach History," http:www.classicalifornia.cim/history.html, accessed June 17, 2008.

24 Grace Kingsley, "Hobnobbing in Hollywood," February 6, 1934, publication unnamed in family collection.

25 "Members of 'The Eskimo' in Ketchikan," March 17, 1933, no publication given, Mala family scrapbook.

26 Ann Fienup-Riordan, *Freeze Frame: Alaska Eskimos in the Movies* (Seattle: University of Washington, 1975), 83.

27 Peter Freuchen, *Vagrant Viking* (New York: Julian Messner, 1953) 268–9; and interview with Maxine Shean.

28 Edwin Schallert, "Hays Office Restricts Number of Film Titles Registered in Year by Picture Concerns," 7.

29 Untitled, undocumented article by Harrison Carroll in Mala family album.

30 "Largest Expedition in Film History Sets Sail," *Los Angeles Times*, February 16, 1935, 5, and

"Cameraman's Daughter Teaches Mala Language of the South Sea Islands," *Last of the Pagans Studio News*, Culver City, California, undated newspaper in Mala family collection.

31 "Trip Thrills Eskimo Star," *Last of the Pagans Studio News*.

32 Aljean Harmetz, *The Making of the Wizard of Oz* (New York: Dell Publishing, 1989), 136, 139.

33 "Last of the Pagans," http: www.imdb.com/title/tt0026609/, accessed July 17, 2008.

34 Interview with Maxine Shean.

35 "William M. Wise," New York passenger lists, 1826–1957, 1937, Arrival: New York, United States, Microfilm serial: T715; microfilm Roll: T715-5956; Lines 29 and 30.

36 Interview with Maxine Shean.

37 " 'Last of the Pagans' Wins Preview," Small Town Girl, *Studio News*, Culver City California, clipping in Mala family scrapbook.

38 *Las Vegas Daily Optic*, January 7, 1936.

39 Last of the Pagans *Studio News,* Culver City, California, and undocumented ad in family collection.

40 Tom O'Neil, "Oscars have 'horrible' record recognizing Asians," *Los Angeles Times*, January 24, 2007, with comments posted by Wayman Wong.

41 Dorothy Lamour as told to Dick McInnes, *My Side of the Road* (Englewood Cliffs, New Jersey: Prentice-Hall, 1980), 54–56.

42 "The Jungle Princess," The Internet Movie Database, http://www.imdb.com/title/tt0027830/, accessed July 17, 2008.

43 Lamour, 49.

44 Lamour, 32–33.

45 Lamour, 54.

46 "Robinson Crusoe of Clipper Island," an undocumented Republic publicity magazine in Mala family collection, 30.

47 Linda S. Graf, "Chapter XII, Rex Goes to Sea," from unpublished manuscript, *Rex, King of the Wild Horses*.

48 Mamo Clark Rawley, *Except Their Sun* (Honolulu: Abigail Kekaulike Kaqwananakoa Foundation, 1994), 175.

49 E-mail interview with James McKee Rawley, son of Mamo Clark Rawley, Redlands, California, February 28, 2009, and autobiography by Mamo Clark Rawley. Also Republic publicity magazine.

50 "John Ward," The Internet Movie Database, http://www.imdb.com/name/nm0911629/, accessed July 5, 2009.

51 "William Newell," The Internet Movie Database, http://www.imdb.com/name/nm0627840/, accessed July 5, 2009.

52 William Whitney, *In a Door, Into a Fight, Out a Door, Into a Chase: Moviemaking Remembered by the Guy at the Door* (Jefferson, North Carolina: McFarland & Company, 1996), 49.

53 Whitney, 50–51.

54 E-mails from Linda Graf, June 18 and 19, 2010.

55 Whitney, 24–25.

56 Whitney, 61–2.

57 Interview with James Rawley, February 28, 2009.

58 Whitney, 52.

59 Valerie Yaros, historian, Screen Actors Guild, 5757 Wilshire Boulevard, Los Angeles, California from microfilmed records via e-mail July 6, 2009. Ray was Guild Member 4739.

60 *Republic* magazine, 4.

61 "Picture Fans Gasp at Parade of Ermine, Silks and Velvet for Chaplin Premier," *Los Angeles Times*, February 16, 1936, D10.

62 "Skates for Health," Los Angeles Times, April 30, 1936, 12.

63 "Hollywood Studio Club," Hollywood, California, http://www.bluffton.edu/~sullivanm/jmhollywoodyw/jmhollywoodyw.html, accessed May 23, 2009; and Kenneth Anger, *Hollywood Babylon*, (New York: Dell Publishing, 1975), 29–35.

64 "Hollywood Happenings," Chicago Daily Tribune, June l3, 1937, F4; and "Russian Princess Comes to Study Us," New York Times, April 6, 1927, 26.

65 Theodor Lissivetz, New York Passenger Lists, Microfilm serial: T715; Microfilm roll: T715_3263.

66 Theodor Lissivetz, Index to Declaration of Intent for Naturalization: New York County, 1907–1924 [database on-line]. Provo, UT, USA, Petition 639, page 349. and Ancestry.com U.S. Naturalization Records Indexes, 1994–1995 [database on-line]. Provo, Utah, USA: The Generation Network. 2007. Series T1220. 1926.

67 Ancestry.com, 1929; Microfilm serial: T715; Microfilm roll: T715_4420; Line: 2.

68 Ancestry.com, Seattle Passenger and Crew Lists, 1820–1857 [database on-line] The Generations Network, Inc., 2006 Microfilm Roll M 1383-83 and Draft registration card 0249, Men born after April 28, 1877 or before February 16, 1897, Fallon Marin, California, 1942.

69 In the 1930 Census, the family is living in Berkeley. "Teodor," 49, is unemployed. Galina is listed as a student. California; Roll 111; Page 19A; Enumeration District: 298; Image: 183.0.

70 Undocumented clip in Mala family collection, dated June 3, 1937.

71 Interview with Shean.

72 "Eskimo Film Player Weds," *Los Angeles Times*, June 2, 1937, A24. The article names the bride as Galina Liss sometimes known as Gadya Liss, a "Russian actress" and former stand-in for Claire Trevor. It also reported she was a graduate of the University of California at Berkeley and gave her age as 24. However the government record of her entry into New York, January 26, 1929, gave her age as 20 (see endnote 66) and the U.S. Census of 1930 lists her as the same age.

CHAPTER 8

1 Signed portrait of Ray to his mother-in-law in the Mala family collection is dated November 12, 1937. The Spurr portrait of Galina is not dated.

2 Records of the Screen Actors Guild show Mala was still living with the Georges on Edenhurst Avenue when he applied for membership in October 1936. His card for 1937–1938 has an address of 6163 Glenn Alden, Los Angeles. MapQuest cannot find this street but suggests the spelling should be Glen Alder.

3 "Pennsylvanian Goes Home After Three Weeks' Whirl," *Los Angeles Times*, September 19, 1937.

4 "Eskimo Film Player Weds," *Los Angeles Times*, June 2, 1937, A24.

5 Read Kendall, "Around and About in Hollywood," *Los Angeles Times*, July 29, 1937.

6 Interview with Maxine Shean, stepdaughter of William Wise, Larkspur, California, 1983; and "Vera Ivanova," The Internet Movie Database, http://www.imdb.com/name/nm0412142/, accessed July 13, 2009.

7 "Milestones," *Time*, March 7, 1938; and Simon Louvish, *Stan and Ollie: The Roots of Comedy: The Double Life of Laurel and Hardy* (New York, St. Martin's Press, 2002), 361–364.

8 Johnny Weissmuller Jr., *Tarzan: My Father* (Toronto, Canada: ECW Press, 2002), 82.

9 Weissmuller Jr., 85.

10 "Jack Oakie," The Internet Movie Database, http://www.imdb.com/name/nm0642988/bio, accessed June 11, 2009.

11 Read Kendall, "Around and About in Hollywood," *Los Angeles Times*, May 27, 1937, A 20.

12 Jane Scott against Ewing Scott for divorce, October 8, 1935, Los Angeles Hall of Justice.

13 Read Kendall, "Around and About in Hollywood," 14. The columnist reported that Scott and Phyllis Loughton, then a talent coach at MGM, had been secretly married. The news is puzzling because according to her official biography, Loughton had just wed highly successful director George Seaton, who started his career as the radio voice for the Lone Ranger, and remained married to him until his death in 1979, The Internet Movie Database, http://www.imdb.com/name/nm0780833/bio, accessed June 11, 2009.

14 "Romance Plays Part in Next Four Star Opus," Los Angeles Times, September 18, 1937, A7.

15 His name is not in the credits of this film, but Maxine Shean noted he went to Washington State to shoot it. Sally Martin Marks, who played a young girl in *The Barrier*, does not recall Mala in that movie, but in an e-mail to the author July 15, 2009, she noted she was very young at the time. Happily, her description of the area is as Mala described it to Miles Brandon year later.

16 "Call of the Yukon," The Internet Movie Database, http://www.imdb.com/name/nm0247484/, accessed June 11, 2009.

17 Sandra Brennan, "Call of the Yukon," The New York Times Movies, http://movies.nytimes.com/movie/86480/Call-of-the-Yukon/overview, accessed June 11, 2009.

18 Hans J. Wollstein, "The Great Adventures of Wild Bill Hickok," The Internet Movie Database, http://www.imdb.com/title/tt0030978/, accessed June 11, 2009.

19 "Wild Bill Hickok [Serial]," The New York Times Movies, http://movies.nytimes.com/movie/153555/Wild-Bill-Hickok-Serial-/overview, accessed June 11, 2009.

20 William Whitney, In a Door, Into a Fight, Out a Door, Into a Chase: Moviemaking Remembered by the Guy at the Door (Jefferson, North Carolina: McFarland & Company, 1966), 133–134.

21 "Herman Brix/Bruce Bennett: 1906–2007," http://www.briansdriveintheater.com/hermanbrix.html, accessed July 8, 2008.

22 "Hawk of the Wilderness: Serial Story," John & Sue on Hillmans ERBzine, Issue 0594, http://www.erbzine.com/mag5/0594.html, accessed June 12, 2009.

23 Weissmuller Jr., 64–65, 70, 85.

24 Weissmuller Jr., 75, 107.

25 Louvish, Stan and Olie: The Roots of Comedy: The Double Life of Laurel and Hardy.

26 "George Seaton," The Internet Movie Database// http://www.imdb.com/name/nm0780833/, accessed July 1, 2010.

27 "Union Pacific," The Internet Movie Database, http://www.imdb.com/title/tt0032080/fullcredits#cast, accessed June 11, 2009.

28 "Christy Cabanne," The Internet Movie Database, http://www.imdb.com/name/nm0127511/bio, accessed June 11, 2009. Film historian Kevin Brownlow is credited the slur.

29 "Mutiny on the Black Hawk," The New York Times, August 2, 1939, 17:2.

30 "Green Hell," review from untitled book in family collection, 1111.

31 Frank Nugent, "Monotony in the Jungle," New York Times, January 30, 1940.

32 "Buster Crabbe," The Internet Movie Database, http://www.imdb.com/name/nm0185568/bio, accessed July 13, 2009, and "The Music of Flash Gordon," http://flashgordon.homestead.com/files/fgmusic40./htm, accessed July 13, 2009.

33 "The Devil's Pipeline," The Internet Movie Database, http://www.imdb.com/title/tt0032392/fullcredits#cast, accessed July 13, 2009.

34 Edwin Schallert, "Paramount Campaigns for Laurette Taylor," Los Angeles Times, July 11, 1940, A11.

35 Ann Fienup-Riordan, Freeze Frame: Alaska Eskimos in the Movies (Seattle: University of Washington Press, 1995), 90.

36 Interview with Shean, and Notice dated July 4, 1940, in family collection.

37 Weissmuller Jr., 89–90.

38 Louvish, 442.

39 Douglas Churchill, "Screen News Here and in Hollywood," New York Times, February 25, 1941, 27.

40 Story with photo of Ray and Galina Wise with the byline of the Seattle Post-Intelligencer staff, dated February 26, 1941.

41 Toronto Star, July 9, 1923, first reported Weissmuller had a heart problem. Son Weissmuller Jr. wrote that the first actual sign of it might have been a stroke in 1973, when Johnny and Joe Louis were working as greeters in Caesar's Palace in Las Vegas, 181. Shean said Mala had known of his condition since he was in his teens and began taking blood pressure medicine in his thirties. She thought the problem had been caused by an early bout with rheumatic fever which is confirmed by his death certificate.

42 Gene Kira, The Unforgettable Sea of Cortez (Torrance, California: Cortez Publications, 1999) 9, 13–16.

43 "Raymond Cannon," The Internet Movie Database, http://www.imdb.com/name/nm0134252/, accessed July 14, 2009.

44 "Mala, Eskimo Film Actor, Does NOT Long for North," undocumented clip in Mala family collection.

45 "Mala, Star of Eskimo Tells of Upward Climb in Picture," undocumented clip in Mala family collection.

46 Undocumented clip in Mala family collection with a dateline of HOLLYWOOD, October 10. Nightmare opened November 12, 1942.

47 Charles Clarke, Highlights and Shadows: The Memoirs of a Hollywood Cameraman (Metuchen, New Jersey: The Scarecrow Press, 1989), 75–76.

48 "Joseph LaShelle," Internet Encyclopedia of Cinematographers, http://www.cinematographers.nl/GreatDoPh/lashelle.htm, accessed July 14, 2009.

49 Internet Movie Database, http://www.imdb.com/title/tt0037008/, accessed June 21, 2010. Commentary by Prof. Jeanine Basinger, Chair of Film Studies, Wesleyan University, Middletown, Connecticut, on Twentieth Century Fox DVD of film.

50 "Thunderhead: Son of Flicka," Internet Movie Database, http://www.imdb.com/title/tt0038172/, accessed July 4, 2010.

51 Interview with Joseph LaShelle, Hollywood, California, 1982.

52 The address on Ray's 1937 Screen Actors Guild application and his application for Social Security was 6163 Glen Alder, Hollywood. His next SAG card showed 912 S. Orange Grove. We know from former neighbor, Jane Handler, that Ray and Galina were living at 4833 Fountain Avenue in 1946 and remained at that address for the rest of their lives.

53 Interview with Jane Handler, October 1981 in Malibu, California; and "Jane Hamilton" (Jane Handler's movie name), The Internet Movie Database, http://www.imdb.com/name/nm0357930/bo0, accessed July 9, 2009.

54 Interview with Miles Brandon, Anchorage, Alaska, 1981.

55 Ronald Davis, Hollywood Beauty: Linda Darnell and the American Dream (Norman; University of Oklahoma, 1991), 89.

56 Hall Erickson, "Lewis Seiler," All Movie Guide, Yahoo! Movies. http://movies.yahoo.com/movie/contributor/1800046235/bio, accessed July 15, 2009.

57 Shean

CHAPTER 9

1 Interview with Maxine Shean, stepdaughter of Bill Wise, Larkspur, California, 1983.

2 Interview with Jane Handler, October 1981, in Malibu, California.

3 Ronald Davis, Hollywood Beauty: Linda Darnell and the American Dream (Norman; University of Oklahoma, 1991), 40–41.

4 "Henry Koster," The Internet Movie Database, http://www.imdb.com/name/nm0467396/bio, accessed July 14, 2009.

5 Interview with Maxine Shean, stepdaughter of William Wise, Larkspur, California, 1983.

6 "Pair Purchase Ranch Estate," no publication given on clipping, October 29, 1947. William Wise file, San Francisco Public Library.

7 Undocumented clipping dated December 7, 1948, William Wise file, San Francisco Public Library.

8 Interview with Shean.

9 Johnny Weissmuller Jr., Tarzan: My Father (Toronto, Canada: ECW Press, 2002), 109–113.

10 Weissmuller Jr., 119, 124.

11 "Gregory Matusewitch," The Free-Reed Journal, http://www.ksanti.net/free-reed/essays/matusewitch.html, accessed June 9, 2009; and Simon Louvish, Stan and Olie: The Roots of Comedy: The Double Life of Laurel and Hardy (New York, St. Martin's Press, 2002), 424–6.

12 Wes D. Gehring, Laurel and Hardy: A Bio-Bibliography (New York: Greenwood Press, 1990), 107–109.

13 J.R.L. "Untamed Fury At the Rialto," New York Times, April 26, 1947.

14 Elizabeth Pallette, "Arctic Movie Adventure," New York Times, May 9, 1948, X5.

15 Terrence Cole, Nome: City of Golden Beaches (Anchorage: Alaska Geographic, Volume 11, 1984), 170–171.

16 Interview with Miles Brandon, Anchorage, Alaska, 1981.

17 Pallette, "Arctic Movie Adventure."

18 Bosley Crowther, "Harpoon," The Screen, Los Angeles Times, December 9, 1948.

19 Ann Fienup-Riordan, Freeze Frame: Alaska Eskimos in the Movies (Seattle: University of Washington Press, 1995), 100–103; and Elizabeth Bernhardt Pinson, Alaska's Daughter: An Eskimo Memoir of the Early Twentieth

Century (Logan: Utah State University Press, 2005), 202. This was the beginning and end of Wilma's movie career, although she did get some work in Hollywood as a model.
20 Fienup-Riordan, 105.
21 Shean
22 While Mala's son recalls his father enjoyed his role as a detective and was excited about getting more work on television, we have yet to learn what show he appeared on.
23 Interview with Shean
24 Lorena Coats, interviewed about 1983 in Fairbanks.
25 Interview with Joseph LaShelle, Hollywood, California, 1982.
26 Interview with Shean.

EPILOGUE
1 Interview with Maxine Shean, stepdaughter of Bill Wise, Larkspur, California, 1983.
2 Interview with Dr. Ted Mala, May 14, 2009.
3 Interview with Shean.
4 Interview with Jane Handler, October 1981, in Malibu, California.
5 "Indian Physician of the Year: Dr. Ted Mala Recognized Internationally for His Work," Inside: The Association of American Indian Physicians Newsletter, Summer 2008, 8.
6 Phone interview with Mary "Betty" Teters, Wilsonville, Oregon, February 2, 2009.
7 Teters, phone interview July 7, and family tree in family collection.
8 Phone interview with Herbert's daughter, Mildred Herbert Richey, Ferndale, Washington, May 3, 2009; and phone interview with Herbert's youngest daughter, Doris Herbert Wright, Seattle, Washington, April 24, 2009.
9 "Eskimo Family Update," The Inkwell, Bradford, Pennsylvania, October 2008, 4–5.
10 October 31, 1933.
11 Letter from Frank Kleinschmidt to Minnie Louise Bismarck (née Wagner-Kleinschmidt) March 8, 1920, from 100 Cathedral Parkway, New York, provided by Mary Katherine Ellison (née Otterbein-Bismarck) for family genealogy by Ruth Sarrett (née Otterbein-Bismarck), Brick, New Jersey.
12 Letter from Frank Kleinschmidt to Minnie Louise Bismarck (née Wagner-Bismarck) June 22, 1939, from 220 West 42nd Street, New York, provided by Mary Katherine Ellison (née Otterbein-Bismarck) for family genealogy by Ruth Sarrett (née Otterbein-Bismarck), Brick, New Jersey.
13 Interview with Olney Webb, Ketchikan, Alaska, and e-mail correspondence dated May 11, 2009.
14 William Thalbitzer, "Knud Rasmussen: In Memoriam," American Anthropologist, vol. 36. 1934.
15 "Alaska Pioneer Visits City," Los Angeles Times, July 26, 1930, A1.

16 Obituary for John Hegness by his daughter, Helga Hegness, from the archives of the Carrie M. McLain Memorial Library, Nome, Alaska.
17 "Capt. Merl LaVoy," New York Times, December 9, 11.
18 "Ewing Scott," The Internet Movie Database, http://www.imdb.com/name/nm0779131/, accessed July 10, 2009.
19 "Biography for Edward Small," The Internet Movie Database, http://www.imdb.com.name/nm0806448/bio, accessed May 12, 2009.
20 "W. S. Van Dyke," The Internet Movie Data Base, http://www.imdb.com/name/nm0886754/, accessed May 5, 2009.
21 Graham Russell Gao Hodges, Anna May Wong: From Laundryman's Daughter to Hollywood Legend (New York: Palgrave MacMillan, 2005), 216.
22 "Iris Yamaoka," The Internet Movie Database, http://www.imdb.com/name/nm0945572/bio, accessed July 2, 2008.
23 1930; Census Place: Los Angeles, Los Angeles, California: Roll: 133; Page 4B; Enumeration District: 45; Image 741.0.
24 "Lotus Long," The Internet Movie Database, http://www.imdb.com/name/nm 0519078/, accessed July 19, 2009.
25 "Peter Freuchen (1886-1957)," books and writers, http:/ www.kirjasto.sci.fi/peterfre.ctm, accessed July 19, 2009.
26 Interview with Gertrude Becker Lundstam, Snohomish, Washington, March 1985.
27 E-mail and phone interviews with James Rawley Jr., Redlands, California, February 2 through July 5, 2009. Like his father, Rawley Jr. served in the military before retiring to teach.
28 Johnny Weissmuller Jr., Tarzan: My Father (Toronto, Canada: ECW Press, 2002), 100–101.
29 Weissmuller Jr., 143,144.
30 Weissmuller Jr., 168–169.
31 A promotional brochure for The Best of John Jobson, edited by Steven Schroeder.
32 "Robert J. Koster," The Internet Movie Database, http://www.imdb.com/name/nm0467405/, accessed July 3, 2010.
33 The legislation is called the Alaska Native Claims Settlement Act.
34 Dean Gottehrer, The Associated Press Stylebook for Alaska, Second Edition (Fairbanks, Alaska: Epicenter Press, 2000), 47.
35 "Look Homeward Simple Eskimo," January 28, 1934, H3.

FILMOGRAPHY
1 "Lost Island of Kioga," Internet Movie Database, http://www.imdb.com/title/tt0060638/, accessed June 23, 2010. Another useful source is the Turner Classic Movie Database, but IMDB has more information.
2 "Something for the Birds," Internet Movie Database, http://www.imdb.com/title/tt0038172/, accessed June 24, 2010.

3 "Les Misérables," Internet Movie Database, http://www.imdb.com/title/tt0044907/, accessed July 8, 2009.
4 "Red Snow," Internet Movie Database, http://www.imdb.com/title/tt0045075/. Ewing Scott used a lot of footage shot for Igloo in 1931 including close-ups of Wise reused for Red Snow. Amazingly, Mala appears to have aged little in the interim.
5 "Run for the Sun," Internet Movie Database, http://www.imdb.com/title/tt0049696/, accessed June 20, 2010. When interviewed in 1982, Joseph LaShelle could not recall whether he and Ray had been working on Run for the Sun or The Conqueror when Mala was felled by a heart attack while lugging heavy equipment up remote Mexican mountains. However Conqueror, with John Wayne and Susan Hayward, was shot mostly in Nevada after an A-bomb test there in 1955, three years after Mala's death. About thirty members of that cast subsequently contracted cancer including Wayne, who died from it. An interesting source on this is The Straight Dope: Fighting Ignorance since 1973, http://www.straightdope.com/columns/read/374/did-john-wayne-die-of-cancer-caused-by-a-radioactive-movie-set, accessed June 20, 2010.
6 "The Outcasts of Poker Flat," Internet Movie Database, http://www.imdb.com/title/tt0045003/, accessed July 6, 2009.
7 "Meet Me After the Show," Internet Movie Database, http://www.imdb.com/title/tt0043795/, accessed June 21, 2010.
8 "Happy Land," Internet Movie Database, http://www.imdb.com/title/tt0035970/, accessed June 21, 2010.
9 "Everybody Does It," Internet Movie Database, http:/ http://www.imdb.com/title/tt0041341/, accessed July 9, 2009. Interview with Jane Handler, October 1981, in Malibu, California.
10 "Come to the Stable," Internet Movie Database, http://www.imdb.com/title/tt0041257/, accessed July 9, 2009. Although there are no credits given for assistant cameraman, both the Mala and Koster families remember Mala's work on this movie.
11 "The Fan," Internet Movie Database, http://www.imdb.com/title/tt0041346/, accessed June 21, 2010.
12 "The Luck of the Irish," Internet Movie Database, http://www.imdb.com/title/tt0040553/, accessed July 4, 2010.
13 "Joseph LaShelle," Internet Movie Database, http://www.imdb.com/name/nm0005766/, accessed July 4, 2010. The films not included are Mother Didn't Tell Me, Under My Skin, Where the Sidewalk Ends, Mister 880, The Jackpot, The 13th Letter, Mr. Belvedere Rings the Bell, The Guy Who Came Back, and Elopement.
14 "Son of Flicka," Internet Movie Database,

http://www.imdb.com/title/tt0038172/, accessed June 21, 2010.

15 "Doll Face," Internet Movie Database, http://www.imdb.com/title/tt0037650/, accessed July 8, 2009.

16 "Laura," Internet Movie Database, http://www.imdb.com/title/tt0037008/, accessed June 21, 2010. Commentary by Prof. Jeanine Basinger, Chair of Film Studies, Wesleyan University, Middletown, Connecticut, on Twentieth Century Fox DVD of film.

17 "The Lodger," Internet Movie Database, http://www.imdb.com/title/tt0037024/, accessed July 8, 2009.

18 "Shadow of a Doubt," Internet Movie Database, http://www.imdb.com/title/tt0036342/, accessed July 8, 2009.

19 "Mala, Eskimo Film Actor, Does Not Long for North," undocumented clip in Mala family collection.

20 "Nightmare," Internet Movie Database, http://www.imdb.com/title/tt0035127/, accessed July 8, 2009. Undocumented clip in Mala family collection with a dateline of Hollywood, October 10, reported Mala was working on this picture.

21 "The Tuttles of Tahiti," Internet Movie Database, http://www.imdb.com/title/tt0035477/, accessed July 8, 2009.

22 "The Girl from Alaska," Internet Movie Database, http://www.imdb.com/title/tt0035477/, accessed July 6, 2009.

23 This funny horror show did not get good reviews. "The Mad Doctor of Market Street," Internet Movie Database, http://www.imdb.com/title/tt0035007/fullcredits#cast, accessed June 23, 2010.

24 "Son of Fury: The Story of Benjamin Blake," Internet Movie Database, http://www.imdb.com/title/tt0035360/, accessed July 8, 2009.

25 According to a clipping in the Mala family scrapbook, dated February 26, 1941, with a Seattle dateline. The name of the publication was not provided.

26 "Honolulu Lu," Internet Movie Database, http://www.imdb.com/title/tt0034867/, accessed July 6, 2009.

27 "Hold Back the Dawn," Internet Movie Database, http://www.imdb.com/title/tt0033722/, accessed July 8, 2009. Family members who have seen the film say Mala is speaking Spanish with an Inupiat accent.

28 "The Devil's Pipeline: Isle of Missing Men," Internet Movie Database, http://www.imdb.com/title/tt0032392/, accessed July 8, 2009.

29 "North West Mounted Police," Internet Movie Database, http://www.imdb.com/title/tt0032850/, accessed July 8, 2009.

30 "The Girl from God's Country," Internet Movie Database, http://www.imdb.com/title/tt0032526/, accessed June 25, 2010.

31 "South of Pago Pago," Internet Movie Database, http://www.imdb.com/title/tt0033082/, accessed July 8, 2009.

32 Edwin Schallert, "Paramount Campaigns for Laurette Taylor," July 11, 1940, A11.

33 "Zanzibar," Internet Movie Database, http://www.imdb.com/title/tt0033294/fullcredits#cast, accessed July 8, 2009.

34 "Flash Gordon Conquers the Universe," Internet Movie Database, http://www.imdb.com/title/tt0032475/, accessed July 8, 2009.

35 "Green Hell," Internet Movie Database, http://www.imdb.com/title/tt0032558/, accessed July 13, 2009.

36 "Desperate Trails," Internet Movie Database, http://www.imdb.com/title/tt0031224/, accessed July 8, 2009.

37 "Mutiny on the Blackhawk," Internet Movie Database, http://www.imdb.com/title/tt0031691/maindetail/, accessed July 8, 2009.

38 "Coast Guard," Internet Movie Database, http://www.imdb.com/title/tt0031163/, accessed July 8, 2009.

39 "Union Pacific," Internet Movie Database, http://www.imdb.com/title/tt0032080/, accessed July 8, 2009.

40 "Hawk of the Wilderness," Internet Movie Database, http://www.imdb.com/title/tt0030219/, accessed July 17, 2008.

41 "The Great Adventures of Wild Bill Hickok," Internet Movie Database, http://www.imdb.com/title/tt0030978/, accessed July 8, 2009.

42 "Call of the Yukon," Internet Movie Database, http://www.imdb.com/title/tt0029961/, accessed July 8, 2009.

43 Read Kendall, "Around and About in Hollywood," Los Angeles Times, May 27, 1937, A20, and Internet Movie Database, http://www.imdb.com/title/tt0028611/, accessed July 9, 2009.

44 "The Jungle Princess," Internet Movie Database, http://www.imdb.com/title/tt0028611/, accessed July 17, 2008.

45 "Robinson Crusoe of Clipper Island," Internet Movie Database, http://www.imdb.com/title/tt0028198/, accessed July 17, 2008.

46 "Last of the Pagans," Internet Movie Database, http://www.imdb.com/title/tt0026609/, accessed July 17, 2008.

47 "Eskimo," Internet Movie Database, http://www.imdb.com/title/tt0023990/, accessed May 20, 2010.

48 "Igloo," Internet Movie Database, http://www.imdb.com/title/tt0023050/fullcredits#cast, accessed June 23, 2010.

49 "The Big Trail," Internet Movie Database, http://www.imdb.com/title/tt0020691/, accessed May 11, 2009.

50 "Girls Gone Wild," Internet Movie Database, http://www.imdb.com/title/tt0019931/, accessed May 21, 2010. No one is credited as assistant cameraman in this film, but Mala sent a photo to his sister during this period which showed him behind the movie camera with star Nick Stuart.

51 "Air Circus," Internet Movie Database, www.imdb.com/title/tt0018633Fox, accessed May 15, 1909. Mala sent a photo of himself working on this film to his sister, according to an interview with Lorena Coats in Fairbanks, Alaska, about 1983.

52 "Two Girls Wanted," http://www.imdb.com/title/tt0018518/

53 Interview with Lorena Coats, and "Nieminen Returning to Kotzebue Brings Report Frantic Search—Rescues," Fairbanks News-Miner, June 5, 1928.

54 "Frozen Justice," Internet Movie Database, www.imdb.com/title/tt0019907/, accessed May 9, 2008.

55 "Heart of Salome," Internet Movie Database, http://www.imdb.com/title/tt0017974/, accessed may 15, 2009. Ray sent a photo of this movie to his sister with a note that he had been working on it, according to an interview with Lorena Coats.

56 "Primitive Love," Internet Movie Database, http://www.imdb.com/title/tt0018280/, accessed June 23, 2010. In 1985, a group of Eskimos at the Nome Senior Center regaled this writer with accounts of Kleinschmidt and Wise's beachfront filming, which had most definitely amused them.

57 Henry Provisor, "Ray Mala Was an Amateur Once," Home Movies Magazine, July 1952, 226.

INDEX

ABOUT THE AUTHOR

LAEL MORGAN is an award-winning writer, historian, teacher, photographer, and journalist. Born and raised in Maine, she moved to Alaska in 1959 where she worked for many years as a photojournalist.

In 1968, she began a five-year stint at the *Los Angeles Times*, and then returned to the Far North for assignments with *National Geographic*, the *Washington Post*, the *Christian Science Monitor*, and *Alaska* magazine. In 1988, she joined the Department of Journalism and Broadcasting, University of Alaska Fairbanks, where she taught writing, photography, and multimedia communications for twelve years.

Morgan became publisher of the *Casco Bay Weekly*, an alternative newspaper in Portland, Maine, in 2001, and remained there until the paper was sold in 2003. She currently teaches web-based courses on writing and journalism for the University of Texas Arlington.

Morgan has authored more than a dozen books, including *Good Time Girls of the Alaska-Yukon Gold Rush*, which in 1998 won her the title of Historian of the Year from the Alaska Historical Society. In 2011, she was inducted into the Alaska Women's Hall of Fame.

Photo courtesy of Lee Warren

www.LaelMorgan.com

Reading Recommendations

for readers who enjoy Alaskan memoirs & biographies

ALASKA BLUES: *A Story of Freedom, Risk, and Living Your Dream*, Joe Upton, $14.95

ARCTIC BUSH PILOT: *From Navy Combat to Flying Alaska's Northern Wilderness*, James Anderson & Jim Rearden, $17.95

BERING SEA BLUES: *A Crabber's Tale of Fear in the Icy North*, Joe Upton, $17.95

BOOM TOWN BOY: *Coming of Age on the Lost Frontier*, Jack de Yonge, $14.95

COLD STARRY NIGHT: *An Artist's Memoir*, Claire Fejes, $17.95

GOING TO EXTREMES: *Searching for the Essence of Alaska*, Joe McGinniss, $17.95

IN SEARCH OF THE KUSKOKWIM & OTHER ENDEAVORS: *The Life and Times of J. Edward Spurr,* Stephen Spurr, $14.95

NORTH TO WOLF COUNTRY: *My Life among the Creatures of Alaska,* James W. Brooks, $17.95

SISTERS: *Coming of Age and Living Dangerously in the Wild Copper River Valley*, Samme & Aileen Gallaher, $14.95

SURVIVING THE ISLAND OF GRACE: *A Life on the Wild Edge of America,* Leslie Leyland Fields, $17.95

Alaska Book Adventures™
EPICENTER PRESS
www.EpicenterPress.com

These titles may be found at or special-ordered from your favorite bookstore or ordered directly from the publisher by visiting **www.EpicenterPress.com** or phoning 800-950-6663.

$19.95 U.S. NONFICTION / BIOGRAPHY

The blazing marquee of the plush Astor Theater in New York City billed the 1933 premiere of *Eskimo* as

"THE BIGGEST PICTURE EVER MADE"

propelling a twenty-seven-year-old Inupiat Eskimo from Candle, Alaska, to overnight stardom.

Handsome Ray Wise Mala became the first nonwhite actor to play a leading role in a Hollywood film. The camera loved him, and so did moviegoers. Mala made more than twenty-five films over three decades, playing Hawaiians, South Pacific Islanders, American Indians, and other "exotics."

This is the fascinating story of a talented, enterprising son of an itinerant Russian trader and an Eskimo mother. Mala was a self-made man who entered the world of whites, but for most of his life searched to find his place in it.

INSIDE: Movie posters, historic black & white photos, Ray Mala's film credits.

EPICENTER PRESS

Alaska Book Adventures™

www.EpicenterPress.com

ISBN 978-1-935347-12-5

9 781935 347125

O Gato de Botas
Puss in Boots

Charles Perrault

Bilingual Portuguese - English Fairy Tale